THE
EVERYTHING
GUIDE TO
RAISING
A TODDLER

Dear Reader,

Raising a small child is one of the most creative adventures you can have. Through the amazing growth of your toddler you will discover everything about life once again for yourself. Whatever you took for granted is suddenly not true from the perspective of this wondrous small person. Your toddler has unusual names for things, quirky categories, and strange and mysterious ways of accomplishing ordinary tasks. Guiding your toddler through this stage of childhood will require more energy than you would ever think is humanly possible, but the result is worth it—a three-year-old who is more conversational, more sociable, more self-disciplined, and in general, quite a pleasant member of your family.

This unique, rewarding responsibility gives you a role in forming the character of the next generation! Have some fun, and realize that at the same time you are creating incredible memories for your family. Take lots of photos and note the details in a baby book or blog, as these short months are irreplaceable.

Ellen Bowers, PhD

Welcome to the EVERYTHING® Series!

These handy, accessible books give you all you need to tackle a difficult project, gain a new hobby, comprehend a fascinating topic, prepare for an exam, or even brush up on something you learned back in school but have since forgotten.

You can choose to read an Everything® book from cover to cover or just pick out the information you want from our four useful boxes: e-questions, e-facts, e-alerts, and e-ssentials.

We give you everything you need to know on the subject, but throw in a lot of fun stuff along the way, too.

We now have more than 400 Everything® books in print, spanning such wide-ranging categories as weddings, pregnancy, cooking, music instruction, foreign language, crafts, pets, New Age, and so much more. When you're done reading them all, you can finally say you know Everything®!

QUESTION

Answers to
common questions

FACT

Important snippets
of information

ALERT

Urgent
warnings

ESSENTIAL

Quick
handy tips

PUBLISHER Karen Cooper

DIRECTOR OF ACQUISITIONS AND INNOVATION Paula Munier

MANAGING EDITOR, EVERYTHING® SERIES Lisa Laing

COPY CHIEF Casey Ebert

ASSISTANT PRODUCTION EDITOR Jacob Erickson

ACQUISITIONS EDITOR Brett Palana-Shanahan

DEVELOPMENT EDITOR Brett Palana-Shanahan

EDITORIAL ASSISTANT Ross Weisman

EVERYTHING® SERIES COVER DESIGNER Erin Alexander

LAYOUT DESIGNERS Colleen Cunningham, Elisabeth Lariviere, Ashley Vierra, Denise Wallace

Visit the entire Everything® series at *www.everything.com*

THE
EVERYTHING®
GUIDE TO RAISING A TODDLER

All you need to raise a happy,
healthy, and confident toddler

Ellen Bowers, PhD

Aadamsmedia
Avon, Massachusetts

This book is dedicated to Janet, who taught
me most of what I know about children and
everything I know about being a mother.

An Everything® Series Book.
Everything® and everything.com® are registered trademarks of F+W Media, Inc.

Published by Adams Media, a division of F+W Media, Inc.
57 Littlefield Street, Avon, MA 02322 U.S.A.
www.adamsmedia.com

Contains material adapted and abridged from *The Everything® Cooking for Baby and Toddler Book*
by Shana Priwer and Cynthia Phillips, copyright © 2006 by F+W Media, Inc., ISBN 10: 1-59337-691-X;
ISBN 13: 978-1-59337-691-8, and *The Everything Toddler Activities Book®* by Joni Levine, MEd,
copyright © 2006 by F+W Media, Inc., ISBN 10: 1-59337-588-3; ISBN 13: 978-1-59337-588-1.

ISBN 10: 1-4405-2585-4
ISBN 13: 978-1-4405-2585-8
eISBN 10: 1-4405-2706-7
eISBN 13: 978-1-4405-2706-7

Printed in the United States of America.

10 9 8 7 6 5 4 3 2 1

Library of Congress Cataloging-in-Publication Data
is available from the publisher.

This publication is designed to provide accurate and authoritative information with regard to the subject matter covered. It is sold with the understanding that the publisher is not engaged in rendering legal, accounting, or other professional advice. If legal advice or other expert assistance is required, the services of a competent professional person should be sought.
—From a *Declaration of Principles* jointly adopted by a Committee of the American Bar Association and a Committee of Publishers and Associations

Many of the designations used by manufacturers and sellers to distinguish their products are claimed as trademarks. Where those designations appear in this book and Adams Media was aware of a trademark claim, the designations have been printed with initial capital letters.

This book is available at quantity discounts for bulk purchases.
For information, please call 1-800-289-0963.

Contents

Acknowledgments

I wish to express a sincere thank-you to Adams Media editor Brett Shana-han for bringing this project to my inbox. Thank you to my friends and family who tolerated my disappearance for a few weeks. I am grateful to the wealth of the Glendale and Pasadena libraries for supporting material. I am grateful to my parents for having unique, enriching views of what it is to raise happy, competent people, to college professors who tolerated my incessant requests for independent studies approaching child development across several disciplines, and to my daughter, Janet Robison, for her knowledge and resources in the areas of technology and early childhood. Thank you to Susan Friend and Jenn Wood for their helpful suggestions, and a warm thanks to two more people for very special support—Orchid Black and Harriet Kaiser.

Introduction

THE TODDLER YEARS ARE far from terrible! In fact, toddlerhood can be one of the most awe-inspiring and magical times in the lives of both parent and child. All a parent needs is a little direction to change these often trying years into terrific memories. Today's toddlers grow up in a world entirely different from the one their parents grew up in, and certainly more different from their grandparents' world. Your eighteen-month- to three-year-old child observes people using cell phones every day and learns from observation that interesting things happen when a finger touches the screen. Life happens faster when surrounded by digital technology.

The cashier at the fast food restaurant notes the order on a touch screen and instantly the meal appears. Touch a particular spot on the phone and you can talk to Grandma. Anything you want to know you can look up on the Internet. For months you have been sending digital photos of your baby to friends and family over the phone or Internet. Everything seems to happen at the flick of a finger.

It is clear that your toddler will grow up comfortable with media of all sorts. You undoubtedly have one to four televisions in your home, one or two computers, and mostly likely cable or satellite TV. You have a cell phone and numerous other electronic devices. How can you mix all this with being a parent? This guide will help you find a middle ground between the past child-rearing methods and the new. You won't have to completely reinvent the wheel, but you can enjoy your toddler with a modern flourish and flair.

You are raising your toddler in an explosion of electronic media. Software and hardware are available for infants even as young as nine months. Your toddler may have already graduated from Baby Mozart and Baby Einstein. The avalanche of software and devices are here to stay. How can you best determine what is good for your toddler and how to use it? What is normal for a toddler anyway? You realize that you definitely cannot refer to Dr. Spock, your grandmother, or in some cases, even your parents, as times have definitely changed. Older relatives and friends may be able to remember at what age toddlers walk and talk, and that is a reassuring help. But no one in past generations will have a clue about recommended apps for your toddler's iPad.

Media is a part of your life, every day. It is part and parcel of the fabric of your being, and you honestly cannot imagine existence without all your gadgets and instant access to anything and everything in your world. How do you raise a toddler in the context of such an instant digital world? How much of it is okay for your little one, and where can you find help with making decisions about your toddler?

Some of the tried-and-true information about toddlers does not change over time, and this book will help you get grounded with some of that. Some things change as generations change, and this book will help you get current on those topics. And some aspects of parenting a toddler are brand new with your generation! You get to be at the forefront of exploring digital life with a small one. This book will help you make some decisions about that, too, that is if your little tyke isn't already showing you the latest applications!

Your toddler will be in the enviable position of being completely comfortable with many forms of technology throughout her life. It is up to you to help her navigate the way. This book will help you. Consider it your GPS for the years between eighteen months and three years old.

CHAPTER 1

One Giant Step

The day your toddler pulls himself up and starts tentatively taking steps around low pieces of furniture will be one of the most exciting days of your life! You will grab your phone or digital camera, and put those captured moments on YouTube, Facebook, and Flickr by the end of the day. Your toddler's world (and yours) is forever changed now that he is upright and mobile. Everything will be upside down and chaotic for about the next year and a half. Brace yourself and take a deep breath!

Getting Around, Toddler Style

The term "toddler" says a lot about what happens during this stage of your child's growth. He has progressed from crawling to standing up, and by the age of three may be jumping and skipping. All these activities of locomotion engage the toddler's large muscle groups—the arms, legs, body, and head—in order to move around in space.

Pulling Himself Up

A toddler should be able to pull himself up to a standing position using furniture, a leg, or whatever sturdy object is handy. To help him get this movement, which usually comes before walking, from a kneeling position, place your child's hand on a coffee table for balance and help him position one foot on the floor and then the other. Gently lift his body, easing his weight onto his legs and feet. You may hear chortles of glee, as the world looks very different from this perspective!

Cruising

Children make their way around the room using furniture to steady themselves. To encourage cruising, put an enticing toy on a coffee table a few inches beyond the reach of the child when he is standing up, holding onto the table. This stage often closely follows pulling up. Your little cruiser will be the life of the party at family gatherings as he moves from person to person holding on to everyone's knees.

Climbing

By twelve months, most babies can climb at least twelve inches at a time. Steps are a great place to practice. With a safety gate at the third step, put your baby into a crawling position at the bottom landing, an enticing toy at the top step, and show him how to extend his hands and slide his knees forward to climb up to it. Once your toddler has mastered climbing, you will need to look around your house and check again for safety issues. It is common for toddlers to fall out of their crib once they've become master climbers. You might let him graduate to a bed lower to the floor.

Walking

Timid toddlers may be reluctant to let go of steadying objects, so they might walk a bit later. While your toddler is standing up holding on to a piece of furniture, sit just out of reach and call him to you. Catch him before he falls and exclaim, "Wow! My baby's walking!" When he's confident enough to let go for half a step, expand the distance by a few inches.

Running

Clear an area in the house where the toddler can practice this important skill. Your decor may suffer if you must push furniture against the wall of a small living room to make space, but your child's development and safety are definitely more important! Eliminate the lumps from the carpeting and use nonslip area rugs to soften hardwood and tile floors. Open areas in a park are wonderful for random running.

ESSENTIAL

If a sedentary toddler shuns physical activity, he may need some incentives to get proper exercise. Parents can enroll themselves and their toddler in a kiddie exercise class. Check online, local parenting magazines, private gyms and spas, and early childhood education programs for leads. Friends with toddlers are good sources of information, too.

Jumping

You may need to demonstrate jumping and help your toddler until he figures out this complex movement. After demonstrating, grasp the child under the arms, lift him up a few inches, lower him until his feet touch the ground, and then quickly lift him back up. Repeat several times. If you jump along with him, he will get the idea more quickly (and it's good exercise for you).

Hopping

Use the same procedure as for jumping, except show your toddler how to extend one leg and keep the other bent. Grasp him under the arms, and help him get the idea by bouncing him up and down. Don't expect him to hop or jump by himself. The aim should be practice, not mastery, at this stage.

Skipping involves combining walking and hopping, so the motion is step-hop-step. By age three, your toddler might be interested in learning how to skip.

Galloping

Galloping is a more advanced skill for toddlers closer to age three. Gallop in slow motion first. The trick to galloping is to make sure that one foot always lands flat on the ground while the other foot remains bent so the child lands on the ball of his foot, without pressing down on the heel. Show him how to step forward, place his whole foot on the ground, then move the other foot forward and step down on the ball of the foot before moving the first foot forward again. Some fun cowboy props and a stick horse might make galloping more enticing.

Collision Course

You might wonder why your toddler runs into so many things as she is learning to walk. Her perceptual system is different and not fully developed. She doesn't scope out everything that is in the way before taking off across the room. She's more interested in where she's going than how she's getting there. As a result, there will be many mishaps.

Think of your little girl as having a one-track mind at this stage. She cannot plot her course and strategize going around things while she's learning to manage those rubbery legs. She just takes off for the sheer exuberance of movement and lets the chips fall where they may.

Toddler bodies are roly-poly in order to cushion those numerous falls. And keep in mind, she's much closer to the floor than you are. You can ease the pain and insult of tumbles by dressing your little one in long pants during the earlier stages of walking. A little fabric over the knee can prevent the skin from getting scraped every time there's a fall.

It might be fun to set up a room in your home with mostly pillows and a soft rug or carpet. Your toddler can explore the space with her new-found skill without hurting herself.

Difficulty coordinating large and small muscle groups and a lack of clarity about physical boundaries cause clumsiness—and both are basic characteristics of toddlers! The usual solution is years of practice. The school of hard knocks will teach them exactly where their body leaves off and the rest of the world begins.

FACT

Controlled rocking in a rocking chair requires subtle flexing movements that are hard for toddlers. Practice sessions are good physical therapy and help develop coordination and motor control. But if rowdiness persists, make the rocker off-limits and substitute an active game to burn off some high-octane toddler energy.

However, some toddlers have a high threshold for pain, so the usual bumps and bruises don't teach them to stop before colliding with the chair, the end table, or the ground—or even with themselves. They step on their own feet and their own hand clunks them in the jaw. They may cry each time it happens, but they are so readily distracted that they forget to watch what they're doing and the same or similar accidents keep recurring. "Careful!" "Look out! "Don't hurt yourself!" "Next time, watch where you're going," their parents repeat as these seeming daredevils continue to knock and scrape and batter themselves in their heedlessly rough-and-tumble play.

But children aren't daredevils if they don't comprehend the risk. Warnings work only if youngsters know what to do to prevent another injury. They learn from their mistakes only if they remember what went wrong last time and can figure out what to do differently to avoid a repetition of the problem when the same situation arises.

If warnings and frequent bumps don't slow your youngster down, provide comfort after she's been injured, and then encourage her to repeat the same movement, but this time without hurting herself. Praise her for being successful. Multiplied over many situations, this kind of concentrated teaching can help toddlers tune in to the position of their body and be more aware of the proximity of their limbs, head, and torso to other objects. Meanwhile, encourage better body awareness by combining song and movement, such as in "The Hokey Pokey." This familiar childhood song helps the toddler isolate particular parts of the body and gain a little more self-control.

FACT

Some experts say swimming lessons before age four don't help children learn faster because of the limitations of their central nervous system and muscle development. Still, water babies' classes can be lots of fun and will encourage them to stretch their little muscles.

Style and Grace

Some toddlers try quite unique ways of getting around once they're up on two feet. Your little one may tiptoe around like a ballerina for days and days. It's nothing to worry about, unless she is unable to keep her feet flat on the floor when she's squatting. She won't be a prima ballerina forever. It's just a way to experiment with various sensations in the foot and leg, while she's learning how it all works.

Your toddler might walk pigeon-toed or waddle with an endearing Charlie Chaplin gait. These phases are temporary as well. If it seems that the unusual style is persisting, you can check with your pediatrician, but usually it's not a problem. Sometimes these ways of placing the feet give your toddler a better sense of balance.

Your little one may goose-step like a head majorette until she learns that such high stepping isn't necessary to take the next stride. When it's all new, it may seem like an extraordinary feat to get those legs to move in an alternating fashion.

Watch Out!

Once your toddler is movin' and groovin' you have to be alert every waking moment, as potentials for mishaps are much greater than when she was on all fours. Perhaps an example will help you understand just how a toddler's mind and body interact. If a toddler is reaching for a freshly iced cake sitting on the table and hears her mother yelling, "Don't touch!" her natural response is to turn her face toward the sound. Then, when she sees that Mother is addressing her, she must figure out what she's trying to tell her. Once she comprehends that her mother's words refer to her hand reaching for the cake and realizes that she wants her to stop, she must figure out which muscles to contract and which to relax to get that little hand to drop to her lap. By then, the hand may well be covered with icing.

ALERT

Walkers do not help babies to walk faster. In fact, most authorities suggest that you not bother with them. An estimated 29,000 children each year have an accident in rolling walkers serious enough to send them to an emergency room! You don't need your baby to be playing bumper cars with everything in the house.

It's understandable that a parent who doesn't have a grasp of toddler development gets very upset in this situation. After all, she said, "Don't touch," and her toddler looked straight at her and stuck her hand in the cake. It's tough enough to have the problem of a ruined cake and an icing-covered toddler. The anger that comes from believing the toddler has purposely misbehaved can cause the mother to punish her child, which leaves the toddler feeling upset without even understanding what she did wrong. So instead of attributing evil intentions to toddlers' misbehavior, be considerate of their inability to process information quickly, and be patient!

Think of the fact that there's a time delay in the child's processing of information. You may see this, also, in a delayed reaction when the child falls down. It takes a few seconds for her brain to interpret the pain signals, which are arriving from a different part of the body than she had expected. It will take another few seconds for the brain to communicate with the throat and eyes so she can let out a large wail and begin to cry. Don't conclude that your child isn't hurt because she didn't start crying at once! If the child isn't injured, provide comfort by helping her up and telling her she's okay. Let her think through what just happened rather than admonishing her to "be more careful." A toddler won't understand what that means, as she has no context for those words. Just comfort her and reassure her in her courageous explorations. To avoid collisions, clear an area of your home where your toddler can run safely, or provide an opportunity each day to play outside.

How to Make Your House Safe for Walking

Whether your child is off and running, or taking his time, there are things you can do to make things a little easier for him and reduce some risks. Open up space in the rooms of your house so toddlers don't have to navigate an obstacle course as they waddle about. Be careful to do the following:

- Remove furniture from high-traffic areas.
- Keep toys picked up.
- Put towels over skid areas to prevent rug burn.
- Pad hard edges of furniture to guard against head injuries. Be especially aware of the corners of low coffee tables.
- Allow toddlers to go barefoot inside whenever possible.

Stairs

Stairs are as dangerous as they are intriguing for toddlers. Until they can negotiate them safely on their own, place a sturdy safety gate at the top and bottom of the stairway. Check to see that its folding mechanism will not pinch little fingers. Remember: What goes up can also fall down! To prevent stairway-related injuries:

- Keep steps and landings free of clutter.
- Secure the edges of carpeting.
- Place skid-proof mats on slippery hardwood and linoleum.
- Keep the stairs well illuminated.
- Place guards on railings, windows, and patios above the first floor.

Finally, when your youngster is old enough to begin practicing climbing up and down (around age two), move the bottom gate up to give him an opportunity to practice on the first few stairs.

Bathroom Safety

Between the cramped space, slippery floors that invite falls, and the unforgiving porcelain fixtures that hurt so much in a crash, bathrooms need special attention to protect wobbly toddlers.

QUESTION

Why has my toddler reverted to crawling again?
If a toddler experiences stress of some sort (parent returning to work, change in environment, a new sibling, or not feeling well) he may regress back to crawling for a time.

Use skid-proof flooring and mats on your bathroom floors, and be sure to place decals or a skid-proof mat on the bottom of the tub and shower. Stick decals on the rim of the tub and shower walls, too. In the event of a slip, that bit of friction may help break a fall.

On Toddler Time

On the day that you have a bunch of errands to do—supermarket shopping, paying bills, returning something at the department store—your toddler seems to want to walk at a snail's pace. Why is this? It could be a little bit of the toddler rebelliousness that creeps in during these months of rapid growth, or it could be simply that your child finds everything quite fascinating along the way. She has a lot to investigate—signs, trees, dogs, other people, stuff in the store, or the changing shapes of the clouds. All this is important work for her, just as your errands are important to you. The difference is, she's not in a hurry. You will learn with experience how much a toddler can be expected to do during a given amount of time. It will be easier for both of you if you maintain a steady, yet flexible pace as you're out and about.

The Well-Shod Toddler

Buying a pair of shoes is an exciting rite of passage, but your little one may not see it the same way you do! Here are some important considerations before you make that all-important trip to buy new shoes:

- Make sure you both are rested and have had a good meal.
- Find a store that is toddler friendly, where the salespeople understand small children.
- Put socks on your child that he will be wearing with the shoes you intend to buy.
- Shop at midday and midweek when the stores are not crowded.
- Have your child stand in the shoes, not sit down. The fit will be different.
- Check for a little bit of room in both the width and length of the shoe, but not too much. Resist getting a size too large for him to "grow into." It will be very discouraging and uncomfortable for him to clunk around in shoes that don't fit.
- Choose nonslip, flexible soles, no heel, and upper construction of canvas or leather. Plastic doesn't breathe and causes a build up of perspiration.
- Choose bright, appealing colors, especially for older toddlers.
- Look for a reasonable price. The shoes will be replaced in just a few months.
- Consider getting two pairs at a time so you can rotate them. That way, they can dry out between uses.

You will probably be replacing shoes every three to four months, and even more frequently if your child has a growth spurt. Resist the impulse to use hand-me-down shoes for your toddler. The shape of the shoe has molded to someone else's foot, and it does your child a disservice to expect his foot to adapt to someone else's shoe. If you decide to get very formal shoes for a special party or wedding, realize that they most likely will be worn only once.

As important as the shoe-shopping expedition is, keep in mind that in cultures where people do not wear shoes at all, people have healthier feet! Yes, in your busy life in Western society, people wear shoes for practical reasons—hard sidewalks and floors, broken glass, and any number of other reasons—but a perspective that it's arbitrary and temporary will keep you from stressing out too much.

Fun Activities for Walking Toddlers

Once your toddler is reasonably steady on her feet, she will love anything having to do with dance. On those days when she's ready to rumble (or rumba) try some of these ideas. Your toddler does not have to take lessons and learn fancy steps to dance. Encourage your child to be free with her movements. Let her use her body to express herself. Don't be shy! Why not kick off your shoes and join in the fun?

Dancing Statues

This game will help your child develop listening skills and self-control while she has fun.

1. Play music and encourage your child to dance. Randomly stop the music and ask the child to freeze a pose. As your child improves, you can ask her to hold the pose for longer periods of time.

Traffic Light

In this activity your child can learn how to follow directions and develop self-control while she dances. You will need:

- Paper plates
- Construction paper in red, yellow, and green
- Popsicle sticks

1. Cut construction paper to the size of the paper plates. Staple paper to plates and attach Popsicle sticks. These are your traffic signals.
2. Play music for your child to dance to. Hold up the different colored signs as she dances. When you hold up the green sign, she should dance fast. The yellow sign means dance slowly, and when you hold up the red sign, she should stop.

Dancing Partner

Dancing with a partner takes extra skill and coordination. Why not pair up your child with someone her own size?

1. Play music for your child to dance to. Provide her with a large doll to serve as her dancing partner. Just about any doll will do, but a large rag doll works best.

Action Plays

Action plays are popular with young children. They are a great way to engage your child's imagination. Just about any story or rhyme can be adapted. Let these activities serve as an inspiration—maybe you can think of other ways to get your child to act out stories.

Birds That Fly

This is a "follow the leader" activity. Much like Simon Says, the object is to fool the player(s). For younger toddlers, just stick with the true directives.

1. Call out an animal and an action for your child to imitate. For example, when you call out, "Birds fly," your child should flap his arms like a bird.
2. There are many possible directives, such as frogs that hop, snakes that slither, or horses that gallop.
3. Try to fool him once in awhile by calling out a silly directive. For example, say, "Fish hop." If you fail to trick him, he gets a turn being the caller.

Jack-in-the-Box

This short-action play is sure to get your child's attention and bring some laughter as well. For younger age groups, you can instead play the song "Pop Goes the Weasel." When the song gets to "pop," everyone can pop up. You may need to cue the children when it is time to do this by yelling, "Pop!" or raising your arms.

1. While your child crouches on the floor, repeat the following rhyme in a slow and suspenseful way:

   Jack-in-the-Box, so quiet and still. Will he come up?

2. The child springs up and shouts, "Oh yes he will!!"

Rescue

Engage your child's imagination while helping him develop balance and large motor skills. You can change the theme of the rescue to suit your child's interest. Perhaps he can rescue the kitten from the dogs or the princess from the dragons.

1. Place a bunch of rags in a small bag or basket.
2. Have your child scatter these around the floor.
3. Choose an object/prop to be rescued. This can be another rag, a stuffed animal, or something else. Toss this object into the center of the others.
4. Challenge your child to walk in and retrieve (rescue) this object without stepping on the others. You might tell him that the dragons are sleeping and that he needs to tiptoe in carefully.

Once I Saw a Bird

This cute action includes a nice variety of actions.

1. Teach your child the following rhyme and corresponding movements:

   Once I saw a little bird come hop, hop, hop
   (hop around)
   So I said, "Little bird will you stop, stop, stop?"
   (hold hand in front of body)
   I was going to the window to say, "How do you do?"
   (wave)
   When he shook his little tail and away he flew.
   (wiggle rear end, then flap arms)

Exercise and Creative Movement

Many adults view exercise as an unpleasant chore. This is not so for young children. You will find that your toddler enjoys exercise just as much as any other movement and dance activities. In fact, she may be even more enthusiastic if she feels that she is doing a grown-up activity.

Jump!

Young children often seem to have boundless energy. This activity will help them burn some of that energy and help them develop large motor skills.

1. Play a lively CD and have your child jump up and down. You can show older children how to do jumping jacks.

Sticky Balls

This is an activity for a group of children that encourages cooperation and helps develop motor skills.

1. Have the children all bounce around in a defined area.
2. When two children meet, they stick together and bounce together.
3. Continue until all the children are stuck in one large ball.

Fun Walk

Children of all ages will want to try this activity. What other surfaces can you think of to include?

1. Tape a strip of clear contact paper onto the floor, sticky side up.
2. Stick a path of Bubble Wrap packing material onto the contact paper.
3. Have your child remove her shoes and socks before stepping on the Bubble Wrap path. You may need to hold her hand to help her with balance.

Flying

This activity is best when your child has lots of room to move.

1. Chant the following rhyme, and teach your toddler the movements to go along with the words:

   The airplane has great big wings
   (arms outstretched)
   Its propeller spins around and sings
   (spin arms)
   The airplane goes up
   (arms up)
   The airplane goes down
   (arms down)
   The airplane goes through clouds all over town.
   ("fly" around)

A Thin Line

A piece of rope is all that is needed to help your child practice balance and coordination.

For this activity you will need:

- Approximately five feet of rope

1. Stretch the rope out straight on the ground. Have your child practice walking along it like a tightrope walker. If you wish, you can have her use a balance bar.
2. Hold one end of the rope. Keeping the rope on the ground, wiggle it around and encourage your child to jump over it. If you don't think it will frighten your child, you can pretend that the rope is a snake.

CHAPTER 2

Language Brain Power

You are the single most powerful influence on your toddler's development of intelligent language skills. The way in which you speak, your tone, style, and content are imprinted on your child's little brain, and it all will be replicated as your toddler first babbles, says individual words, and then creates original sentences. This part of your toddler's growth is among the most exciting and rewarding! Communication opens up new ways of cooperating within the family and with people of the larger world outside the home.

Childish Imitation

Your toddler is taking in language at a silent level before you will hear her speak clearly distinguishable words. She will be taking in the lyrics of hip-hop, arguments from TV dialogue, and slogans from commercials. She will hear your outburst as you drop something or forget something important. If you are undiscriminating about the language your toddler is exposed to, you may be in for some colorful surprises when he starts putting sentences together. It might be humorous at first, but off-color language will not impress the day care instructor or your mother-in-law.

Building Blocks for Language

Every day you are adding to your child's language development, even if you don't realize it. In fact, the process started in the womb, as your little one became accustomed to the sound of your voice. What are some specific things you can do now to add to your toddler's speaking skills?

- Read to her every night. Make the time with a book warm and cuddly, so she will associate language, ideas, and books with loving times with you.
- Sing to her every day. You probably remember children's songs from your own childhood. You will never again have as appreciative an audience as your little toddler. The rhythm and rhymes of simple music help a child learn the rhythm and rhymes of speech.
- Answer your child's questions and respond to what she says.
- Speak in a normal tone of voice, respectfully.

Add a Little Something

When your toddler speaks a small sentence or even puts together only two words, use that as an opportunity to expand the sentence, right on the spot. For example if your toddler says, "red truck" you can expand it to "Here's your red truck." This gradual process of adding on just a little bit expands your child's awareness of how language works.

It can be a lot of fun, noticing how toddlers learn to become conversant. First they will name objects, a lot of objects. They will name verbs, a lot of words about things to do. It can be amusing to notice how they form generic groups. For example, for several weeks all animals may be doggies. Your child probably sees very well that a cow and horse do not look like a dog, but the word "doggie" is suitable for the time being, sort of like a placeholder. Don't do a lot of correcting, but you can add a helpful word.

Possession

Toddlers are very interested in what belongs to whom, especially when it's theirs. It can be fun to talk with your toddler, helping him to name things that belong to him and things that belong to you. You can say "my coat" and "your coat" indicating by touching which is which. This is a good time to talk about parts of the body every day. Make a little game out of it as you touch your child's nose, hands, head, and feet, over and over again. Your child's language development thrives on repetition, and he will never be bored.

FACT

Twins will often learn to speak at a somewhat slower rate than children who are not twins. They tend to have their own private lingo and find it not as enticing to learn everyone else's language. They always eventually catch up.

What about cute words that a child invents for various things? Sometimes younger children in families of multiple children make up words for things and don't let them go because the other children reinforce the cute substitutions. There's no harm in this, but it does tend to slow things down in the child's language development. Perhaps you can get everyone in the family to agree to use the normal words. Then the littlest one will be encouraged to join in.

Lots to Talk About

Interesting activities make interesting topics of conversation between you and your toddler. It can be simple things around the house—folding laundry, opening and closing drawers, setting the dishes on the table for lunch. Each object and motion is named, and your child joins in. This is how language is learned. When you get ready to go outside, name each item of clothing and each thing you take along. You might think of it as a lot of speaking out loud your normal thought processes. "I want to take my cell phone. Here are the car keys. Let's take along your crackers. You might get hungry later."

In the supermarket there's a lot to talk about. Everyone's interested in food, including your shopping assistant. Give her something to hold while you're going up and down the aisles. Some toddlers like to be in charge of a box of cereal. Talk about what you're getting from the shelves and bins. "Here are some potatoes. I want three. I think I'll get some tomatoes. These are a nice bright red."

When you get home, if your little shopper isn't too worn out, you can reinforce again the name of each thing. "Here are the potatoes. I'll put them in the sink to wash. Let's put the tomatoes in the sink to wash." You may find yourself speaking in shorter sentences than usual. That's your natural adaptation to your child's learning. Keep the tone low and at a normal pitch. No need to shout or be too sing-songy.

Talking with Toys

No doubt, every day you will be helping your child to put away things and get out other things. Name each one as you go through the process. In this way, your child learns the names of each object and words of location, such as "in the box," "on the shelf," "in the wagon."

Most toddlers love to talk about their dolls and stuffed animals. It's a way of vicariously learning about themselves. You will have daily conversations about putting the animals down for a nap, dressing them, fixing them some lunch, taking them for a ride, and reading them a story. If you treat all this as serious business, your toddler will rapidly learn ways of talking about all these daily processes. Playing with stuffed animals and dolls is another opportunity to talk about parts of the body again. Your child will be highly motivated to show you the bear's ear, tummy, foot, and hand.

Whether to Walk or Talk

Some child development experts believe that toddlers choose either walking or talking as their first priority, trying to master one before taking on the other. In other words, if your child walks first, then speech may be a little delayed. Don't worry about it, as he is very busy learning how to physically navigate in the world. After a certain degree of mastery, he will take on speaking a lot more. The same is true in the reverse. Some children learn to speak in rather complex sentences and still are not walking very well by seventeen or eighteen months. Again, not to worry. It's one task at a time. After the language is relatively well mastered, he will become motivated to become seriously mobile. Walking and talking are the major tasks for a toddler to learn, and it seems a lot for them to take on both at once.

FACT

At twelve months old about half of all children can say six or more words. By three years old, the toddler's vocabulary has ballooned to 1,000 words, along with the expression of thousands of ideas. A child's facility with language is an important aspect of doing well in school and in social relationships.

Concrete to Abstract

Why are books and reading so important? Won't there be plenty of time for that in school? Time shared with books is very important because your child learns that language and ideas are highly pleasurable. Even more, with the repetition of favorite stories, your little one learns that each object in life has a name, and furthermore, pictures of things have the same name as the actual thing! This is a major mental leap, a large factor in a child learning to read. You probably take for granted these conceptual tasks, but a tree is not quite the same as a picture of a tree. Yet one uses the same word for both. As your child learns this, she will move forward in leaps and bounds, very soon discussing everything there is to discuss and eagerly asking for stories about each thing of interest.

The Language Ladder

It doesn't work to apply the averages to individual toddlers, of course, because the age at which a child begins talking is governed by physical maturation. Typically, however, the language progression is:

- Cooing
- Gurgling
- Babbling
- Gibberish
- Individual words
- Two-word sentences
- Complex sentences

The most common progression is for children to begin with one word, gradually add others, and then combine them into two-word sentences before creating more complex sentences. This is not the only pattern, however.

When it comes to saying those first dozen words, researchers say that simply practicing doesn't make speaking perfect. Toddlers will be able to get the words out when the speech centers of the brain mature. But vocabulary comprehension grows quickly. Don't judge your toddler's progress with language by his ability to speak, because the amount youngsters understand is a much better predictor of later language ability. Just keep talking to your toddler, even if you don't receive a reply!

Toddler Speak

Some youngsters mouth rapid-fire streams of gibberish. Their voices rise and fall as if they were expounding on the state of the universe. Their facial expressions are as serious and their gestures as dramatic as Shakespearean actors, yet they don't utter a single recognizable word. This apparent delay can be worrisome to parents, but when toddlers finally start saying words people can understand, they usually begin with short sentences rather than individual words, and continue to progress rapidly.

When your toddler talks to you in gibberish, with a lot of inflection and gesture, treat it as a real conversation. You can reply, "Well that's interesting. I hadn't thought about it that way." The respect you give her utterances helps her learn that conversation is important, and what she says is important.

On average, girls start talking at an earlier age than boys do, if only by a few months. Some children speak later than others because there is simply no need for them to talk—their parents and older siblings are all too adept at figuring out the meanings of their grunts and whimpers. They fulfill their toddler's requests without letting them know that there are other, better ways to communicate.

Encourage, Gently

The best way to encourage youngsters to use words rather than gestures to communicate is to demonstrate the correct way to ask for an item. For instance, when your toddler points at a glass of water and grunts, you can respond, "Water? Can you say 'water'?" After a brief pause to let the question sink in, hand over the water whether or not she attempts to say the word. Your child may be unable to speak because her brain is not sufficiently mature.

ALERT

Cooing seems to be innate. Even deaf infants coo. But if babies cannot hear their parents' responses and feedback, instead of progressing to gurgles, babbles, and gibberish, the coos will gradually disappear. Even if your state mandates newborn hearing evaluations, seek a second opinion from a speech and language expert.

Trying to force her will only make her feel bad. Pushing toddlers is a definite "no-no." There will be plenty of times when you find yourself using the "just tell me what you want" line when you really don't know what your toddler is trying to communicate. But there's no point in creating a scene when you do understand the gesture. Too much pressure makes children tense, and she may stop trying to speak.

Children who have delays in several areas, as premature babies often do, may have language delays, too. Parents can expect toddlers with slower overall development to begin talking later rather than sooner. There's no need to be concerned about exactly when children start talking as long as the child is younger than two, or the following signs are present:

- Gibberish and babbling continue
- Attempts to imitate sounds continue
- Comprehension continues to improve
- Responds to your hearing tests

Still, if you can't shake the feeling that something's wrong, talk to your pediatrician.

Words, Words, Words

Besides normal hearing and listening in general, children need to hear words spoken in context. You've been uttering streams of them since day one, so by twelve months your toddler has had continuous exposure to millions of words. But if you've been less verbal with your child, begin now to make up for those lost months.

Pediatricians warn that TV dialogue does not substitute for conversation with you, although you may occasionally hear your toddler repeat a word heard on TV, especially from commercials. The crucial ingredient in television talk is missing—the association of the sounds of language with the objects to which those sounds refer. In fact, the TV shouldn't even be playing in the background, since the noise can keep toddlers from hearing language that is being spoken.

First Sounds

The first discernable sounds embedded in English-speaking youngster's gibberish are *b*, *p*, *m*, *t*, *d*, *n*, *h*, *k*, and *g*. Although parents celebrate the arrival of the word they've been longing to hear—"Mama" or "Dada"—they usually first occur by accident, as random sounds tucked in the youngster's babbling. It may take several more months for toddlers to use the words consciously and attach meanings to them.

FACT

Don't be surprised if a bilingual baby is somewhat behind in speech. Her brain has more to process! The opportunity for foreign language fluency is up to six years old. It's best to expose babies to the second language very early, and it often is recommended that each adult in a child's life speak to the child only in one language.

During the gibberish phase, some parents have been known to exclaim, "She's speaking a different language!" There is an element of truth to this. Babies are born with the capability to learn any language and emit sounds from every language in the world. As they imitate adults and receive praise for repeating certain sounds while other sounds are ignored, the variety of the sounds they make diminishes. They gradually lose their ability to make the sounds needed to speak other languages. That is why learning to speak a foreign language like a native becomes harder after age six, and impossible for most after ages twelve to fifteen. Certainly the remarkable ability of young humans to go from completely nonverbal to fluent is the envy of any adult who has tried to learn a foreign language.

Life Lessons

Although maturation dictates when children will be able to talk, parents are crucial partners in helping to develop language skills. The amount of exposure to language toddlers receive is critical, and it is associated with intelligence as measured by IQ tests at age three.

Share Your Thoughts

To spur your child's language development, verbalize your thoughts whenever your toddler is around, not just when you have something specific to say, like "Let's get your coat. We're going out now." Instead, try this: "It's about time to run errands. Let's see, I need to pick up some food for dinner, but where did I put my coupons? Oh, here they are. And I need to stop at the bank on the way to the grocery store to get some cash. Well, maybe I'll just use the debit card. Okay, let's get your coat. We're going now."

When parents speak their thoughts aloud in an ongoing, running narrative, youngsters hear words in context and in grammatically correct sentences. They are also exposed to a host of other important information. By hearing a parent think out loud as he gets ready to go to the gym, for example, the child learns how to prepare for this kind of outing, which actually involves quite a bit of planning and organizing: "Where is my gym bag? Oh, it must be in the closet. Oops—I forgot to wash these socks. No wonder this bag smells!" To teach children to think ahead, you need to show them, again and again, task after task, the kinds of things to think about.

Teaching Meanings

As you go through your day, dedicate yourself to helping your child grasp the meaning of individual words. Saying, "Do you want milk or juice?" while holding up a carton of milk and a bottle of juice is a way to teach children that different objects have different names. If your child points to the juice, only to get upset after taking a drink and frantically pointing to the milk, this isn't necessarily a sign he's being negative. He simply may not have learned to associate the word "milk" with the carton. By hearing their parent say a word and having the chance to experience the object, children learn what things are called.

First Conversations

Some parents have a hard time remembering how very important it is to continue talking to their child when they don't get a verbal response. Parents need to speak directly to toddlers about daily affairs, leaving pauses to teach them about the normal give-and-take of verbal exchanges—no matter that the tykes are still too inexperienced with language to hold up their end of the conversation. For example, you might say, "I was thinking I'd make tuna casserole for lunch. What do you think about that? . . . No, it looks as though I'm out of tuna. Perhaps we'll have tacos. Would you like tacos for lunch?"

A child's inability to respond with words doesn't mean that nothing is going on. It is quite the contrary. When the parent pauses, youngsters formulate responses in their mind long before they can demonstrate their knowledge by speaking.

Parents can focus their toddler's attention by getting down to their eye level and speaking directly to them. For instance, you might say, "We're going to visit Grandma. Do you want to show her your new hat? (Pause.) Come on, let's find your hat." Even if your tot doesn't know what a "hat" is at the beginning of the conversation, by the time you've said, "Here's your hat. Let's put it on you. It's cold outside. Your hat will keep you warm" (to teach about the purpose of a hat), and later, "Grandma, how do you like Jonathan's new hat? Jonathan, show Grandma your hat," he should associate the word with the object.

Explaining the World

As you go through your days, concentrate on telling your child about the world. "See the brown truck?" "That's called a stop light. When it's red, all the cars stop." "This is the aisle where they keep all the cereal." "The lady who rings up our groceries is called a cashier." "This yellow flower is a dandelion. See how it tickles your nose?"

And don't forget to repeat yourself . . . again and again and yet again. Toddlers love repetition. It makes them feel more secure because the world feels more predictable; when they hear about things they already know, it gives them a sense of mastery.

First Words

By the time toddlers can say twenty-five words, they can understand about 170. At that point, their spoken vocabulary is apt to consist of a few names of family members, foods, body parts, and animals; a smattering of actions like *up* and *open*; some adjectives like *soft*, and *pretty*; the adverbs *where* and *there*.

When beginning speakers point at an object while saying its name, they usually mean, "I want it." After youngsters are able to say about fifty words, somewhere between sixteen and twenty-two months, they realize that everything has a name. This is a magnificent discovery! Then the pointing changes from a demand to a question. They don't want the item; they want to know what it is called. Suddenly their vocabulary explodes as they flit from object to object, asking to know the name of everything they see. Parents' responsiveness pays off in a big way. Toddlers going through this stage can master several new words each day.

First Sentences

After accumulating a store of individual words, the next developmental step is to combine them into sentences. At first toddlers use two words to create short sentences, such as "Want juice!" for "I want some juice" and "What dat?" for "What is that?"

Expanding Language Skills

When your toddler is able to signal her desire for a drink by saying "water," you can encourage her to take the next step to more elaborate sentences by saying, "Can you say 'Water, please'?" Or you can respond with a full sentence ("You want some water.") or with a grammatically correct question ("Do you want some water?") to help move her toward the toddler version of a complete sentence, "Want water." Again, you should hand over the cup even if the only reply is a nod, which means, after all, that she has heard and understood the question.

Similarly, if a toddler sees a cat and starts a conversation by pointing to it and saying, "Cat," a caregiver can engage in conversation by expanding on the subject she brought up. To do this, the adult might say, "Yes. It's a cat," or "Yes, it's a big, white cat. And look at its long tail!" By giving a verbal response as opposed to simply nodding when toddlers speak, adults encourage them to say more.

After all, if toddlers don't receive a response when they initiate a conversation, there is no reason for them to talk! By responding with longer, more complex, sentences, adults help build toddlers' vocabularies.

Pronunciation Errors

New speakers make many "errors of articulation"; that is, they mispronounce words in predictable ways. Although articulation problems may stem from hearing problems, cerebral palsy, cleft palate, or dental problems, all toddlers make many errors. The vast majority improve with a little time and a lot of practice.

ALERT

By age three, strangers ought to be able to understand your child's speech. If they cannot, it's time to talk to your pediatrician about a referral for a speech and language assessment. By age eight, children should correctly produce all the sounds of the English language.

Common errors include (1) omitting sounds, saying "at" for "hat" or "muhk" for "milk"; and (2) substituting easier sounds for more difficult ones, saying "danks" for "thanks," "medsur" for "measure," "wabbit" for "rabbit." The letters *s*, *r*, and *l* are especially difficult for toddlers to pronounce, and many children take several years to get them right. It is not unusual to hear students say "wunning" for "running" in the early grades of school. The same goes for lisping—substituting the *th* sound for the *s* so that "sand" becomes "thand."

Correcting Errors

You must continually demonstrate the proper way to speak so your child has a good model to copy. At the other extreme, continually correcting toddlers can produce self-consciousness and frustration that increases shyness and reticence about speaking. After all, if a child says, "Wa-wa" and points, it's probably because she still lacks the physical ability to coordinate tongue, breath, and lips to produce all the sounds in the word water. So instead of saying, "It's not 'wa-wa'; it's 'water,'" which can discourage a beginning speaker, emphasize correct pronunciation and grammar by responding, "Do you want some water? Here you go—one glass of water coming right up." Producing the water lets your toddler know that she is successfully communicating, which encourages her to continue to speak to get her needs met. Repeating the correct word several times in grammatically correct sentences encourages toddlers to pay attention to correct pronunciation and usage.

ESSENTIAL

If you teach vocabulary by saying an object's name while moving it, toddlers learn the words faster, experts say. Somehow it helps to roll the toy truck when you say "truck," bounce the ball when you say its name, or make Barbie dance as you say "doll."

Most toddlers, just like adults, are sensitive about having their speech corrected. Hearing language spoken correctly and having opportunities to practice speaking is what improves verbal skills. After all, people receive more benefit from feedback telling them they have done something right, because then they know exactly what to do. Receiving feedback that they have done something wrong doesn't clue them in as to exactly what they should do. Being told, "It's not 'wa-wa'; it's 'water'!" doesn't tell a toddler how to make all the complicated mouth movements needed to say the word. But when she finally says "wah-tuh," point it out and encourage her to practice while the memory is fresh by exclaiming, "You did it! You said 'water'! Can you say it again? Wow! My baby's growing up!"

Naming Parts of the Body

Besides talking directly to your toddler, voicing your thoughts when your toddler is within hearing range, and responding when he initiates conversations, set aside some time for helping him learn specific vocabulary. A good place to start is naming the parts of the body. This is basic vocabulary that toddlers need to know, the words are easy to teach, and the lessons provide an opportunity for fun parent/toddler interaction.

Simply say, "This is Mommy's nose" while touching your nose. Then say, "This is your nose" while touching your child's nose. Then ask, "Where is Mommy's nose? Here it is!" and place your child's hand on your nose. With repetition, children learn not only the word nose but also those important phrases: *this is, where is,* and *here it is.*

FACT

It is common for tykes to talk to themselves when they are playing, falling asleep, or lying awake in bed in the morning. Don't discourage them; they are practicing their language skills! Once they've got all the mouth movements down pat and have matured, they'll be able to think their words without getting on your nerves by saying them.

Once the nose has been mastered, begin adding other parts of the body, such as ear, mouth, hair, eye, hand, and foot. Once toddlers can talk, they can take turns asking their parents to point to different parts of the body. Keep it fun by incorporating these suggestions:

- Squeeze your nostrils when you say, "This is my nose," to make your voice sound nasally.
- Smack your lips when you say, "This is my mouth."
- Bat your eyelashes wildly when you say, "These are my eyes."
- After you ask, "Where is your tummy?" quickly answer your own question by saying "Here it is!" and giving your toddler a quick tummy tickle.

Parents as Teachers

As any school principal can tell you, the best teachers spend as much time entertaining as they do teaching. Developing a positive attitude toward language and learning and being receptive when a parent steps into the role of teacher is more important than any individual lesson. Learning (and teaching) requires a clear head, so if your child can't attend to the task at hand or you're feeling frustrated, don't push it. Also, avoid drilling at all costs. Lessons should be enjoyable enough to make you both smile and short enough that you'll both look forward to playing again. If your toddler isn't finding it fun, forget it!

ESSENTIAL

Teach vocabulary by asking your youngster to hand you clothing when you're dressing her ("Please hand me your sock."), kitchen items while you set the table ("Please get a cup."), things you need to go out ("Where is your diaper bag?"). Remember, it's never too early to teach manners, so include "please" and "thank you."

Here are some simple ways to boost your toddler's verbal skills:

- Let her talk to relatives on the telephone.
- Ask her to tell you about her favorite activity at day care.
- Write down the details of a trip or outing and read them back to her.
- Turn off the TV at mealtime and talk.
- Turn off the MP3 player in the car and recite nursery rhymes. Or sing!

Grappling with Grammar

Many routine grammar errors may actually show that toddlers correctly comprehend very complex grammar rules of the English language. For instance, the past tense in English is usually formed by adding -ed to the present tense of the verb, as in reach/reached; seat/seated; hope/hoped; jump/jumped. When toddlers say, "She teached me," they demonstrate their grasp of this basic rule. They are making an irregular verb regular, which is a very smart thing to do! The best way to teach the correct forms of irregular verbs is to correct the errors each time they occur by restating the sentence correctly.

Unlike trying to get toddlers to pronounce words properly, which may be impossible until they mature physically, correcting grammar is important to keep bad speech habits from developing. So, if your child says, "It's bended," respond by saying, "Yes, it's bent." You should respond to "I done it," with, "Yes, you did it."

CHAPTER 3

Gender and Sexuality

Toddlers are sexual beings, and taboos around childhood sexuality remain strong. The past practice of admonishing toddlers that touching "down there" would land them an eternity in hell has largely disappeared to be replaced by the myth that only youngsters who have been sexually abused display a keen interest in sexual matters. Thus, instead of considering toddlers' sexuality to be immoral, many view it as an indication of "sickness," a symptom of post-traumatic stress. In truth, toddlers are sexual beings, though not in the adult sense. Parents may wonder about gender issues—how boys become boys and girls become girls, in their behavior and identity. What activities, toys, and family attitudes contribute to a child's sense of femininity or masculinity?

"Where Do I Come From?"

One day, precocious thirty-three-month-old Jamie asked the question many parents dread: "Mom, where do I come from?" Jamie's parents had promised each other that when The Question arose, instead of resorting to the stork story, they would give an accurate recounting. And since Jamie was a boy, they decided his father would be in charge of teaching him the facts of life. With a red face and occasional stammer, Dad began fumbling through the tale of Daddy's seed and Mommy's egg, praying Jamie wouldn't ask exactly how Daddy puts the seed there. Mom listened for a bit, then interrupted. "Jamie, you come from Hawaii," she said. Jamie nodded and returned his attention to his toy piano. There are three morals to this story:

- Find out exactly what information your toddler is requesting before trying to answer his question.
- In general, less information is better. Let toddlers ask if they want to know more.
- Don't overwhelm either of you by serving up more information than your tyke is ready to hear.

Gender Issues

A few differences between the sexes seem to be innate. For instance, toddler boys tend to be more active and fussier than girls. Although boys don't actually cry more, their sleep tends to be more disturbed. As a group, girls' language skills develop faster than boys'. Girls also develop bladder and bowel control a few months earlier. Of course, these are tendencies and group averages. The differences vanish when individual children are considered.

When twelve-month-old boys build towers out of blocks and zoom toy cars across the floor, for example, research has shown that parents nod, smile, and praise them more than when little girls do the same thing. The older that boys get, the more support they receive for playing with "boy" toys, and the more they are subtly or actively discouraged from playing with toys such as dolls. Parents are less upset and react less intensely when girls cross the gender line in their choice of play activities.

Teaching the Stereotypes

It is not possible to predict what sexual orientation a toddler will ulti-mately adopt. It is normal for toddlers of both sexes to imitate the behavior of both parents. Sensitive boys with tastes that run more to the artistic than the athletic will have a harder time developing comfort with their masculin-ity if their parents cannot accept these traits, and instead try to push them into more macho roles.

FACT

Adults typically talk to boys and girls very differently. They subtly en-courage boys' independence, offering more support when they head off to explore and providing the kind of guidance that helps them solve problems themselves. In contrast, adults typically provide girls with fewer problem-solving tools by ignoring them more or by solving problems for them. Studies show that adults are more likely to use baby talk with girls than with boys, employing diminutive forms like "doggy" or "dolly" nearly twice as often.

When children of either sex play with baby dolls, they are doing what they see parents, sitters, and day care staff do: take care of babies. Baby dolls can be helpful to boys as well as girls in several ways. They provide practice nurturing and taking care of a baby, enhance feelings of closeness to parents, and prepare toddlers for coping with uncomfortable situations.

Dolls can also help older toddlers resolve their feelings about trying situations and traumas. After imagination has developed and before chil-dren can talk effectively about their problems, re-enacting upsetting events through play helps children work through anxieties and come to terms with troubling emotions. Playing with dolls doesn't turn boys into homosexuals any more than it turns girls into lesbians.

Gender Identity

Core gender identity is formed during the toddler years. Children may go through phases of being a Mommy's boy or Daddy's girl and regularly mimic the behaviors of both men and women, but by age two they should have a conception of themselves as being male or female. Three-year-olds usually identify with the same-sex parent, which is often reflected in their stance, the way they walk, their gestures, and some of their speech patterns.

Toddlers typically identify people's sex by their peripheral characteristics, such as clothing, hairstyle, or use of makeup; they don't have a real conception of what it means to be male or female. To increase identification, the same-sex parent should:

- Spend more time engaging in activities the child enjoys, since this can strengthen the parent-child bond.
- Be more accepting and less critical, since children emulate people they feel close to.
- Be kinder toward a spouse. (Children are protective of both parents and commonly align themselves with the one they feel is being picked on or unfairly attacked.)

Sugar and Spice Stereotypes

Most modern parents want to avoid raising their children in accordance with old gender stereotypes. They want their daughters to have a positive self-image, be comfortable asserting themselves, and have wider career aspirations. They want their sons to be able to express a range of emotions, nurture others, and cooperate as well as compete. However, researchers say it is almost a given that parents will pass on the sexism they've absorbed from the culture at large because so much of it is unconscious. Other research has demonstrated the following:

- Parents react differently to videotapes of toddlers engaged in routine play. For instance, subjects describe a child's response to a jack-in-the-box as "fearful" if they're told the little one is a girl, but "angry" if they're told the child is a boy.
- Most parents are now okay with little gun-toting Annie Oakleys and are far more comfortable than in decades past when little females oversee Tinker Toy, Lincoln Log, and building block construction

sites. But many still get squirmy when a boy expresses more than passing interest in a doll or dresses up in a girl's clothes.

- Parents display more pleasure and spend more time interacting when their little boy tosses a foam rubber ball in the house than when their little girl does the very same thing.
- Girls get more encouragement for staging tea parties and playing house.
- When the daily dose of words and hugs are tallied, day care center teachers respond far more often to boys than to girls.
- Gender stereotyping on TV remains intense; it doesn't take kids long to figure out who is supposed to want My Little Ponies and Hot Wheels.
- In disputes over toys, adults commonly urge little girls to "share" and reprimand them for taking a boy's toy. Adults help little boys "protect their turf" by helping them fend off interlopers who try to take their toys.

That's So Cute!

The differences in the way adults respond to cutely dressed kids shows how subtle but powerful sexist stereotypes are transmitted. When one little girl entered a day care center dressed to the nines, the staff clucked, "Aren't you sweet!" A moment later a little boy entered the very same center. He, too, was all dressed in a coordinated outfit. The same staff members clucked, "What a darling little sweater!" The messages conveyed to these children were clear: When she dresses up, she is cute; her clothes merge with her and together form her identity. When he dresses up, his clothes are cute, but the clothes remain separate from him and he continues being who he is.

Parents as Role Models

It's not just the differential treatment from adults that instills sexism at such a tender age, researchers say. All toddlers need to do is observe the daily household routine to see that mothers devote more time to food, clothing, cleanliness, and children's feelings, while fathers are chiefs when it comes to maintaining yards, cars, and rules. (If spouses argue about who doesn't do enough of what around the house, watching who-does-what when their child starts playing house can settle it.)

Even when "Mr. Mom" is responsible for the household and the mother is the breadwinner, men relate to children differently than women do. For example, women tend to carry infants facing in, toward their chest, while men more often carry them facing out so they can see the world.

ALERT

Given that most youngsters are exposed to adult sexuality via TV shows, music videos, and commercials, it isn't surprising that curiosity runs high, or that many try to mimic the behavior they see. This is yet another reason to monitor—and limit—children's TV viewing.

It should come as no surprise that by twenty-four months toddlers are adhering to their sugar-and-spice versus puppy-dog-tail roles. If they're not, she's probably being labeled a "tough cookie," rather than a self-possessed little girl, while adults are probably running out of patience with his tendency to wear his heart on his sleeve and are searching for ways to help him develop a thicker skin.

Seeking Sexual Identity

Throughout the toddler years it is not unusual for children to cross gender lines in playtime activities. Little boys like to play with dolls because they see their mother and other adults caring for babies. Girls may prefer hero action figures.

By about the age of three, most children have a sense of who they are and what they will grow up to be. Boys will exhibit a preference for traditionally male toys. However, these days, unlike in past generations, more boys will continue to prefer to play house and make a nice honey stew for Winnie the Pooh. More households are dual career, and toddlers observe their father doing more of the housework and child care. If your little boy continues to enjoy caring for dolls, applaud him for being a good daddy.

Today's toddlers of both sexes have a wider range of behaviors to choose from and real men do paint, cook, and care for their households. Many parents are uneasy about a son being homosexual if his behaviors are too effeminate, but it usually is too early to tell.

The toddler years are a time for exploration and experimentation—dropping food on the floor, painting with juice, and turning things upside down. Gender experimentation is just as normal. Your daughter may want to use tools, help you build a bookcase. Let her, and try not to confine her in clothes that are too fussy and frilly. Don't fight or comment on a child's experimentation with the opposite gender, even if she blurts outright, "I want to be a boy!" Toddlers have learned the power of words and may try to shock you. Just stay calm.

If after the age of three your toddler expresses consistent displeasure with his or her sex, consult a doctor. For example if your little boy only plays with dolls, does not want to play with boys, and regularly wants to dress in girls' clothing or your little girl emphatically does not want to be female, it is time to request the help of a professional.

Societal expectations of boys and girls are deeply ingrained. Even enlightened parents find that as they try to be broadminded and provide gender-neutral toys for their toddlers, the boy will throw the doll up in the air as he does gravity experiments and the girl will take the doll family for a ride in the toy car. No one really knows how much of gender identity is biological and how much is environmental. Research shows that adults talk differently to boys than to girls, and boys act somewhat differently from girls, even in infancy.

Set an Example

Do what you can to offer a wide range of choices in toys and activities, but don't push. If the father shows ease in doing a variety of activities, including hugging little ones who are scared or hurt, this sets a good example for boys. If you do not have that type of man at home, it is healthy to seek out role models in the community or church group, so that your toddler has good examples to follow.

Broader Cultural Values

During past generations, men followed the desperado examples seen on the screen, believing that's what it took to be a man. Today's culture more openly supports the gentler traits, expressive emotions, and a wider range of professions. Be aware that research shows that adults tend not to coddle boys as much, and sometimes they need it! If your little boy falls down, hold him and soothe him. Support him warmly. Such well-rounded nurturing produces an adult who is a sensitive, compassionate individual, someone who is capable of loving and caring for others.

Feminist Toddlers?

Raising a girl in a non-stereotyped way might include encouraging her to thoroughly investigate the worm on the sidewalk. It probably is very interesting to her, not yucky, just as her future biology classes will be deeply engrossing. The most important element in how a girl structures her identity is the mother in the home. If the child's mom is secure, self-confident, and able to negotiate the boardroom as well as the supermarket, the little girl will grow up to have a wide range of choices.

Child development experts recommend that to set an egalitarian example in the home you can do the following:

- **Set equal examples.** Divide up the housework fairly, keeping in mind which person is good at which tasks.
- **Display nurturing.** Either parent can offer a warm lap or a friendly shoulder. Don't admonish little boys to "Be a man." Emotions expressed in a healthy way lead to a better-balanced adult life.
- **Encourage strength.** Cheer when children of either sex are able to climb high or master something especially difficult. And at the same time, if children are afraid, don't push them.
- **Gender-free toys.** Let children of either sex play with the dolls, houses, tea sets, blocks, trucks, and fireman's hats however they choose. Your little girl may grow up to be an engineer or an anthropologist, and your little boy may become the most exquisite chef.
- **Explore wide options.** Help the toddler see that whatever work is chosen, the role of being a parent is of equal importance. Try to cultivate a social life that includes positive role models so that your toddler sees loving people in a wide range of competent activities.

Most of all relax! Your common sense will serve you well in most instances. It's wise to be informed, and at the same time, trust your own judgment about sexual and gender considerations.

Let Me Be Naked!

Lots of toddlers decide clothes are something they'd rather do without. Every time parents turn around, they find their little one has managed to wriggle out of her clothes again. The dislike of clothing isn't surprising. If children are warm enough, they will feel much more comfortable with the freedom of movement that comes from being in bare skin. It may not be a problem if toddlers want to run around the house in their birthday suit, though this can get pretty messy if they're not toilet-trained. (That's an incentive some parents have successfully used with determined strippers: If you use the toilet, birthday suits are allowed at home.)

At Home and Away

Regardless of what policies are in force at home, parents should insist that toddlers observe the social niceties of keeping their clothes on outside the house. Even if you don't care, other parents will be offended. Dressing toddlers in blouses that button up the back, pants with belts, and double-knotting shoelaces can slow down little strippers so parents can catch them before they completely disrobe.

However, there's no need to be upset or to shame them about it. Since they're too young to comprehend adult views on the subject, instilling guilt might make them feel that their body is bad or dirty. It should be enough to firmly state, "Undressing outside the house is a no-no!" and to put their clothes back on again and again until they get the message. Don't comfort them if they howl; there are times when staying dressed is nonnegotiable. Also, avoid attempting to make dressing fun. Otherwise, they may conclude that removing their clothes is a way to initiate a great game.

Penis Curiosities

If your little boy notices that baby sister does not have a penis, he may become worried that he will lose his too! Keep in mind that a toddler's world viewpoint is about having things and keeping them—cookies, toys, and penises. Your little girl may notice that a playmate has a penis and want one for herself. These commonplace situations are calmly explained like this. "Girls have vaginas and grow up to be women, like Mommy, and boys have penises and grow up to be men, like Daddy. Say that boys and girls are different, and that's the way it's supposed to be. There are helpful books that explain the basics of anatomy, and you might want to include them with bedtime stories.

Potty Mouth

Children only use words they have heard someone else say. If the naughty words have come from outside the household, the best strategy is simply to ignore them, which ups the odds that they'll go away. Otherwise, you'll spark your toddler's curiosity about the magic of a word to make you laugh or get angry, increasing the likelihood he'll use it more often. Even if naughty words don't bother you, they can upset teachers, other parents, and children enough to dampen your youngster's social life.

If the offensive words don't disappear on their own, or if she's using words she's heard at home, eliminate these no-nos from the family vocabulary before they become a habit. Tell your child that saying that word is a no-no and provide a brief time-out. To help yourself and other family members clean up their vocabularies, say, "Oops, somebody just said a no-no," and put your child in charge of walking the offender to his or her bedroom for a brief time-out.

Parental Nudity

There's nothing to indicate that young toddlers are in any way harmed by exposure to parental nudity. However, they will undoubtedly have questions and may want to touch, too, so be prepared. As children approach age three, many become uncomfortable about witnessing the nudity of the opposite-sexed parent. Whether this is because they are experiencing conflict about their emerging sexual feelings toward that parent, as many psychologists believe, or because the societal taboos they have absorbed conflict with what is happening at home, it is important to respect their wish for boundaries. Eliminate joint father-daughter and mother-son baths, and close the bathroom door and oust little ones of the opposite sex from the room before changing.

Toddler Genitals

Children's genitals are very sensitive, so they readily discover that the physical sensations produced by touching and rubbing are pleasant. Fondling the genitals for comfort is also common. Some youngsters may also hold themselves in hopes of stopping themselves from urinating. It also is common for little boys to have erections. When little girls see naked boys, many express concerns about their own lack of a penis. To reassure them, parents can simply explain that little girls have a vagina instead.

Too Much Touching

Sometimes when children progress from diapers to training pants they have a heightened awareness of their genitals, and their hands may wander more often. For your toddler, exploration of all parts of the body is normal. Touching the genitals brings pleasure, and the child repeats the action. This is not masturbation or sexuality in the adult sense, even if a little boy has erections, when they do. Too much attention given to the matter will teach the child that there is something forbidden or especially enticing about "down there."

ESSENTIAL

Some children hold their genitals when they need to go to the bathroom. You will be able to learn the distinction from the circumstances and calmly ask your toddler if he needs to go to the potty.

The best approach to handling the touching? At home, simply ignore it. At play dates, try to direct the child's attention to something else. However, touching in public settings should be discouraged, as it is considered socially inappropriate. Gently teach your toddler that some things are fine to do at home in private but not out in the world. If she forgets, just quietly say it again. Take hold of her hand and suggest that she's big enough to wait until she gets home.

Parents will have to handle sexual issues in accordance with their personal beliefs. The best approach seems to be to teach youngsters the social rules: masturbation is something to be done in private. Telling toddlers that they should only touch themselves when they are in the bathroom or bedroom and must refrain when around other people can be as straightforward as telling them it's not nice to belch at the dinner table. If parents can be calm and matter-of-fact in discussing sexual issues, children will feel freer to turn to them with future questions.

Sexual Abuse

The definition of sexual abuse accepted by most child welfare professionals includes acts of exposing youngsters to sexual stimuli that are developmentally inappropriate. Parents place themselves at risk of being accused if they allow toddlers to witness parents having sex, touch parents' genitals, watch R-rated movies, or view pornographic materials. Symptoms commonly displayed by sexually abused youngsters include:

- Mimicking adult sexual behavior
- Possessing sexual knowledge and vocabulary beyond what is normal for the child's age
- Engaging in persistent sexual play (commonly with dolls, other children, pets, or themselves)
- Having abrasions, pain, bleeding, or swelling of the mouth, genitals, or anus
- Having an obsession with touching or poking objects into the genitals or anus
- Incurring unexplained urinary or vaginal infections
- Suffering from a sexually transmitted disease
- Making direct or indirect comments about having been molested
- Displaying a sudden, exaggerated upset over being touched when having a diaper changed, being bathed or helped to the potty, or during physical examinations
- Suddenly manifesting phobias or exaggerated fearfulness around particular people or in specific locations

If a parent suspects sexual abuse and there is no physical evidence, discovering the truth can be difficult. Given children's propensity for saying what they think parents want to hear, and the ease with which false memories are implanted, it's best to consult a professional with expertise in interviewing children and let him or her ask the questions.

ALERT

Youngsters need not be physically injured during molestation to suffer severe psychological repercussions. The aura of secrecy can be upsetting. Threats of retaliation against the child or a loved one for revealing what has transpired can produce significant trauma. If you suspect sexual abuse, consult a professional immediately.

Protection Against Sexual Predators

It is so easy for adults to manipulate and physically overpower toddlers that trying to teach them about bad people who hurt children won't enable little ones to protect themselves—and it can terrify them. In 90 percent of sexual molestation cases, the abuser is well known to the child.

The concept of keeping secrets is hard enough for toddlers to grasp. Don't complicate it by urging them to keep secrets about birthday surprises or anything else. It will be impossible for them to differentiate secrets that are okay from secrets that are not okay. When youngsters are old enough to understand, they can be taught that some secrets are okay and others are not, and that they must inform you immediately if someone tries to get them to keep a secret from you. In the meantime:

- Keep track of his whereabouts at every moment, and leave him with trustworthy caregivers.
- Instruct your older toddler to be sure to tell you if anyone touches her in a way she doesn't like.
- Teach your child the correct names of all body parts, including "penis" and "vagina," so if something untoward does occur, he will have the words he needs to communicate.

Societies Differ

Exactly what constitutes abuse? In societies where families sleep in the same room, youngsters routinely witness parents' sexual intimacies without ill effect. However, children are born imitators, and their playground re-enactment of bedroom scenes may be a problem in countries with more conservative sexual norms.

FACT

In most states, citizens are obligated to notify the authorities of any kind of suspected child abuse. Failure to report abuse is punishable as a misdemeanor. By making a report you are not acting as judge and jury. You can ask to remain anonymous. The police or child welfare workers will decide whether the reported suspicions warrant an investigation. For further information, or to obtain the phone number for reporting in your state, call 800-4 A CHILD (800-422-4453).

In Western societies any unnecessary touching of genitals is regarded as abuse. When youngsters reach adolescence and reflect on what transpired, they realize that a sacred parent-child trust was broken. Many spend their lives trying to heal from the devastation.

PDA—Parental Displays of Affection

How do you draw the line about what is okay for your tyke to observe and what is not? Hugging, kissing, and a pat or caress is warm and healthy for your child to see. It makes the home feel loving and secure, that everyone is cared for. Stop at the point that the embrace becomes a groping, smoldering lip-lock, steaming up the room. Such fierce passion can frighten a child and isn't really appropriate for a toddler's observation.

Toddlers may occasionally express jealousy of the parents' affection for each other. You can enfold the child into your parental embrace, so he is included. You can say, "Daddy and Mommy love you, and Daddy and Mommy love each other." Realistically, there is the private, sacred element of the adult bond that is apart from the child, and that is necessary for the strength of the family unit. Your child probably senses that, but you do not have to dwell on it because it is out of the range of comprehension of a toddler.

Caught in the Act

What do you do if your toddler catches you making love? According to Arlene Eisenberg, author of *What to Expect, The Toddler Years*, it's best to treat the interruption calmly. Ask her to wait outside the door for a moment, while you slip into some clothes. Calmly return the child to her bed. You didn't do anything wrong, and neither did she.

If your toddler seems alarmed, perceiving aggression in the adult sexuality, just provide reassurance that Mommy and Daddy were being very close in the ways that Mommies and Daddies do. No one is getting hurt. Most likely, he will be sleepy and will not require that explanation.

It's best to have a lock on your bedroom door, or at least a hook and eye so your child will not surprise you. Such incidents are usually quickly forgotten if you handle them calmly, answering any questions with age-appropriate information.

CHAPTER 4

Brainy Toys

Although putting toys in a separate category is not really how your toddler thinks, you, as the adult will sometimes trudge to the toy megastore to select something fantastic for your little one. From your child's point of view, everything around him is quite interesting and fascinating. In his mind a pan from the kitchen cupboard, something from the household repair toolbox, or clothing from the hamper are things to be investigated.

Choosing Toys and Materials

Stores today are filled with literally thousands of toys and educational items for toddlers. You have probably already discovered that not all are created equal. There are many considerations to keep in mind when purchasing learning materials and toys for your child.

Safe Toys

The first concern must be safety. Even a sturdy, well-constructed toy can be a danger for a child too young to use it. Look at the label on the item for a suggested age range. This is a not a guarantee that the toy will be appropriate for your child, but it does serve as a useful guideline. Toys for children under the age of three have special restrictions that need to be followed. They must be large enough so that a child who puts it in his mouth will not choke. Be on the lookout for larger toys with smaller parts that can fall off or be easily removed. Avoid toys with sharp edges, points, or hinges that can pinch.

ALERT

Watch for feelings of competition and keeping up with the Joneses in your toy shopping. You live in a complex culture, under a barrage of constant advertising about having more and doing more. Ask yourself if a two-year-old really needs a laptop, the latest digital gadget, or clothing with cool logos.

Worthwhile Toys

It is a common scenario. You go from store to store, desperately seeking the latest "hot" toy that your child has been demanding for his holiday gift. You wrap it up with fancy ribbons and are eager for him to open it. The moment arrives! He is thrilled when he removes the toy from the box. However, ten minutes later, when he has pushed all the buttons and rung all the bells, he's already bored with it. Then he finds a new toy that captures his interest and imagination. Sure enough, he spends the rest of the morning playing with the box!

Too many toys that are on the market today are tied into popular television programs or pop culture. While they may be very attractive to your child, their usefulness can be limited. A worthwhile toy encourages your child to use it in a variety of ways. It inspires creativity and engages his imagination, inviting him to pick it up again and again. He will find new and exciting ways to play with it as he grows.

Building a Toy Collection

As your child grows, you will be adding more and more toys and learning materials to his collection. Try to provide a wide range of items that will help your child develop in many ways. Purchase toys that will help your child practice motor skills and coordination. Good toys for toddlers include push toys, wagons, balls, and simple puzzles. Do not forget to include dolls, large action figures, dress-up clothes, and props. These toys help your child work though his emotions. They also let him try out different roles and encourage his imagination. Other toys will help your child with problem solving, and language and cognitive skills, such as blocks, games, puzzles, books, and puppets.

What the Experts Say

Jim Silver is an analyst for the toy industry and an editor for a toy magazine. As an expert, he has noticed a large increase in toys that involve viewing a screen. In fact the toy industry is not strictly called the toy industry by insiders. It is the "family entertainment and leisure business."

Of course you want to be up on the latest trends, but keep in mind that such trends are driven by the market. Know, logically, what drives the appearance of various things on the shelves and on the websites you might use for shopping. You might decide that in fact, yes, Barbie needs an MP3 player, but make it a conscious choice.

Fun and Games

Toys designed especially for kids are a relatively new invention. Just a few generations ago, toddlers played with everyday household objects and material from the outdoors. Getting modern youngsters to confine themselves to items that have been especially purchased for them can be difficult. Their favorites will probably turn out to be very different from what toy manufacturers would like them to choose!

The Best Toys

Perhaps children are programmed to master the world they will one day inherit, and that is why they automatically gravitate toward the everyday household objects their parents use. Today's toddlers live in a world of digital wonders. Their parents have been surrounded by electronics their entire lives, and it is likely that the tots of today will become technology sophisticates of tomorrow.

In any event, until TV ads and trips to the store change their minds, it won't matter to youngsters that the house doesn't contain a single store-bought toy. Toddlers' attention spans are short, but they are easy to entertain. Since everything is new to them, every room is filled with objects they find fascinating. You must watch them constantly, as they will find their own toys, pots and pans, shaving cream, and shoe polish equally fascinating.

FACT

Toddlers like toys that *do* something. If you decide to go the big-box retail store route, you might want to look at a currently popular toddler toy, The Fisher Price Learning Home. This toy plays twenty-one songs, features a doorbell with a chime, a mailbox for toddler letters, and a flower that grows. The two-sided structure teaches numbers, letters, shapes, and colors.

Parents already have all they need on hand to keep their child busy for the next two years. As every toddler knows, the pots that parents only consider useful for cooking make wonderful drums, hats, dollhouses, and containers for filling and dumping. The plastic lids from frozen juice cans are fun to stack, and the sound they make when smacked together is music to little people's ears. Before you buy lots of manufactured toys and trail your toddler around the house with long litanies of no-nos, ask yourself if the household object she's chosen to investigate must really be off limits:

- Could she actually ruin it?
- Would it be dangerous if she mouthed or chewed it?
- Does it have sharp edges or rough surfaces that could cause abrasions or cuts?
- Does it have dangling cords that could strangle?
- Could small parts be bitten off, swallowed, or cause choking?
- Could moving parts or hinges catch a hand, pinch a finger, or smash a foot?

If not, maybe it's okay for your toddler to play with it. Try not to inhibit learning! With supervised independence, your toddler will find plenty of safe items in your kitchen or bathroom to keep her entertained for hours.

ALERT

Is the toy small enough to fit through the middle of a toilet paper roll? Then it's small enough to fit into a toddler's throat . . . meaning it's really not a safe toy! Your toddler could choke on the item. Consider it dangerous.

Kitchen Utensils

Take a quick look around the kitchen, and you'll see lots of items a toddler would be delighted to manipulate, bang, stack, and, inevitably, taste:

- Beaters from electric mixers (kids love the shape)
- Ladles (show them how to use one to scoop up a ball)
- Tongs (useful for picking up small objects)
- Spatulas (show them how to slide them under a small object; see if they can move from squatting to standing without dropping it)
- Pie and cake tins (for filling, dumping, banging, and clanging)
- Cookie cutters (to put in and dump out of pie tins or cardboard boxes; check for sharp edges first)

Plastic Containers

So many foods come in plastic containers and they make great toys. Just wash them and hand them over. Be sure to save the containers from cottage cheese, whipped topping, soft-spread margarine, and yogurt. The colorful plastic tops from cans of cooking spray, and other nontoxic aerosol products also make pretty toys.

Nesters and Stackers

It's not easy to stack a few metal spoons, but toddlers practice visual/motor skills when they try. And they learn important information about shape, size, and volume by fitting items inside one another. Try nesting plastic bowls, measuring cups, measuring spoons, and plastic funnels.

ESSENTIAL

Don't short-circuit learning by providing the answer. Let their brain do the work! Toddler learning (and fun!) comes from exercising mental muscles by experimenting again and again until a puzzle problem is solved.

First, give a nesting demonstration. Next, turn the cups upside down and give a stacking demonstration. Then let them do their own thing. Just don't hover and try to dictate how toddlers play. Stacking three objects is a challenge for an eighteen-month-old. It may take days, weeks, or months to figure out how to fit nesting objects one inside the other or how to stack a group from biggest to smallest.

Little Drummers

Toddlers love to drum, and for many, their high chair tray is their favorite instrument. For safety's sake, you must draw the line if they begin beating on something breakable. Drumming can also become dangerous if they create enough vibration to cause hot liquid to slosh or spill or a bowl to topple over. Say, "Don't bang the plate. It might break!" while removing it, but don't except young toddlers to understand. If you prefer the serenade of toddler banging to toddler wailing, trade a breakable plate for a sturdier item.

Natural "Toys" from Outdoors

Some of the most enjoyable things to play with are right outside your door! For a toddler, rocks, bugs, sticks, and butterflies are enormously interesting. There is nothing as marvelously squishy as real mud. After a rain, take your toddler outside and investigate puddles, plants, flowers, and rainbows. Let your child "paint" with a paintbrush, using water on a surface that is dry. Toddlers can be happy for long periods of time collecting rocks and washing them, counting them, and categorizing them. You can join in, engaging the child in conversation about sparkles, texture, and shape.

FACT

Play is the work of young children. Play is the most powerful way for young children to learn. Some scientists have found evidence that play can sculpt the brain and build denser webs of neural connections. When children play, they literally exercise their brain cells and make them expand—a physical development that happens as your child learns.

Ordinary leaves are appealing for your toddler to play with. They offer an amazing array of shapes and types. If you live in a place where fallen leaves are raked in the fall, your toddler will enjoy playing with the piles of leaves before you dispose of them.

Other items to hunt for in nature include pinecones, nuts, birds' nests, and flowers. After a warm rain you might find earthworms on the sidewalk, which your tot will find endlessly fascinating.

Art Materials

Art materials are wonderful for your toddler to play with, as the results are expressive and open-ended. Some of the classic, tried-and-true art supplies that are always appealing include the following:

- Crayons—Take off the paper, and choose the fatter size for your toddler
- Construction paper—Keep lots of colors on hand
- Poster board—Wonderful for collage and more durable constructions

- White craft glue—Choose a washable type
- Old magazines—Good for cutting and tearing
- Scissors—Beginner's safety scissors are available for small hands
- Felt-tip markers—Choose washable markers
- Food coloring—Note: It does stain
- Recycled household materials—Cardboard tubes, egg cartons, fabric scraps
- Tempera paint—A good basic type of paint, and it is washable

Blocks

Blocks help your child develop an understanding of spatial relationships, create something from a mental concept, and refine motor skills. Block sets come in natural wood finishes or a colorful painted finish, and you can add a basic storage cart or wagon, even with your child's name on the side.

ESSENTIAL

Who says blocks have to be square? Show your toddler how to build a giant tower from a variety of household items, including pots, pans, books, cardboard boxes, or cardboard tubes.

Homemade Blocks

Cut a clean quart- or half-gallon-size cardboard milk container in half cross-wise. Push the two halves together to make a square block. A few dozen gallons later, you'll have enough blocks to keep a playgroup of toddlers happy for a year. To jazz the blocks up, cover them with plain paper or fabric and color the sides with different shapes (triangles, circles, and squares), capital letters, or numbers. Or glue on pictures of animals cut from magazines.

Hardwood Blocks

Your child's day care center probably has a cart of blocks. Spend some time there to investigate their sizes and sensory qualities. You might like to have a set at home, complete with a rolling cart, or suggest that a grandparent spring for some blocks at the next birthday or Christmas.

Shakes, Rattles, and Rings

Sew dried beans, rice, or peas into a sock or a piece of stocking; and put some sand or pasta into a plastic bottle (topped with a lid that stays secure)—your toddler has a start on a percussion band. Stitch jingle bells onto a cloth (sew them well—if the bells come off, they're small enough to swallow!), and let the tambourine music begin. What about cymbals? Why, pie tins, of course!

Pull Toys

Tie a short cord to a box or stuffed animal to make a pull toy, or tie several boxes together with string for a train. But beware! Sixteen inches is the maximum length for cord; which reduces the chance it will create a strangling hazard. A toddler's ability to get entangled in seconds is amazing.

Bubbles

Bubbles are usually a good choice for entertaining young children. Toddlers especially love to watch them float, to chase them, and to pop them. All you really need is a nice outdoor breeze and a vial of bubble solution, and everyone is happy.

Homemade Bubble Solution

Makes 5 cups. You will need:

- ½ cup liquid dish soap
- 2 tablespoons glycerin or light corn syrup
- 5 cups water

Save money and have fun at the same time. You can make as much bubble solution as you need when you need it. Just adjust the proportions to make the amount of solution you desire.

1. Mix all ingredients together. Don't be afraid to alter the proportions and experiment to create the perfect bubble solution.
2. Store in a spill-proof covered container.

For a real bubble extravaganza, on a hot summer day, make the bubble solution in a wading pool and experiment with hoops and rings of various sizes to make very large bubbles. Even playgroup parents will want to get into the action!

Puzzles

Standard wood puzzles for toddlers and preschoolers are available in beautiful colors, shapes, and levels of difficulty. Do the puzzles with your child, one at a time. If several are dumped out at the same time, you will have your work cut out for you! Your young toddler may need some explanation of the object of puzzle play, and don't be surprised if she enjoys putting them together face down or upside down. A toddler's worldview is quite different from yours!

Make Your Own Puzzles

To make a beginner's puzzle, cut several holes of different sizes into the top and sides of a shoebox so your toddler can fit blocks, small cars and other geometric shaped toys inside.

To make an intermediate board puzzle, cut a large circle from the center of a heavy-duty cardboard box with an X-ACTO knife (using every precaution around both young fingers and your own). Glue the piece of cardboard from which the circle was cut onto another square of cardboard, which will create the backing. Show your child how to fit the circle into the puzzle. Using other pieces of cardboard, make more puzzles in the shape of a square, a diamond, an arrow, and a cone. Paint them bright colors to add to their eye-catching appeal.

More Puzzles

To make more advanced puzzles, cut the front of a cereal box into three pieces and show your toddler how to put them together. Or glue a colorful picture from a magazine like *National Geographic* onto a piece of cardboard. Cut it into three to five pieces. Rubber cement is preferable to white glue, as the pictures will lie flat. Don't let your child breathe the fumes, though.

Make Your Own Finger Paints

To make your own finger paints you will need:

- ½ cup cornstarch
- 3 cups cold water, divided
- Food coloring

Pour ½ cup cornstarch into a large bowl. Blend in 1 cup of cold water; then add 2 more cups. Microwave the liquid for eight to nine minutes, stirring every two minutes until thickened. Pour it into six separate bowls and stir in food coloring. Let it cool. Then roll up your child's sleeves, give him some paper, and let your little Matisse begin. Demonstrate how to smear a layer of a single color over a multicolored drawing, and then use a fingernail or plastic spoon to scrape through the top layer to expose the colors beneath.

A Fiberglas serving tray makes a nice container and frame for finger paints. Explore with your child different ways to use the hand, fist, and knuckles to make various impressions. Older toddlers might enjoy having a print of a finger painting they made. Lightly press a piece of newsprint or butcher paper over the painting. Pat it down, and gently peel it up. Lay aside to dry. Young toddlers will not be interested in the finished product.

For a real sensory adventure, surprise your toddler with pudding for finger paint. Don't mention that it's edible, and see what happens. The fragrance will give away the secret. You will have to make it clear, after that, that not all paints are edible.

Dramatic Play

Visit your neighborhood garage sales and gather an array of wardrobe items befitting a queen, princess, mermaid, superhero, pirate, cowboy, or anything else your child likes. Keep your eyes open for cloth remnants, costume jewelry, hats, purses, scarves (pin them to shoulders; don't tie them around little necks), and shoes.

FACT

Pretending develops social skills (cooperation, turn-taking, and sharing), language and vocabulary development, imagination, and emotional expression. When toddlers engage in dramatic play, they are practicing what is entailed in being a person in the world. They try on roles and practice what to say and do in various life situations.

Kids will also appreciate things to put in a purse, such as an old comb or wallet. Applying a bit of color from half-used tubes of lipstick, eyeliner, and powder is a great accent for any outfit. (Make sure you supervise this part.) Turn your child into a superhero by pinning a pillow case cape to your child's shirt, bestowing a pizza pan shield, fashioning a tinfoil hat and wrist bands, providing a pair of gloves, and adding a plastic spatula to fend off the bad guys.

Props

Other things around the house will make dressing up more fun and engrossing—plastic dishes for a tea party, pictures of food or plastic food, furniture, a sheet over a card table for a house or hideout. Your little thespian can have a tea party for you or his favorite stuffed animals.

Down 'n Dirty

Toddlers know they've landed in heaven when they're given a garden spade or some plastic kitchen utensils, a bucket or a few plastic whipped-topping or soft-spread margarine containers, and a chance to play in the dirt. Add to that a bucket of water, and they'll probably be more contented than with any other toy. It's a given that they'll end up with some around their mouth; the challenge is to keep younger ones from getting too much in their mouth.

FACT

Children work out their understandings of relationships through dramatic play. If you step back and listen, you will hear how you speak to your spouse and your child, perfect in every tone and inflection! If you're surprised by what you hear, you can always change how people speak to each other in your home.

Of course they'll get dirty—make that filthy—but it's got to be better for kids to wallow in nature than to stare passively at television. Certainly it's easier to clean up their bodies than their minds.

Make a Sandbox

If you prefer a down-'n-far-less-dirty experience, sand is cleaner and can be more fun for toddlers to play in than dirt. If a traditional sandbox is too expensive, you can make your own:

- Dig a hole six inches deep and line it with plastic. Punch holes in the plastic for the water to drain through, and fill the hole with sand until it's level with the ground. Cover it with another sheet of plastic weighted with rocks to help keep out the rain.
- If the homemade kind is too much work, look for a rectangular plastic storage bin at a discount store, pour six inches of sand in the bottom, and pop your toddler inside—leaving the lid off, of course!

Repurpose a Wading Pool

For a quick and easy sandbox, fill an inexpensive plastic wading pool with sand.

Keep the sandbox covered, as neighborhood cats or your own cat will think it's a bathroom. And there are myriad summertime opportunities for water play with a wading pool. Keep it safe, though. Do not leave your toddler for a minute, even with just an inch of water in the pool.

Forbidden Toys

Some seemingly harmless objects that toddlers love are too dangerous to allow. Don't try to teach them that these are no-nos; to do so would be to risk an accident. Instead, simply keep the following items always out of reach:

- Any toy marked "not suitable for children under age three"
- Glitter, which has edges sharp enough to damage eyes when they're rubbed with glitter-speckled hands
- Plastic wrap and bags
- Small toys and objects that could be swallowed, such as buttons, marbles, Lego's, and deflated balloons
- String, yarn, cords, and long thin objects such as necklaces and bracelets, which can choke or strangle children
- Styrofoam products (cups, plates, bowls, and packing materials) that could be eaten

Check It Out!

When shopping for toys, be sure to look for the targeted ages noted on the box. That should help ensure that the toys are developmentally appropriate and safe. Also consider whether the toy needs batteries. If so, are they included? So many toys require them that investing in a battery charger can save not only money but also the headache of making frequent runs to the store.

Keep in mind that a lot of the fun of toy shopping is for you, the parent. Your toddler is more than likely happy with whatever there is around the house, so be aware that your emotions and perhaps nostalgia about your own childhood play into what you want to buy. You may want to be the best or coolest parent and get the newest digital gadget. That's fine, but be aware of why you make those choices.

The award-winning toys listed for this age group include Fisher Price Pull Up Ball Blast for ages nine months to three years, Brio Builder System Robot Set for ages two and over, and the Big & Small Chime Ball for ages six months to three years. Some of their recommended toys, like Imagi-bricks Giant CastleBlocks, should provide hours of educational fun for toddlers.

Toys, Toys Everywhere

There are a number of compelling reasons why toddlers need to learn to pick up their toys—and not just to fulfill your desire for a neat house. Not only will toddlers break the toys by walking on them, but also possibly hurt themselves tripping or stumbling amid the rubble. In the process of learning to care for their possessions, toddlers learn to sort and organize. Little ones won't know how to do that, so plan on doing most of the work for quite some time.

ALERT

Because toddlers slow things down to a snail's pace, it's often easier for parents to pick up everything. But when parents look ahead and consider that playthings will need to be picked up every day for the next eighteen years, they'll realize how important it is to work actively on teaching this skill now.

Toddlers do like to go back and forth between toys, playing with one for a while, moving on to another one, then returning to the first, so the strategy of insisting that one toy be put up before the next is taken out is too rigid. But to hold the chaos in check (which makes many toddlers, like many adults, feel scattered), to keep toys from becoming trampled on and broken, and to teach organizational skills, consider these guidelines:

- Have out only two or three different toys at once, not counting that special blanket or bear he wants to keep close at hand at all times.

- Keep the quantity down to items that can be carried to his room or piled into a container he can drag to the toy storage area in a single trip.
- Store toys that aren't being used much out of sight. Bring them out for a surprise on a day when you're both in the mood for something different.

Cleanup Games

When your toddler is looking for something new to play with, say, "Let's pick these up and find you a new toy." Then make the picking up of toys into a game. Ask, "How many of these can you carry?" Place one toy in her right hand, one in her left, tuck one under her arm, and another under her neck if she's a practiced walker. Keep up the fun by giving a quick tummy tickle and seeing if she can manage not to drop them.

If you're putting away toys in a carrier that a toddler can drag from room to room, toss a toy inside and then hand her one to toss inside and continue taking turns. Count aloud as you alternate placing toys in her box. Have a race and see who can pick up toys the fastest. Make the trek to her room pleasurable—this is a great time for a hiking song or a chorus of "Ten Little Indians."

A Place for Everything . . .

Designate a special spot in the toddler's bedroom or toy storage area for each toy. Show young toddlers where to put each item, handing her one item at a time, while giving verbal instructions. "The clown goes on your bed." "The ball goes in this box." "The blocks go in this basket." When the toys are put away, exclaim your congratulations ("You did it!") and help her select a new toy or activity.

When a child is old enough to want to have a say in the matter (i.e., when she's going through the stage in which when you say, "Let's pick up the toys," she refuses, and if you say, "Don't pick up the toys," she proceeds to pick them up), defer to her need to make some decisions by asking her what goes where: "Where should I put the blocks?" "Where does your clown go?" If she's being "terribly two" and refuses to put away her toys, don't argue.

But hold firm that no other toys can be played with until the other ones are picked up. Be calm and firm about this, but not punitive.

ALERT

Avoid placing toys on high shelves that toddlers might want to climb. Also avoid the board and brick storage solution from your college days, as it can easily fall over on your little climber. If you live in earthquake country, have your storage units firmly secured to the wall.

Storage Solutions

Now that traditional toy chests have fallen from grace, you can be more creative about designing toy storage that solves some of the problems big chests posed. For instance, consider these solutions to typical problems:

- Use a shallow storage box.
- Use a number of smaller containers rather than a few large ones to keep toys separated and organized. Remove the lids so toddlers can see inside. Try clear, plastic containers.
- Place toys on open shelves low on the wall so toddlers can easily see and reach their toys. You might opt to have some dishpan-sized containers on the lowest bookshelves in the family room or living room.
- Use small- to medium-size cardboard boxes, lightweight laundry baskets, or pillowcases to transport toys from one room to another.
- Make a stuffed animal holder from a fishnet or see-through beach bag and hang it on a low hook or hooks.
- Attach Velcro dots to the wall and to toys so your child can pull them down and stick them up.
- Store books in a plastic dish drainer on the floor or a low shelf.
- Attach wicker baskets to the wall (low so children can reach them) and drop toys inside.
- Place favorite dolls and stuffed animals in a low doll bed. You and your toddler can make a game out of tucking them in for "night night."

CHAPTER 5

Nos and Tantrums

Not every toddler has tantrums, but most do. Tantrums are most common between ages two and three, when there can be as many as one to two daily for several weeks. Not all tantrums were created equal, and telling them apart can be tricky. The toddler years are stereotypically known for tantrums, due in part to the fact that toddlers can be very opinionated. They have learned the true power of the word "no" and enjoy exercising their verbal prowess in no uncertain terms. For parents it can be exasperating.

Red Alert Tantrums

The toddler years are a time of rapid and sometimes uneven growth. Your little guy is busy developing a sense of separate identity, exploring his environment, and learning about life in general. Tantrums occur when he is overwhelmed. He has played for hours and hours and doesn't recognize that he is tired. He wants cookies instead of a normal dinner. He has accompanied you on several errands and has run out of patience for one more. All his various systems are on overload, and there is nothing left to do except scream with outrage.

Communication Tantrums

Sometimes toddlers throw tantrums out of sheer frustration over their inability to communicate their needs. For instance, it's very clear that your toddler wants something. It's clear to your toddler that you have it. Try as you might, you can't figure out what your child is asking for. He tries every way he can think of to get the message across, and then dissolves.

ESSENTIAL

To help your toddler feel better about the wildness within her, read *Where the Wild Things Are* by Maurice Sendak. It can comfort her to know she's not alone. She may also enjoy hearing *Alexander and the Terrible, Horrible, No Good, Very Bad Day* by Judith Viorst.

Or it is all too clear what your toddler wants: ice cream. He is sure it is in the freezer, because that's where it's kept. Except that there isn't any ice cream there or anywhere else because you're fresh out. He's sure you're withholding it, and you can't find a way to explain it to him. Maybe he wants to watch a particular movie, but the DVD is broken. Or he wants his pacifier, but it's lost. The only recourse is to provide reassurance that you would give him what he wanted if you could and let him rage at the injustice of it.

It's not easy being any age, but it can be particularly hard to be a toddler. Parents who remain sympathetic as children struggle through these trying moments may also feel helpless. Remember that by demonstrating your love for your youngster when he is at his very worst, you are in fact helping a lot.

Stress Tantrums

The toddler is stressed (tired; hungry; ill; or cranky due to a number of small disappointments, changes, and/or defeats), when some unpleasant thing happens. Perhaps he hates to have his diaper changed, and Dad insisted on it. Or Mom kept her hands on the grocery cart when he wanted to push it himself. Or his toy broke. That one small incident becomes the straw that broke the camel's back, and suddenly the toddler loses control. The screaming and carrying-on is out of proportion to the problem at hand because the upset isn't about a single event. It's the result of an accumulation of stress that has taken its toll on a tyke who, because of his age, doesn't have a lot of emotional control to begin with.

Trying to sidestep a stress tantrum may merely be postponing the inevitable. As things heat up, it becomes increasingly clear that the toddler is trying to provoke a struggle.

To manage stress tantrums:

1. Hold the child firmly but lovingly and provide reassurance that he'll be okay in a bit. This assumes you can hold him. Children may thrash too wildly to be safely held.
2. If he's endangering himself, other people, or property as he rolls about the floor, clear the area if you can. Otherwise, move him to a safe place, like a carpeted floor.
3. Let him cry it out. Tears are a great tension reliever.
4. Empathize with the fact that he's having a hard day.
5. When the tantrum ends, ask if he'd like to sit on your lap and have you rock him, or lie down and have you rub his back.
6. Provide reassurance that things will get easier for him when his new tooth comes through, he's rested, he's adjusted to his new day care center, or the stressful situation has passed.

Holding It Together

The last thing enraged toddlers may want is to be held and comforted, especially if they are furious with the person who is trying to do the comforting. Even if out-of-control youngsters attempt to pull away, it can help them to be physically held. They are relieved that someone can contain the anger that feels so huge and overwhelming to them. It is as frightening to a toddler to be out of control as it is to an adult.

ALERT

In an effort to assert this desire for autonomy and control, some toddlers may become defiant. They start to challenge limits and say "No!" to your requests. If you recognize that these behaviors are not made out of spite, you will be better able to manage them with patience and humor.

Hugging and holding by force is a no-no, however. Like infants, toddlers signal their desire for emotional distance by looking away. They may break eye contact and try to escape. They may go limp (since the dead weight makes them harder to carry). Then they try to slide to the ground. And if that doesn't work, they whimper, cry, scream, stiffen, and arch their back in an effort to free themselves.

These kinds of physical struggles make toddlers more wary of being held, as well they should. Imagine if someone five times your size, even if it were someone you loved, had you locked in an embrace against your will and wouldn't let go, no matter how much you begged or pleaded! It's not surprising that toddlers with overbearing parents or relatives become increasingly standoffish.

On the other hand, physically containing an out-of-control toddler by holding him firmly can reassure him immensely. It helps to know that a big person can safely contain those scary emotions that have taken him over.

When it comes to stress tantrums, the best cure lies in prevention. Consider them a signal that your toddler is under more pressure than he can manage and see if there's a way to help lessen it. Remember that toddlers are already under a lot of stress because they are struggling with their personal sense of inadequacy that comes from wanting to do things and being unable to do them, having lots to communicate and being unable to say much, and wanting to be independent while being emotionally needy.

FACT

In a stress tantrum, the child isn't trying to get something; instead, she is trying to get rid of the unpleasant feelings that have accumulated. Having a momentary whim gratified helps a stressed toddler feel better, but not for long. The next small crisis produces another upset of similar or even greater intensity because the real problem—feeling generally overwhelmed—remains.

Manipulative Tantrums

Some children learn to tantrum to get something. Their manipulative tantrums are their way of saying "I want something and I want it now!" Once their end is achieved—freedom to run around the store, liberation from the car seat, permission to eat the cookie or to have a toy—they settle down. Tantrums in public are common because many children have learned if they stage a big one, they will immediately be taken home, which is exactly what they want.

It can be hard to hold firm in the face of manipulative tantrums. Their fearsome intensity can quickly melt parental resolve. But of course, every time you appease the child by giving in, you drive home the lesson that screaming, hitting, kicking, thrashing, breath-holding, fainting, and even head-banging and vomiting are workable ways to achieve goals.

If the behaviors during manipulative tantrums are particularly dramatic, discuss the problem with your pediatrician to satisfy yourself that the quickest, most effective way to end this kind of tantrum—ignoring it—is a safe option. Behaviors that warrant a professional opinion include banging his head or other self-injurious behavior, or holding her breath to the point of turning purple, passing out, precipitating an asthma attack, or vomiting.

To end manipulative tantrums:

- If he's a raging puddle on the floor, tell him you'll talk to him when he's settled down.
- Carry him to an open space where he can't harm himself or something else, preferably with carpet to soften the blows, if he's flinging himself around.
- Step over him and busy yourself nearby (but out of kicking range) by studiously ignoring him.
- Remain alert to what is happening so you can intervene if he tries to hurt himself or something else.

ALERT

If the tantrum is causing a public, and disruptive, scene in a store, movie theater, or restaurant, remove the child if you can. You can deal with the tantrum, and the issue behind it, once you're in a calm and private area.

The challenge is not to take manipulative tantrums personally. See them for what they are: a child's rage at rules and limits. By failing to give in and not paying attention to him, you're showing what happens when people are assailed by crushing disappointments: life goes on.

When a tantrum ends and the child has settled down:

- See it as the victory it is—the child regained control on his own.
- Don't attempt to discuss what transpired before or during the tantrum—let the subject drop.
- Be warm enough to show him you're not angry with him—respond to his desire to be held, hear a story, or have you participate in another quiet activity once he's settled down.
- Don't try to compensate for having held firm by being overly solicitous.

If throwing a tantrum has worked in the past, the predictable short-term result when parents don't give in is an increase in both the intensity and frequency of tantrums. Confused youngsters work harder to employ the strategy that has worked so well in the past to get their way. It may take a number of scenes before they grasp that tantrums are no longer a useful method for getting what they want.

You're the Adult

During tough outbursts it may be extremely difficult to remember that you're in charge. Although the situation is trying, you do actually have a lot more maturity, knowledge, and capability than the small screaming person. Do your best not to take it personally. All children have uncontrollable moments. Your child is not behaving badly on purpose. In fact, the behavior is not directed *at* you, although you may feel that it is. The calmer you can remain during the event, the sooner it will end.

ESSENTIAL

Don't resort to hitting an unruly child. Take a behavior management course to learn physical containment ("holding") strategies. Many mental health professionals and therapeutic foster parents enroll to learn to contain volatile youngsters. Contact the Crisis Prevention Institute at 800-558-8976 or check their website at *www.crisis prevention.com.*

Resist the temptation to give your child a cookie or some other reward to calm down. This will have the opposite effect of what you want. He will learn that having a tantrum brings something desirable and will become conditioned to keep having tantrums.

"The Big Kahoona"

Harlan was angry because his grandmother wouldn't take him outside to play. "Shut up, dummy!" he exclaimed.

"Harlan," she said gravely. "Have you forgotten? I am the Big Kahoona. You must never say 'shut up' or 'dummy' to the Big Kahoona."

"What dat Big K'oona?" Harlan asked nervously.

"That is me. I am the Big Kahoona."

"Why?" he asked.

"Because that's what I am," she answered. Harlan nodded gravely. "Why don't you play in the family room until it's time to go outside?"

Later, when Harlan began asking to go outside again, he was irritated and impatient but not disrespectful. At lunch when Harlan's grandmother told him not to pour milk onto his plate, he persisted.

"What did I tell you?" she asked.

He smiled. "Big K'oona," he said. He stopped pouring the milk.

Every toddler needs a Big Kahoona—a caregiver who is authoritative, firm, deeply secure, and absolutely in charge.

Street Brawlers

Some children escalate to the point that even time-out doesn't settle them down. They leave the time-out area or destroy property. Parents must not allow destructive behavior. If children are out of control, parents need to control them. Biting cannot be allowed. The easiest cure is to give your little Jaws something he can safely sink his teeth into, like a sock or a thick rubbery something he can't shred or bite through.

Children must not hit parents, either! Sometimes it helps ground their energy to place your hand firmly on their forehead to hold them away from you. With your feet, and their feet, planted firmly on the ground, let them flail away. Don't smile at the "cuteness" of their impotent rage or otherwise reinforce this forbidden behavior. If they persist:

1. Firmly say, "No! Biting/hitting me is not allowed!"
2. Send them straight to time-out.
3. Do not give them any additional attention; some children thrive on being yelled at, so don't waste your breath.
4. Do not comfort them when you release them from time-out.

Cry Babies

Toddlers are still babies, and some are more sensitive than others. Lots of crying is to be expected. Here are a few tips to help a little one who is sensitive:

- Encourage him to use words to express his feelings.

- Recognize that crying doesn't always signal sadness. Many children cry when they are angry. Model how to express frustration and irritation by using words when you are upset and by helping him say the magic words, "I'm angry!"
- Just let him cry! Tears can relieve tension. They're only a problem when parents work overtime to make them go away.

Your Own Anger

There will be days when you think that you are just not cut out to be a parent of a toddler. You are basically at the end of your rope and do not have it in you to tie a knot and hang on. Rest assured, every parent has those days.

Dealing with toddlers is very tiring and utterly exasperating. They are rebellious and irrational. They are demanding. Once you have something worked out, they grow and change, and there is a new issue to contend with. On a particularly horrible day you may yell and scream at your toddler. That's understandable and forgivable. It does not mean that you're a horrible parent.

After an outburst like this, stop and apologize to your child. Don't go on and on. Just say simply that you're sorry for yelling and that you were tired. Go on to something pleasant together and put it behind you. This is not a time to reward your toddler by going all out with something indulgent, as that sends a confusing message. Keep the normal house rules, but do what you can to even out the emotional tone between you. Children can be very forgiving.

Hitting

If your anger has escalated to hitting your toddler, it's time for outside help. Call your child abuse hotline and speak to a worker. Then arrange for support from a clergyperson, physician, or counselor. Arrange the same for your spouse if violent tendencies are becoming apparent. Your toddler's physical and emotional well-being is at stake. If addiction to drugs or alcohol is a part of the picture, get help for that as well, as substances tend to blunt the normal control of impulses. You need an absolutely clear head to manage your frustrated emotions around the terrible two's.

If you are cooped up at home for long periods of time, seek out support groups online or over the phone. There are many such programs available to parents, and most are free or set on a sliding fee scale. Babycenter.com is a good example. Look for forums and chat groups that can support you. A lot of young parents experience the same frustration, and you don't have to be isolated with it.

Depression

If you're feeling low, it's okay to tell your toddler in a simple way, "I'm feeling sad today." This teaches her that life consists of ups and downs. It's better to be honest about it than to teach her that everyone is happy all the time. It is impossible for anyone at any age to keep up that façade.

At the same time, consider what is appropriate to tell a toddler. Don't mention that you've just been diagnosed bipolar and that your significant other was fired. A child cannot comprehend such large issues.

Try to track down what is making you feel depressed. Do you need to share honestly with an adult who will understand? Has it been weeks since you've had some time out of the house on your own? Has your social life diminished because of being a parent? Try to pinpoint the root cause and take some action. Maybe you need to pick up an interest that you've set aside. Take an art class or get back into tae kwan do. Maybe you're grieving the loss of your work identity. It might be possible to get something part-time to refresh your burned-out brain.

Communicate honestly with your spouse about the depression and together come up with a plan that is workable for the family's resources and schedule. You might need to budget more time for yourself so that you can meet friends for lunch or dinner. Maybe you want an entire afternoon at an art gallery or a night at the symphony. These are legitimate adult needs, and depriving yourself in too many ways for too long does bring on anger.

Even if it seems that the toddler is the problem, maybe you can creatively do some things together that will enrich both of your lives. Plan a trip to the zoo and take along your camera or sketch book. Indulge in creative photography of the animals to add to your mountains of photographs of your child. Fun will revitalize you and your relationship with the little one.

More exercise always helps to moderate depression and anger. Can you sneak a workout session into your week? Walk the dog in a beautiful park—alone? You might establish a regular time when you take your toddler out in a stroller, only you jog instead of stroll, perhaps with Fido on a leash running along with the two of you. You will be with your child but not interacting as much, and she will be happy with the breeze blowing through her hair. You might sneak in some time with your own iTunes while you're running.

Occasionally order out for food, put up your feet and enjoy a DVD that is perfect for your own taste. A steady diet of Barney and SpongeBob Squarepants is sure to give you media diabetes. Maybe an adult book club, in person, would invigorate your mind and spirit. Maybe envisioning a plan for a new career direction would provide some energy and hope. Investigate classes and degree programs that will take you a new direction. Could you do an online college class or even an entire degree while your toddler is sleeping?

Consciously plan your own style of time-out when you are really boiling. Walk a few dozen paces around the yard, with your toddler in full view. Don't leave your toddler alone while you're venting your steaming emotions. If you can, say out loud what you are doing. "I'm very angry right now and I'm walking a lot until I feel better. Please stay over there while I'm doing this." As much as possible, do what is appropriate so that your toddler sees good ways to handle anger. This is not the time to throw dishes or kick through the wall.

Sometimes playing music will set a new mood for you and the child. Listen to music that you love, not toddler tunes. It's your heart and soul that needs replenishing. The child is doing quite well on what you have provided up to this moment, and now it's your turn. Play grunge, hip-hop, or punk if it makes you happy, but be careful about exposure to words or violent ideas that are not right for a child. If you need to detach even more, plug into your headset and iTunes and be in your own world, but keep your child within visual range.

Write in your journal when you have time, trying to see patterns in your difficult moments. See what you can change and correct so that the hurricanes are not always hitting your house. It may take time and a little diligent tracking to fix the roots of your problems with anger and depression. You can do it. Others have managed such difficulties, and so can you.

Journaling can help you find triggering factors. Do the angry episodes occur when either you or your toddler are especially hungry or tired? Are there underlying issues? Are you angry about doing double duty—working a full-time job and handling a lot of the household responsibilities? Are there financial pressures or debt? Are your rules for your toddler too strict and unreasonable?

Time to Unplug

You may have gradually become isolated with your parenting responsibilities. True, you are connected with online communities, instant messaging and texting every day, but sometimes one craves an in-person conversation with a real live human being. Without realizing it, a lot of your time may be spent interacting with machines. Combat isolation by making a date with a friend. Some in-person shared time, especially if you can laugh and cry together, will make you a more amiable parent.

Activities to Calm Your Toddler

It is often very difficult for young children to shift gears. They are unable to go from being active and wound-up to calm and restful without a transitional time. In other words, it is unrealistic to expect that your toddler will be able to go directly from a tantrum to a long and peaceful nap. Try to have a few routines with calming activities in place to assist your child in quieting down.

Back Blackboard

Try this to help calm your child down. You can also massage your child's hands and feet this way.

You will need:

• Body lotion, if desired

1. Ask your child to lie still on his stomach. Direct him to pay attention to what he feels.
2. Use your finger to draw on your child's back. For younger children, make shapes and spirals. For the older child, you can draw specific shapes,

letters, or numbers and ask him to guess what they are. Use lotion with a nice fragrance for a variation. Ask your child what he thinks about the fragrance. Sometimes fragrances are very calming by themselves.

Blanket Burrito

Tucking in your child like this can be part of a soothing ritual. Sometimes being firmly contained like this will calm an overwrought toddler. For this activity you will need:

- Bed
- Extra blanket

1. Spread the blanket out on top of your child's made bed.
2. Have your child lie on top of the blanket on one side of the bed.
3. Tuck the near side of the blanket over him and gently roll him across the bed until he is wrapped up in the blanket roll. Unroll your child before you leave him to rest quietly or go to sleep.

This Is the Way

Just about anything goes better when you are singing.

1. Make up different verses to the tune of "Mulberry Bush." Here's an example:

This is the way we quiet down,
Quiet down, quiet down.
This is the way we quiet down,
So early in the morning.

Other potential verses might involve how to "dry our tears" and so on, adapted to whatever seems to be the child's difficulty.

CHAPTER 6

Emotional Intelligence

A large part of your responsibility as a parent is to encourage your toddler to feel good about herself. This, of course, is an ongoing endeavor throughout the years of child-rearing. However, the important building blocks of self-esteem are set in place during the youngest years. Make it a point every day to let your little one know how very precious and loved she is. Even on the loudest of tantrum days, hug your child and tell her she's wonderful.

Toddler See, Toddler Do

You and the other adults in the household set the emotional tone. Make it positive, optimistic, humane, humorous, and tolerant. Children who scream and hit have observed that in others. Children who speak compassionately to their stuffed animals and tuck them lovingly into their little bed are mimicking what they see in the adults in the home.

Growing Experiences

Between ages one and three toddlers make great strides in mastering their intense emotions. In this case, "familiarity breeds content," so toddlers encounter fewer new things that inspire fear. They know what to expect and how to behave in many situations, and they have learned to follow most of the family routines and rules. Still, even older toddlers may become upset when confronting events they find especially distressing—for instance, when Mom and Dad leave them with a sitter and walk out the door. If the toddlers have been raised in a secure and stable environment, experience will have taught them that they are not being abandoned. Although youngsters nearing their third birthday still break lots of household rules and resist routines at times, they bump into fewer unexpected no-nos while toddling through the house each day. That alone makes parenting far easier.

Emotional development during the toddler years means that as they approach age three, they shouldn't routinely dissolve into tears while having to wait to have their needs and desires satisfied. Although waiting is still hard for them, they react less intensely to small stresses but still frequently become overwhelmed and remain overly emotional by adult standards.

Growing Bodies, Growing Minds

The increased maturity of the frontal lobes of the brain plays a role in children's ever-improving emotional control, too. These physical changes render older toddlers less impulsive and more able to plan ahead, tolerate frustration, and delay gratification. Further, as youngsters develop physically, their skin becomes somewhat less sensitive, their digestive system works better, and their sleep patterns stabilize. Perhaps hunger pangs don't strike with such intensity at age three as at age one, so a minute spent waiting seems less like a year . . . and more like only half a year!

Learning to Trust

Learning to trust others is a major developmental task that has ramifications carrying over into adult years. You may have friends or have known people who cannot trust, no matter what, and they tend to have miserable lives. You have the ability to create an emotional environment for your child that will enable him to be a happy adult. It's an important job!

Being able to trust caregivers enough to accept their comfort, help, rules, and guidance is critical for toddlers' overall emotional well-being. This foundation of trust should have been established during infancy through the unwavering love and nurturing devotion of parents and other caregivers. Toddlers' growing trust in themselves complicates their trust in parents, which wanes as toddlers put more trust in their own feelings, thoughts, and ideas. Emotional swings intensify as youngsters try to balance their trust in themselves and in their parents. In order to maintain a strong relationship when trust wanes during the toddler years:

- Be true to your word.
- Invite toddlers to participate in decisions that affect them by giving them choices.
- Soothe upsets by cuddling, kissing, and speaking kindly.
- Communicate your understanding that some rules and limits are upsetting.
- Let your child's upset be her own. In other words, be aware of what is your child's emotion and what is your emotion.
- Let your child know you love her even if you dislike some of the things she does (criticize the behavior not the child).

- Show with your actions that your love and respect for her continue even when you are angry with her.
- Apologize if you become harsh and critical—this will help your child learn it is okay to make mistakes and to apologize for them.

Time Out from Multitasking

Before becoming a parent, you may have been accustomed to going everywhere with earbuds in place and managing your online accounts while texting a friend. Your toddler does not have that kind of digital sophistication, and will do best with one thing at a time. You may find that from time to time it works well for your family to turn off *everything* electronic and focus on listening to your little one, one sentence at a time. Answer each question, and follow the flow in toddler time. This orientation may seem odd in your warp-speed life, but it will ultimately create an atmosphere where your child realizes that he is more important than any digital device.

Adults who have trouble with self-assertion, feel overwhelmed by conflict, or look to their youngster to affirm their sense of self-worth may find parenting a toddler a special burden. It is draining to tangle with a power-tripping youngster several times a day—not to mention every hour. It's hard for parents not to take the struggles personally when they are the targets of toddler wrath. It's important for parents to remember that the stage of development is driving the behavior—children are not "choosing" to create problems—and that their toddler is not railing against them but against the injustices of life itself.

Just when a youngster is feeling oh-so-powerful, he finds he can't do a simple task like put his shoes on by himself. He can't float his toy car in the toilet without a big person appearing at the door to stop him. Life keeps reminding him he's not powerful at all.

It's Complicated

A parent may feel her youngster doesn't trust her to know what's best, given that the tot works hard to reverse so many of her decisions. In a sense, that's true. Toddlers often trust their own knowledge about what is in their best interest more than their parents'. Realizing they are still dependent on others to make decisions and handle even the most basic aspects of their care delivers continuing blows to a budding ego.

At the same time the fear that "If I can do it myself, Mommy might stop taking care of me" looms large. Thus, failure highlights their inabilities while success threatens their relationship with parents. Accepting the disappointing reality that their newfound power to walk hasn't transformed them into an all-knowing god, and that being able to do more for themselves doesn't mean they will lose their parents' love, takes time.

Bonding

When children can make a parent a target of their bad moods, then turn to that same parent for comfort, it usually means that they trust the parent not to retaliate. In the past, parenting experts were adamant that caretakers should avoid being too solicitous or indulgent. With the recognition of the importance of trust, the advice has changed. Rather than spoiling infants and toddlers by giving them too much time and attention, it is now believed that lots of attention makes children more emotionally secure, enabling them to tolerate more independence sooner. Experts also believe that toddlers more readily cope with rules, disappointments, and frustrations from a trusted caregiver who is loving and kind when enforcing limits.

Parents as Safe Havens

Psychologist Harry Harlow conducted groundbreaking research that demonstrated how critical a nurturing parent is for children's emotional development. His studies on young monkeys have important implications for child rearing. Harlow separated newborn monkeys from their parents and raised them in cages that were barren except for a wire mesh structure. When the little orphans nursed from a baby bottle, they would cling to the wire mesh as if it were a mother.

Despite adequate nutrition, it soon became evident that the emotional development of the little ones was seriously distorted. When Harlow placed something frightening in a cage, such as a noisy wind-up toy, each orphan would flee to a corner, hide its face, and tremble in terror, unable to summon the courage to approach the object for a closer look. Later, when other baby monkeys were placed in the cage of a little orphan, it didn't know how to play or interact with them. When the deprived orphans grew up, their emotional development was so stunted they couldn't even figure out how to mate.

Young monkeys raised with their mother were much more able to cope with the wind-up toy trauma. They fled to their mother for comfort when the frightening toy first appeared but soon became brave enough to approach it. Each time they lost courage, they ran back to their mother for support and to regroup. Within moments they were happily playing with the new toy.

The parent-child dynamics of these monkeys, Harlow realized, mirrors what happens in the human world. A caregiver to whom the toddler is attached serves as the child's island of safety when a stranger comes into the house or when she feels frightened for any reason. Once a frightened child has spent a few moments with her human security blanket, she ventures forth with renewed courage.

Stranger Anxiety

Shy, fearful behavior around strangers (meaning anyone other than the immediate family and trusted caregivers) intensifies around twelve months of age. It gradually lessens and disappears by age three except in the shyest youngsters. Negative reactions during this period tend to be more pronounced toward men than women, and least pronounced toward other children.

ESSENTIAL

Support your child's desire not to be touched by saying, "He doesn't want to be touched right now. He'll let you know when he's ready." Give your child the words to hold others at bay by instructing him, "Can you say, 'I don't like that. Please stop.' Can you say, 'Stop'?"

When a child is distressed about a "stranger" (who can actually be a relative or neighbor the child has met many times before), hold her on your lap to help her feel safe and don't pressure her to interact. Once out of the limelight and given time to observe, most toddlers grow bolder about approaching household guests. Tell Aunt Emily and Uncle Bob not to take the rejection personally.

This is not the time to teach toddlers about "dangerous" strangers, or "good" versus "bad" touching. They're too young to understand these concepts, and emphasizing the issue may make them more afraid of people than they already are. Instead, begin teaching limits by helping children ward off any intrusive actions, including hugs and kisses from "strangers," like Aunt Tanya and Great-grandpa David, and either kisses or blows from a toddler friend.

Contact Comfort

Harlow's studies on young monkeys yielded another important finding: Little orphans deprived of the warmth of a live mother monkey were less healthy than their peers. Researchers have found that this, too, has parallels in the world of humans. Youngsters in orphanages often have poor weight gain. Some sicken and die if they are not held and cuddled regularly, even if they are otherwise cared for. This medical condition is called "failure to thrive."

Experts now agree that loving human touch, "contact comfort," is a basic need, as important as food and water for physical and emotional development. Contact comfort has important health benefits for people of all ages. By learning to reach out for a hug, toddlers learn a skill that will help them stay healthy!

Soothing Touches

When young toddlers are upset, words alone aren't enough to comfort them because of their limited comprehension of speech. They need:

- A shoulder to cry on when they are sad
- A lap to bury their face in when they are afraid
- Arms to hug them and provide comfort and reassurance
- Back rubs to soothe them when they are ill
- Tickles to cheer them up

Hugging, kissing, rocking, rubbing, and cuddling have relaxing and soothing physical effects. A toddler's pulse rate slows and respiration becomes more even. Endorphins released into the bloodstream provide a sense of well-being. Soothing touches are also important for building trust and strengthening the child's emotional attachment to the primary caregiver. Studies show that youngsters in intensive care recover more rapidly if they are regularly massaged, stroked, held, or otherwise able to reap the benefits of human touch.

QUESTION

What is a comfort object?
A comfort or transitional object is the popular term for a blanket, piece of clothing, toy, or other object that serves as a child's "surrogate mother." If your child derives comfort from one, respect this important relationship! It has deep, emotional meaning to the child, just as your favorite items have deep, particular meaning for you.

Comfort Objects

Did you have a special teddy or blankie when you were small? If you can remember that far back, you can empathize with how important those special objects are to your toddler. Having them nearby can make transitions from home to car to day care to the store and back home manageable. Without, it's a disaster. It's common for toddlers to become so attached to a particular object they can't bear to be separated from it. The object doesn't have to be something soft, like a blanket. Some youngsters develop affection for a toy truck or flashlight. What matters is the bond the child has formed with it. These special objects help toddlers cope with situations that require a separation from their parent, such as going to day care or to bed.

Parents may be frustrated if their toddler insists on having the same toy at his side every moment of the day and sleeps with it at night. As the months go by and their child's grip on Mr. Teddy or his "blankie" remains as tight as ever, they begin to picture their toddler walking up to the podium at high school graduation clutching the bedraggled toy under his arm. Fortunately, no such incident has ever been recorded, and there's no reason to believe your child will be the first!

The social pressures of kindergarten can be counted on to bring a quick end to the love affair with an inanimate object—at least in public. Lots of teens still cuddle their teddy at night, so don't worry about your child's need for a comfort object, and don't push your child to relinquish it. If your child seems overly attached to a comfort object, try to give more hugs and spend more time cuddling.

Feelings 101

Much of the improvement in emotional control that takes place during the toddler years is due to youngsters' improved ability to communicate. As toddlers become more adept at labeling their feelings and communicating their needs, they react less impulsively. Youngsters who cannot talk out their feelings can only act them out. As they become more able to express their feelings in words, they don't have to rely on crying to signal their hunger, thirst, need for a diaper change, desire to be held, or wish to play with a particular toy.

ALERT

Do not ridicule, shame, or tease frightened toddlers. Otherwise, they learn to hide their fears, not overcome them. Fears may also be relayed in nightmares, or the child may lose the ability to sense danger. The goal should be to develop courage, not to create a thick-skinned daredevil.

Toddlers are not able to identify their feelings with much accuracy. They simply experience a physical or psychological discomfort and they react.

Parents and other caregivers need to teach toddlers to recognize their emotional and physical states and to use the vocabulary of feelings to express discomfort. What is obvious to an adult is not at all obvious to a little person. Parents need to make it a habit to tell toddlers what they are feeling before attempting to help with whatever is upsetting them.

Unhappy Feelings

Unhappy feelings serve a useful purpose. They let human beings know that something is wrong or that something needs to be changed. These feelings help people determine the source of their distress with greater precision. Once they know exactly what is wrong, they are in a better position to figure out how to get their needs met and desires fulfilled. Unhappy feelings indicate that something is wrong, but toddlers may not know what that something is. They may be bored but think they are hungry. They may be tired but think they are angry at a toy. They may be feeling ill and think they are sad because their parent is talking on the telephone. Parents must constantly provide corrections. Once they are able to correctly identify their feelings, toddlers will be more able to figure out what to do to feel better.

Words of Comfort

As toddlers' language skills improve, words alone are often enough to help them feel better. Whether or not words are combined with hugs, parents should apply regular doses of soothing words when calming upset children. Children eventually learn to comfort themselves by being soothed and comforted by parents. With time and repetition the comforting words parents say become so much a part of their toddler, he will use them to comfort himself.

ALERT

Always respect your child's feelings—even the unpleasant ones. Since the words you say will echo in your child's mind for the rest of her life, be kind so your child can learn to be kind to herself! Humans have a way of internalizing those earliest parental voices. Make sure they're kind, as the tape will run for decades.

Tapes of crib monologues made after toddlers have been put in bed for the night show that, to comfort themselves, they repeat the words they've heard from parents, such as "It's okay" and "Go nigh-nigh now." Other soothing phrases parents can say to their child include the following:

- "We're going home soon."
- "You'll feel better after you eat something."
- "You'll see her again tomorrow."
- "You're more scared than hurt right now."
- "It may taste bad, but this medicine will help make you well."

Trusting others to provide verbal comfort will enable children to reach out to day care teachers, sitters, and other caregivers for help and solace. During their teenage years, a phone call to share troubles with a friend or a talk with an understanding teacher will provide emotional support. By sharing feelings with trusted family members and friends, adults have access to a lifelong source of important moral support. People never outgrow their need to be nurtured!

Words That Hurt

Normal children will try to fend off criticism to maintain a sense of dignity and self-worth. The problems are likely to escalate if parents shame them for being upset. If a parent routinely heaps criticism on an upset toddler to try to settle her down, the harsh words will eventually begin to echo in the child's mind in an effort to ward off unhappy feelings whenever she is upset.

FACT

There is some evidence that emotional IQ is a critical ingredient in long-term success and happiness. Studies show that when it comes to delaying gratification and controlling impulses, children who wait their turn are more popular with peers, students who refrain from talking and getting out of their seat without permission do better in school, and young adults who go to work although they'd rather not are better able to hold down jobs.

Needless to say, that doesn't work very well. Toddlers' turmoil increases as they battle the belief that they are bad for feeling unhappy in the first place. Harsh comments made in an attempt to contain upset youngsters too often have the effect of compounding their distress. Critical comments may teach children not to verbalize their unhappiness, but that doesn't make the distress go away. The unhappiness lingers. Derogatory statements erode self-esteem. Statements that deny the reality of children's distress increase their confusion about what they are actually feeling. Instead of learning to use their feelings as a guide to getting their needs met, they end up feeling worse and don't know what to do to make things better.

Learning to Wait

One of the important things for your toddler to learn is how to wait. Life will be so much easier for him and for you when he understands that the shopping trip will be over soon, that Daddy will come home after naptime, and that the cookie will be available after eating broccoli.

One result of the information age is that people of all ages expect to get, find, and have things instantly. Most any type of information is available with a few taps of your finger and communication is speedy and to the point via text, e-mail, or cell phone. Even before your child was born, you were able to know his sex, a luxury unavailable for previous generations.

Some experts, such as writer Neil Postman, believe that having so much information available so quickly is not good for society. Past societies were able to weigh situations and people in a larger context of philosophy, culture, and history, whereas technocrats believe that something is true, simply because it's on a screen.

Patience in the Digital Age

Such immediacy is the opposite of patience, and you will need a lot of patience, as your toddler masters various tasks. You, yourself, will need to take a deep breath from time to time and realize that it takes a lot of time and repetition for your little one to master pulling on socks, eating with utensils, and waiting in line at the bank or post office.

In *Generation Text: Raising Well-Adjusted Kids in an Age of Instant Everything*, psychologist Michael Osit warns that in an immediate-gratification world your child has to learn the difference between wants and needs. Your toddler may insist, "I need the iPod" with the same insistence that she wants something to eat when she's hungry. As the parent, you help her learn the difference. Everyone has to learn that delay is a part of life and nobody always gets what he wants.

Accepting the disappointments of life, like not being able to play with the iPad one more time, is a part of gradual maturity. Osit describes it as learning to exercise a muscle. Little by little, parent and child get through the anguish of realizing that life does not always provide what is wanted. Clear, firm guidance during the toddler years prevents later nightmares, such as an adolescent demanding an A in a class or assuming that the parents will fix a traffic ticket.

Parents Set the Example

You, as the parent, need to exercise the patience and strength muscle as much as the child, as it's certainly no fun attracting the stares of other library patrons while your child is in the throes of a screaming tantrum. During such difficult times, remember that you're both learning and exercising the patience muscle. The child needs for you to be the wise, experienced adult and to help contain the rage and frustration of being unable to wait.

How do you teach a toddler to hold it together and wait?

Be calm, not angry. Parental anger triggers more emotional upset in tots, making difficult situations all the more taxing for them. Remember that there is nothing wrong with a child wanting something. When guilt and shame are added to toddlers' frustration over not having their desires fulfilled, their stress increases and that makes it more difficult for them to wait.

ESSENTIAL

Explaining "why" may be one way to give toddlers the tools they need to work out conflicts without resorting to a blowup. One study found that 75 percent of toddlers' aged twenty-one to twenty-four months tried to negotiate to get parents to alter their demands. By thirty months this figure increased to 93 percent.

Give reasons. Explain why your toddler must wait. It is all too easy for toddlers to conclude that their parent is withholding things and privileges capriciously. That compounds their frustration.

Furthermore, reasonable explanations enable toddlers to apply what they learn in one situation to another. Tots in church may not understand when a parent says, "You must be quiet now. People are talking to God with their hearts and you're disturbing them. You can talk later." But as their language skills improve and they continue to hear explanations, they will eventually understand. Then they can use their knowledge to figure out how to act in other situations where people are concentrating, such as at a live performance, instead of needing an adult to tell them what to do at every moment.

Sometimes parents can't give explanations because they aren't clear about the reasons for certain rules themselves. They only know they must be observed. If you can't supply a reason at the moment, think about it later. When you come up with a reason, share it with your toddler: "Remember yesterday when I said you couldn't use the computer until later? That's because too much computer isn't good for kids. Kids need to play to exercise their bodies and minds." There is sometimes a benefit to sharing reasons later rather than during a contentious moment. Children are more able to listen and consider the parents' words more objectively.

If children are admonished when they have difficulty waiting and hear nothing when they do wait patiently, they won't recognize that they are capable of delaying gratification of their wants and desires. When your toddler finally calms down after a scene over wanting something now, remember to point out his accomplishment. An hour after calm is restored, say, "I'm proud you were able to stop crying when I told you that you couldn't paint until after lunch. I'll make sure you get to do it after we eat."

Maybe your child's tantrum was so violent you were still trembling an hour later. Maybe complimenting your toddler for waiting seems like complimenting Dracula for having such a charming effect on women. But toddlers need to know they are in fact capable of waiting. They prove it every time their wish isn't gratified and they live to tell the tale!

ALERT

When pointing out a child's success at delaying gratification, focus on his achievement. Save the "thank-yous" for when your child has done you a favor. Children aren't doing their parents a favor by developing patience. This is a hard-won gift they are giving to themselves!

Temperament has a hand in dictating how toddlers react to frustration. Some concentrate long and hard on that tiny button as they struggle to fit it into the little buttonhole on their shirt, watching carefully to move all those little fingers just so in order to get the button lined up and in. Others have far less patience with these nerve-wracking situations. Their feelings of frustration overwhelm them, and when they are upset, they can't think clearly enough to work effectively. Work with your toddler to break the cycle of difficulty, frustration, upset, and giving up.

Me Do It!

Coping with the toddler's drive for independence can be hard for parents, and it's even harder for toddlers. Mother Nature can be capricious. She pushes youngsters to be independent even when they lack the skills needed to do things by themselves. The same child who is determined to put a puzzle together by himself may lack the fine motor coordination needed to do it. One minute she is raging at the parent who dares to try to help; the next minute she recognizes her inadequacy and rages at the parent for not helping. Then, when the parent once again tries to show the toddler how to do it, Mother Nature whispers in the toddler's ear that she must do it herself, and she is again raging at the parent for having touched her puzzle. Now that the parent has defiled it, the youngster wants nothing to do with it.

ALERT

Allow more time for getting ready in the morning and before going out in case your toddler suddenly decides she must handle some of the preparations herself, but don't allow your child to become a little dictator. Seize control when your child's attempts to be independent are inappropriate.

Children in the throes of an independence struggle put their parents in no-win situations because toddlers are caught in a series of no-win situations themselves. Their emotions vacillate wildly and their behavior becomes erratic as they insist on being independent one minute and regress to helpless dependency the next.

Toddlers in this stage may revert to the familiar comforts of thumb sucking and demand their long-discarded baby bottles back, but then treat parents' attempts to help them cut their meat as a major affront to their dignity. Long-resolved issues such as the need to wear a seat belt and hold Mommy's hand while crossing the street may become battlegrounds once again.

Although toddlers must be allowed to try to do more for themselves, having too much power frightens them. They are not ready to be independent, and they know it.

CHAPTER 7

Potty Training

Today's toddlers tend to complete potty training much later than prior generations. Twenty-five years ago, 90 percent of toddlers were trained by age two and a half. Now, one-third of children are still in diapers after their third birthday. Parents who wish to pursue a more lenient approach should prepare themselves for later completion of toilet training (or "toilet learning"), as well as questions and an occasional raised eyebrow from older friends and relatives.

Early Learning

By providing a potty before age twelve months, noting children's schedule of elimination, and having them sit on it several times a day (perhaps while you read a story to encourage them to stay put), toddlers may accept the potty as a part of life. With lots of praise for an occasional success and compensation for the loss of the pleasurable time having their diapers changed, some youngsters can be trained very young—if they are physically capable of stopping and starting the flow of urine.

Few children have this ability before age one, however. In some cases, parents who claim their youngsters were trained at a very young age may in fact have trained themselves to predict their toddler's need to use the potty and get them there at the right time. Most children will be in diapers throughout most or all of their toddler years, so parents should consider all the diapering options.

The Lowdown on Diapering

Today's toddlers will call the earth their home for many decades to come, and the only way to protect it is for each family to do its part with ecology. When the environmental toll of disposable diapers is considered, the cost is much greater than even their price tags suggest.

The Cotton Advantage

Cloth diapers can help potty training by making it easier for youngsters to feel wetness, which enhances awareness. If toddlers dislike the sensation of a cold wet diaper, cloth can increase their motivation to use the potty. Cloth diapers and plastic pants won't leak if they're 100 percent cotton and don't contain synthetic batting to give them that thick and fluffy feel. Unfortunately, polyester-filled discount brands fool lots of parents into believing that cloth doesn't work well. To ensure that the nap doesn't end up lining the dryer, avoid flannel and terry cloth. Choose cotton with long fibers. You might try cotton diapers and a diaper cover with Velcro tabs to eliminate the need for old-fashioned pins.

Easing Diaper Cleanup

Contrary to popular belief, there's no need to dunk dirty diapers in the toilet or lug water-filled pails to the washer. Drop the stool into the toilet (it's easier with diaper liners), and then toss the diaper directly into a covered pail. Store wet diapers in a separate covered pail.

FACT

If you hate the toilet-dunking routine for messy diapers, there is an alternative. A product called Little Squirt functions like a high-powered sprayer. It attaches to the water supply of the toilet—and it's outside the wall so you don't have to cut through your wall to install it. Spray the contents of the diaper or reusable liner into the toilet; then toss the diaper into the diaper pail without ringing it out. The valve contains a safeguard to keep youngsters from rinsing down the entire bathroom.

Professional laundry services put diapers through as many as sixteen wash cycles, but they can be laundered at home with fewer cycles. Here's how:

1. Besides your regular dose of laundry detergent and bleach, for extra help neutralizing the uric acid, add ½ cup of baking soda to each cycle.
2. Run the dirty diapers through the cold cycle of the washing machine to prevent the stains from setting.
3. Add the wet diapers and put them both through a warm-water cycle.
4. Run them through a third cycle of very hot water.
5. Give them an extra rinse.

Down with Diapering!

If changing time is turning into a battle of wills, check for diaper rash. If you discover a chronic or acute rash, check with your pediatrician. If nothing is physically wrong, it's probably just toddler independence asserting itself. Here are some tips to ease diapering struggles:

- Let your toddler be the official helper, handing you each item as you ask for it.
- Change the location. Spread a towel on the floor or on a bed instead of using the changing table—which may also be safer if your child is thrashing about.
- Have everything ready and laid out so you can finish fast.
- Choose easy-to-put-on diapers—cloth with Velcro tabs or disposables.
- Provide a novel toy that can only be played with during diaper changes.
- Play the "Where is Daddy's nose?/Where is your hair?" game.
- Sing a song or recite a familiar nursery rhyme. But instead of delivering it at normal speed, vary the cadence from very fast to very slow and provide a surprise burst of tickles.
- Tell your child that when he is old enough to use the potty by himself, life will be oh-so-much better!

ESSENTIAL

If your child hates having her diapers changed, play "magic tickles." Bet your child that you can make her laugh without touching her. Slowly move your hands over her bare tummy, getting as close as possible without touching her, and wiggle your fingers while telling her not to laugh. Most toddlers will soon explode into giggles!

Fearless Potty Training

It's not surprising that many parents approach potty training with such trepidation. Psychologists once thought that the methods they used had a major hand in children's personality development. Sigmund Freud went so far as to state that parents' toilet-training methods dictated a child's eventual career choice! The good doctor believed that overly lax methods would result in the kind of sloppiness that would prompt adults to enter careers like painting. Harsh training methods would lead to controlled youngsters who would enter fields emphasizing the traits of frugality, obstinacy, and orderliness, which Freud considered typical of bookkeepers and accountants.

There is absolutely no evidence that a parent's approach to potty training has anything to do with forming personality, much less career choices. Yet people still refer to exacting, over-controlling adults as having "anal personalities," and many believe these traits stem from their potty training experiences. Indulge their fantasy if you wish, but know that the research suggests that they're wrong.

Who's in Charge?

In potty training toddlers, parents can do absolutely everything "right," but youngsters won't be successful until they are physically ready, are intellectually capable, have mastered the complex mechanics involved, and decide to refrain from wetting and soiling. In many families, the last point is the stickler. Since readiness tends to occur at the time toddlers are entering a particularly oppositional stage, the foundation for difficulties is laid if parents are very anxious to say goodbye to diapers. Starting potty training very early can be a way to lessen conflict—assuming the child is physically ready. The time to begin is before the actively oppositional period begins. On the other hand, starting potty training very late also lessens conflict—assuming parents can resign themselves to dealing with diapers.

You Are Powerless!

Even if parents are very strict and insistent, potty learning offers parents potent lessons in accepting their fundamental helplessness. When it comes to deciding when and where to go to the bathroom, all the punishments and praise and presents you offer may not make much of a difference. For once, toddlers are in control. All parents and caregivers can do is teach children what they need to know to be able to use the potty, help them acquire the specific skills, try to increase their motivation, and remain confident that if nothing else, the social pressures of kindergarten (if not preschool and day care) will provide an incentive powerful enough to zap the thorniest resistance.

Physical Readiness

In order to be potty trained, children must be physically capable of controlling bladder and bowel, which means their central nervous system must have matured to the point that they can control the sphincter muscles that stop and start the flow of urine and expulsion and retention of stool. To achieve nighttime control, the child must be awakened by the sensation of a full bladder, so staying dry at night typically comes later.

It's not possible to be certain whether a youngster's muscles are still automatically giving way when the bladder fills to a certain point. A toddler may have enough physical control for successful potty training if he:

- Remains dry for three to four hours at a time
- Awakens from a nap with a dry diaper
- Passes a substantial quantity of urine at one time
- Has bowel movements that occur at predictable times
- Has well-formed stools
- Routinely goes to a specific place to urinate or have a bowel movement (e.g., a corner of the living room)
- Is able to stop the flow after urination has begun

ALERT

There is no way to be certain that after experiencing the urge to urinate, the child has the physical control of the sphincter to stop the flow. Punitive methods can cause youngsters who cannot comply with demands to feel incompetent, ashamed, and humiliated. Parental kindness and patience are in order.

Cognitive Readiness

Using the potty is a complicated affair. In addition to being able to recognize and communicate the need to go to the bathroom, and follow instructions on where and how to use the toilet, children must be able to:

- Understand how urinating and passing stool happens (that it comes from inside the body)
- Understand the purpose of the toilet (that they are to go to the bathroom there)

- Discern when their bladder is full (recognize the physical sensation of the urge to urinate)
- Recognize the urge to have a bowel movement (recognize the physical sensation of the urge to pass stool)
- Consciously contract the muscles of the abdomen to push out urine and stool while simultaneously relaxing the sphincter muscles

Psychological Readiness

Youngsters must also be emotionally up to the challenge. Psychological readiness includes:

- Being proud of their accomplishments
- Enjoying independence
- Wanting to wear underwear
- Disliking wet or soiled diapers
- Being able to sit quietly for five minutes
- Not being in the midst of a phase of toddler negativism
- Not being distracted by other major stresses
- Has a good relationship with adults he wants to please

ESSENTIAL

Reading can facilitate potty training in several ways. Read toddlers a story to prepare them. Then, after buying a potty, read to them daily while they sit on it. Check out *Everyone Poops* by Taro Gomi or the *Once upon a Potty* series by Alona Frankel.

Parent Readiness

Parent readiness matters, too! Choose a time when you aren't under a lot of stress so you can be patient. You should feel very comfortable with your baby taking yet another giant leap toward independence, and have the time to be on call for at least two days. Children need far more than two days to learn, but working parents can at least help toddlers have some concentrated practice to get them started. Then the methods being used at home need to be discussed with day care center staff and babysitters so potty training can continue during the week.

Seeing Is Believing

Before toilet training can begin, toddlers must be aware that their urine and stool come from them, and that elimination is an act on their part. If they are always in diapers, they may think all those wet and soiled clothes happen by magic. They may have better luck making the connection by:

- Having the opportunity to watch others use the bathroom. Some parents aren't comfortable with this, but it can really speed things along! Sometimes an older sibling is willing to demonstrate. Many children have opportunities to witness peers using the potty at day care.
- Being repeatedly told that they are having a bowel movement when they are grunting or straining. If you can tell when your child is going in his diaper, be sure to point it out!
- Observing themselves in the act. Letting them go around the house without clothes is messy, but toddlers simply must be able to observe that urine comes from their own body. Letting them be naked in the backyard in summer is a solution for some families.
- Watching the contents of their diaper being put into the toilet. This doesn't guarantee they'll make the connection, but may help some youngsters make sense of what is supposed to happen.

What's in a Name?

What's in a name? Far more than some parents might anticipate. Toddlers need to learn the vocabulary of the bathroom: potty or toilet, clean and messy, wet and dry. They need words for urine and stool, too. Parents may think it's funny when their toddler refers to bowel movements as "shit" or "crap" and to urine as "piss." But professionals from pediatricians to teachers will find such language unpleasant, and most other parents will be appalled.

Older children can learn that certain words are too offensive to be used in school and other social situations, but for toddlers it's an all-or-nothing proposition.

Alternative acceptable words for "number 1" are variations on pee, pee-pee, tinkle, and wee-wee. For "number 2," it's things like BM, poop, poopy, and do-do.

Some child development professionals urge parents to avoid words like "stinky." They point out that negative terms can make youngsters feel ashamed of what is a normal bodily function. And if they feel ashamed, they might not want to admit when they need to use the potty. That makes toilet training difficult indeed!

Get Ready

Buying a potty seat can be an opportunity to begin generating enthusiasm for training, but no matter how excited toddlers seem, parents shouldn't expect miracles. Once it's out of the box, they may be more interested in wearing the seat on their head than in sitting on it. It's better to start toilet training with a self-contained potty unit that sits on the floor. Sitting on a toilet so far from the ground can be scary for toddlers. Later, parents can provide a stepping stool and a specially designed toilet seat insert. The insert offers additional security by ensuring they don't fall in.

FACT

Musical potty chairs are intriguing during the initial stages of training. Some play a little tune when the child sits down. Others have a moisture-activated sensor, so that when children tinkle, they receive instant positive reinforcement: a chorus of "Old MacDonald." No tinkle, no tune. It provides toddlers with that all-important sense of personal control—only they can make it work.

Parents will need to explain what the potty is for: "This is where people put their poop and pee so they don't have to wear diapers. I'm going to teach you how." Having a teddy bear sit on it and discussing the bear's pride in being a big boy with a potty all his own can give a toddler a chance to observe and become comfortable with the situation before she tries it. Here are some other tips:

- Unless a child wants to remove her clothing, it's a good idea to suggest she remain dressed so the feel of the cold, hard plastic doesn't alarm her. The goal should be to get the child to sit on it every day for a week with clothes on. (But of course, if she wants to remove her pants and/or diapers, so much the better!)
- Some children are more amenable to sitting on their potty while their parent uses the toilet or while being read a story, singing songs, or playing with an iPad. Forcing them to spend time sitting on the potty can lead to power struggles, so parents should decide in advance whether they're going to adopt the firm "you need to do this now" approach or let the child proceed at her own pace, although later they may decide to switch tactics.
- Whether or not their youngster sits on it, parents should be sure their toddler understands that she can use it whenever she wants, and should ask if she wants help. Take your toddler with you to the bathroom after each diaper change, and reinforce the message: "Your pee goes here" (point out the potty). "Your poop goes here" (scrape it into his potty so he can see it).

ALERT

When buying inserts, parents should beware of brands that have a raised splashguard. Eventually most toddlers bump into it, and that can be painful enough that they refuse to use the toilet again. Some potties can be moved onto the toilet when the child is ready, and the continuity can make the transition easier.

Put down the potty lid, but don't transfer stool to the toilet for flushing until the toddler has left the room. Children may enjoy flushing, and the chance to pull the handle on the tank may serve as a big incentive to use the potty. But unless parents are certain that their youngster isn't afraid of the sound and motion, it's better not to let them do it. Flushing can take on a whole new meaning when youngsters realize that it causes something of theirs to disappear—a fact they may not have grasped when parents cleaned or discarded their disposables. They may think that their stool is a part of their body, and it could be distressing to see it go down the toilet drain.

The Next Steps

After toddlers have become comfortable sitting on the potty fully clothed, the next step is for them to become accustomed to the feel on bare skin. This is a good time to introduce training pants that can be pulled on and off.

Disposable training pants may prevent children from feeling the wetness. Since they need to be able to distinguish the difference between wet and dry, cloth may be a better choice while they're awake. However, disposable training pants may be more convenient at night while children are still bed-wetting.

Small, electronic sensors are available that can be attached to diapers to indicate when they are wet or becoming wet. The sensors make a slight beeping sound or emit a light to let you and your child know what is happening inside the diaper.

Teaching Hygiene

Using the potty will be messy for little boys who insist on standing to urinate. Learning to aim takes practice, and splashing is inevitable. If they won't sit, have them climb onto a stool to urinate into the toilet. Make sure the stool is stable and doesn't slide. Teach children basic hygiene.

- Show them how much toilet paper to use.
- Teach girls to wipe from front to back so they don't introduce bacteria into the vagina.
- Consult your pediatrician for ways to care for an uncircumcised penis as your son goes through the potty training process.

- Provide a stepping stool so they can reach the sink.
- Help them turn on the cold water, apply soap, rub their hands together, rinse, and dry them with a towel. Explain the danger of turning on the hot water.

Many stomach and intestinal upsets that parents believe to be a mild case of flu are actually bacteria from poor bathroom hygiene. Toddlers spend a lot of time with their hands in their mouth; they must be taught to wash carefully every time they go to the bathroom.

Rewards and Praise

Lots of parents recognize that their personal interest in potty training is much greater than their youngster's, so they happily invest in a quantity of Hot Wheels, stickers, cookies, or other items to make the potty experience worthwhile. At first, rewards can be given for simply sitting on the potty for five minutes. Later, the parent can up the ante a bit. Keep in mind, though, that a small toddler does not have an adult conception of time.

ALERT

Many toddlers are content to wet their diapers, but try to avoid piddling on the floor. Many also love to run around the house naked. Allowing them to go without clothes can serve as an incentive for them to use the toilet, but you must be willing to clean up accidents patiently.

Target Practice

When parents turn potty time into a game, most kids can't wait for the chance to play. The standard procedure is to draw a bull's eye with a magic marker on a circle of tissue paper. Drop it into the potty, and see if your toddler can take aim, fire, and score a hit. Alternatively, drop a Cheerio or a square of marked toilet paper into the potty and see if the child can hit it. (This is easier for boys, but fun for all.) Boys can also try to roll a Ping-Pong ball around the bowl. (Disinfect both the ball and the hand that retrieves it afterward.)

FACT

Although the interruption of usual family routines during a trip or vacation can set potty training back, it may be better not to worry about it until returning home. Otherwise, it's a good idea to pack up the potty since strange bathrooms, which many toddlers find scary, can cause a setback. For a truly portable potty you can use in the car, try a plastic ice-cream bucket for girls and a plastic jar for boys.

But if parents lose interest in the games before their toddler and decline to participate, the child may decide diapers are preferable. As much as toddlers are determined to prove their independence by opposing every parental suggestion, they need all the attention of a little baby. If forced to choose, most toddlers would probably decline to grow up.

Up with Undies, Down with Diapers!

Have your child help select underwear that can be worn as her reward for sustained continence. Let her break out her new attire when she's made it through a full day without an accident.

To increase interest in using the potty for toddlers who are intently working on independence and autonomy issues (that is, going through a very oppositional stage), parents can try making a studied show of having lost interest in it themselves. Employing a bit of reverse psychology works best if a youngster has demonstrated some enthusiasm for learning, but the pattern has been for enthusiasm to quickly fade. Some of these strategies are a bit harsh; parents need to beware, since by using them they risk creating still more control struggles:

- Suggest your tot relinquish pull-on training pants and return to diapers.
- Allow the youngster to experience the discomfort of wet and soiled diapers by being less responsive to changing them. (Delaying a few minutes is enough—the point isn't to torture little ones or to cause diaper rash!)

- Pick her up for a diaper check or change when she's engrossed in a fun activity.
- Eliminate the fun and games when changing her.
- Be less solicitous and more businesslike.

Bed Wetting

At age three, an estimated 50 percent of three-year-olds still wet the bed. Within six months, the figure drops to 25 percent; at age four, it's down to 20 percent. Bed-wetting is considered normal until age six, but the figures remain high for young adolescents, too: 8 percent of boys and 4 percent of girls. The reasons for bed-wetting are not well understood. Genetics may play a role, since studies show children who achieve nighttime continence late often have a parent who had a similar problem. Sleep patterns of hyper-active and depressed children are such that they may not awaken when they need to use the bathroom.

To help eliminate bed-wetting, try the following:

- Limit fluid intake before bedtime.
- Have youngsters use the bathroom right before going to bed.
- Try to determine the time at which the bed-wetting usually occurs, set an alarm, and walk your toddler to the bathroom during the night.

Compassion and Kindness

Children who wet the bed need to be handled with compassion. Parents need to trust that children don't like to wake up in a cold damp bed, and should avoid using shame, humiliation, and punishment. Instead, parents should use a sturdy plastic sheet and involve older toddlers in the cleanup. They should be able to help with removing the sheets and putting them into the laundry basket. Older children can sometimes overcome the problem by using a moisture-activated device that awakens them.

Bowel Problems

Many toddlers continue to have a bowel movement everywhere and anywhere, except the potty. Some are trained for a time and then regress. Is this yet another sign of the uncanny affection toddlers have for their poop? Is it a reaction to the discomfort or embarrassment of sitting naked on a potty for an extended time? Could it be a last-ditch effort to hang onto babyhood? Or perhaps it's an assertion of toddler autonomy?

Most parents never do decipher this puzzle. One thing is certain: If it's a struggle for control, parents are probably doomed to lose. Those who become angry and punitive may find themselves dealing with chronic soiling, known as *encopresis*. If this condition persists, you may have to start over with toilet training, or in the extreme—wait for kindergarten peer pressure to solve the problem.

FACT

How would you feel if your insides fell out and disappeared forever? This simple misunderstanding is what causes so many toddlers to work overtime to prevent disaster by becoming constipated or secreting their stool around the house. Many potty-resistant toddlers have made a dramatic turnaround after hearing the simple explanation: "When people eat food, their body uses what it needs. Then it gets rid of the part it doesn't need, which is the poop."

So why do some children insist on having bowel movements anywhere but the toilet? In the absence of an underlying medical problem, resistance that develops into full-blown *encopresis*—constant soiling—often develops from a predictable chain of events. The child is slightly constipated, and it hurts to go to the bathroom. When he does manage to pass a hard stool, it splashes cold water, startling the child. He becomes afraid and withholds stool. Eventually liquid passes around the hardened stool, making a rather continuous mess.

To break this difficult cycle, increase his intake of fruits, vegetables, and fruit juice, and keep him well hydrated with water. If that doesn't help, check with the child's pediatrician about administering a stool softener such as mineral oil. A good stool softener will make it impossible for children to contain bowel movements once it takes effect. Since mineral oil can interfere with vitamin absorption, it may be necessary to add a multivitamin; mixing it in juice can make it more palatable.

QUESTION

Can a child stop having bowel movements for psychological reasons?
The book *Dibs in Search of Self* by Virginia Mae Axine describes an interesting case in which a young, highly sensitive and intelligent child completely stopped having bowel movements. The child and play therapist work together to understand and overcome the distressing problem.

Once the child has been having regular soft bowel movements for ten days, rectal soreness should be completely healed. At that point, it is time to work on having bowel movements on the potty. For starters, have the child sit on the potty or toilet for five minutes every day at the time he usually goes, wearing pull-on training pants while seated. Wearing the training pants should add to his feelings of safety and ensure no splashing occurs if he is on the toilet and does have a bowel movement.

If his resistance is too strong to be overcome by reassurance and pep talks alone, offer stickers, toys, or special privileges. Set a timer and engage in a quiet activity he enjoys, such as reading a book, listening to iTunes, playing with an Etch-A-Sketch, or reciting nursery rhymes. Reassure him that the point isn't for him to have a bowel movement; it's to learn to relax while sitting on the toilet.

Once he's sat for five minutes without a struggle for at least three days in a row, it's time to up the ante. Make rewards contingent on having a bowel movement there. Ask him to tell you when he needs to go. After a week of having regular bowel movements on the potty, his memories of the trauma are fading (You hope!). At that point, have him remove his training pants and try having a bowel movement in the potty or toilet. Continue to set a timer to ensure that he sits for five minutes, but only provide a reward after he actually uses the potty, which may be later in the day.

CHAPTER 8

Safety First

What can toddlers get into? The obvious answer is, everything within reach. But how far, exactly, can they reach? Much farther than you might think possible! Consider everything that can be climbed on, fallen off of, pulled open (or over), and used to extend their reach. The list of hazards is endless. Use common sense and watch carefully to see the kinds of danger your child might get into. Your child is rapidly growing, and what was safe one day might be unsafe the next.

Instant Trouble

Faster than a parent can dash to the next room to answer the doorbell, run to the kitchen to remove burning food from the stove, or hurry to pick up the phone, a toddler can get into serious trouble. After an accident, the common parental refrain is, "But I only turned my back for a moment." Parents never dream their child would eat Grandpa's medication lying on the table, or that their toddler, in the midst of having a bath, would turn on the hot water.

ALERT

If you suspect your child has ingested something he shouldn't have, call Poison Control immediately. Keep the phone number posted by every phone in your home: (800) 222-1222. For serious injuries, call 911. Make sure babysitters and other members of your family know the location of emergency numbers.

Safety at Home

Some basic safety precautions should be obvious to every parent. In fact, child welfare departments consider them so basic and obvious that if parents don't adhere to them, they could be charged with "child endangerment" or "failure to protect," which means that their toddler could be placed in foster care while the parents attend court-ordered counseling sessions and parenting classes. Here are some ways to toddler proof the home:

- Cover unused electrical outlets with plastic guards or heavy furniture.
- Replace frayed electrical cords.
- Install safety latches on cabinet and appliance doors and toilets.
- Keep plastic bags out of reach. (Use cloth bags or boxes for storing toys; store food in waxed paper.) Suffocation can occur very quickly.
- Place small items that could be swallowed out of reach, including buttons, coin collections, and marbles. (Don't forget to hide the dish containing hard candies, too.)
- Lock up knives and other sharp or pointed objects.

- Unplug small appliances such as hair dryers, blenders, and toasters; and don't let the cords dangle from countertops or dressers.
- Beware of uneven carpeting and rugs that slip. (Put skid-proof mats on tile and hardwood floors.)
- Lower the thermostat on the water heater to prevent scalding.
- Keep garage door openers and other gadgets out of reach.

Firearms

Parents must keep guns and ammunition locked, and they must store them separately. Hiding them isn't enough, and here's why: An investigative news reporter interviewed youngsters in their homes about where the family's gun was located. As the cameras rolled, the common response was, "I'll show you, but you have to promise not to tell. I'm not supposed to know." One youngster after the next then led the reporter to a suitcase stored under the parent's bed, to the bottom of the stack of clothes at the back of a dresser drawer, or to some other "secret" location. In one case, the reporter examined the gun and said, "But there aren't any bullets in here." "Up there," the little one said, opening the closet door and pointing to a shelf high above his head. He indicated he'd need a chair to reach the box.

Teaching preschoolers about the dangers of guns made no difference. Immediately following the talk, the children were placed in a playroom with a box that held toy guns and a real one. They didn't even pause before going straight for the steel. The moral for their astounded parents was clear: Hiding firearms isn't enough. They must be locked up. (And if you have youngsters, consider not keeping any firearms in your home at all.)

Bathroom Safety

Bathtub seats are a factor in many toddler accidents, so if you use them, keep these points in mind:

- Collect everything you need—towels, shampoo, soap—before filling the tub.
- Don't trust an older sibling to supervise. According to a study, eleven deaths occurred when a big brother or sister was left in charge.

- Ignore the doorbell, the incoming text, and the soup boiling over on the stove.
- Ignore your other child's call, too. Studies show that 24 percent of the deaths occurred while a parent ran to check on the other child.
- If you leave the bathroom for even a second, take your dripping baby with you!

ESSENTIAL

For questions about the safety of any product, call the U.S. Consumer Product Safety Commission hotline at (800) 638-2772. They will give you recommendations about which items are best for your child.

Toy Chests

When the toddler reaches inside a toy chest and the lid falls on her hand or head, the result can be serious injury or even death. When a child climbs inside and lowers the lid, the result can be asphyxiation. The safety standards for a toy chest include the following:

- A hinged lid that will stay open rather than falling shut with gravity
- No latch, so a child who has crawled inside and lowered the lid can push it open
- Air holes for ventilation

When shopping for a toy chest, check for all three safety features, especially check the lid's hinge or select a box with a lightweight top. If you're using a metal trunk or another box to store toys, remove the lid.

Safe Strollers and Playpens

While in a stroller, toddlers are apt to lean out to look, rock from side to side when excited, and hurl themselves about when angry. To guard against tips and spills, choose a stroller with wheels set far enough apart to provide a wide base and with rear wheels positioned behind the weight of the toddler. Before making the purchase, check to make sure the stroller doesn't become unstable when the toddler is in a reclining position. The latches should also be secure enough not to open by accident. When your toddler is in the stroller, keep her seat belt on, even when she is sleeping. And be careful when opening and closing strollers. This is a prime time for parents and toddlers to pinch their fingers.

When purchasing a playpen, check to be sure that the holes in the mesh are small enough so toddlers can't step into them and climb up the side. Don't leave toddlers unattended in mesh playpens with a side down. Tots can become caught and strangle in the loose mesh. The bars on wooden pens should be no more than two and one-half inches apart so toddlers can't get their head caught.

Poisonings

In the event of chemical poisoning, have the container by your side when you call poison control so you can answer questions by reading the label. If the poisoning is from a plant and you don't know its name, take a piece with you to the phone so you can describe it, or to the emergency room so you can show it. Be ready to provide the following information:

- The brand name and ingredients (for medicines and chemicals)
- The species name (if you know it)—the shape, size, and color (if you don't)—for a plant the child ingested or the insect or animal (such as a snake) that bit him
- An estimate of how much material was ingested
- How much time has elapsed since the poisoning
- The child's condition—behaviors and symptoms
- Any medical problems or allergies the child might have

In the event of a poisoning emergency:

1. If your child has collapsed, is having convulsions, has stopped breathing, or you feel that the amount or kind of the ingested poison is going to require a trip to the emergency room, call 911.
2. Don't wait to see if accidentally ingested medication actually has an effect before calling poison control. It's better to be safe than sorry!

3. Keep a one-ounce bottle of syrup of ipecac for inducing vomiting on hand for each child in the home, but *do not* induce vomiting unless a medical professional says to do so. You can double the problem if the ingested poison is the kind that burns the throat.

4. Call a neighbor for help while waiting for an ambulance so you'll have a cooler head on hand, and someone to help with your other children.

Chemical Potpourri

Modern households are filled with substances that parents may never have thought of as being particularly dangerous . . . but that's because they never considered eating them!

ALERT

One of the more dangerous substances for toddlers is lead, which has been linked with lower IQ, aggression, and antisocial behavior. Since lead is commonly used in paint, especially in older homes, parents should be especially careful about sweeping up chips and flakes from walls and window frames. Check your blinds, too; some newer models have lead-based paint. If you discover lead in your home, alert your pediatrician and see about having your child tested.

When parents are childproofing the house, they should be careful that all of the following potentially hazardous substances are beyond children's reach:

- Ammonia
- Antistatic products
- Batteries
- Bleaches
- Boric acid
- Caulk
- Cigarettes and nicotine
- Cleansers
- Dishwasher detergents and rinses

- Disinfectants
- Drain cleaners
- Dyes for fabrics and foods (And unless that Easter egg dye says "non-toxic," watch those eggs like a hawk!)
- Fabric finishers and softeners
- Fertilizers
- Fire extinguishers
- Fireworks
- Floor cleaners and polishes
- Gasoline
- Herbicides
- Incense
- Indoor plant foods
- Ink
- Insect repellants
- Insulation
- Kerosene
- Laundry detergents and additives
- Lighter fluid
- Matches and lighters
- Mothballs
- Oven cleaners
- Paints (including watercolors)
- Pencil lead
- Pesticides
- Photographic chemicals
- Polishes and waxes
- Room deodorizers and air fresheners
- Rust removers
- Soldering flux
- Stain removers
- Starch
- Stripping agents
- Toilet bowl cleaners
- Typewriter correction fluid

Poisons via the Eye

If a child gets a dangerous substance in her eye, call 911 or poison control to see if there is a need for professional medical attention. Recommendations typically include the following:

1. Fill a pitcher with tepid (not hot!) water.
2. Keep the child from rubbing his eyes by wrapping him in a blanket, sheet, or towel that is large enough to keep his arms at his sides.
3. Do not force the eyelid open.
4. Pour the water into the eye from a distance of two to three inches.
5. Repeat for a full fifteen minutes.
6. Encourage the child to blink as much as possible.

It's wise to inform yourself about poisonous plants, or better yet, do without houseplants while you have a toddler. Become aware, also, of various kinds of insects whose bites and stings could be drastic for your toddler. Also, purge your drawers and cabinets of perfumes and cosmetics, as these are dangerous if your toddler swallows them.

Dangerous Gases

The following gases are hazardous: carbon dioxide, carbon monoxide, chlorine, methane, natural gas, and propane. In the event of an accident:

1. Avoid breathing the fumes yourself.
2. Get your toddler to fresh air fast.
3. Open doors or windows (if this can be done without spreading dangerous fumes)
4. Administer artificial respiration and chest compressions if the child isn't breathing and call 911.

Buckle Up . . . Carefully

The leading cause of death in children ages one to four is unintentional injuries, and the vast majority of those are incurred during automobile accidents. Don't even think of starting your car engine until your toddler is securely fastened into a car seat or, for children over forty pounds, until she is buckled into a seat belt. But first, be sure to have done your homework:

- Check with the car seat's manufacturer. There have been numerous recalls in recent years; more than 10 million models have been deemed unsafe. The handles break on many that double as carriers, tumbling children to the ground.
- Install car seats in the backseat in accordance with the directions. Unless properly installed, car seats can't be counted on to protect your child.
- Check the fit of the seat belt. Standard seat belts can be dangerous for little people, so booster seats are recommended for youngsters weighing in at forty to eighty pounds.
- Consider purchasing a clip that changes the angle of the seat belt so it runs across the shoulder instead of the neck and fits securely across the lap.
- Failing to use the shoulder strap can cause the lap belt to be pulled too tight during a deceleration accident, causing abdominal injuries.
- Tucking the shoulder strap under the arm can prevent the strap from engaging properly during a sudden stop, rendering it useless.

ALERT

Beware of air bags in your car. Although they can save lives, the explosion as they inflate has resulted in massive injuries and even death for children. Many parents of young children have had them deactivated. Check to see if your car has air bags for the rear seats.

While driving, consider turning off your Bluetooth. Your parent instinct will make you alert to sounds coming from the back seat, and you must concentrate on the road as well. Adding a third thing to do at the same time could be too much.

The dangers of drinking and driving are well known. However, when a toddler is on board, even one drink is too many. Depending on an individual's tolerance for alcohol, just one or two drinks can significantly slow down your reflexes, and driving with an active or cranky toddler requires optimal concentration and reflexes. A common side effect of alcohol is that it convinces people they are fine when they may not be fine at all.

Swimming Pools

Swimming pools—and that includes kiddie pools—are lethal for unattended children. The greatest danger is of a toddler gaining access to a swimming pool without the parents knowing they are capable of doing so. Even sturdy fences with tall gates and big locks are ineffective if they are left unlocked or propped open! Keep the following cautions in mind:

- Just because a swimming pool gate is locked today doesn't mean it will be locked tomorrow.
- Just because a pool gate is locked doesn't mean a child won't find a way to climb over it.
- Supervision is the primary preventative measure against drowning.
- Water safety training for you doesn't improve children's poolside behavior.
- Swimming lessons decrease children's fear of the water, making them more likely to enter water when no one is present to supervise. Beware.

Kitchen Safety

In the kitchen, install knob covers on the range so toddlers can't turn the stove on. Then, when cooking, make it harder for your toddler to reach hot pans or skillets by using the back burners of the stove. Always turn the handles of pans and skillets toward the back so they are less likely to be bumped by the cook or grabbed by a little hand with a long reach. And, since fires can and do happen despite everyone's best efforts to prevent them:

- Buy fire extinguishers that can be used against both electrical and liquid flames. Get the kind that shows the remaining pressure. When it's reading low, replace the unit.
- Create a fire escape plan by walking into each room and figuring out how you could get yourself and your child to safety if you were trapped there.

ALERT

When shopping for safe pajamas, look for the brands that are flame-resistant and fit snugly. Loose-fitting cotton T-shirts catch fire easily and burn quickly. The main culprits, responsible for 200 serious sleepwear accidents each year, are candles, matches, lighters, and stove burners. Beware of dangling sleeves!

Keeping Your Cool

It's one thing to be alarmed, scared, or frightened. It's quite another to be panic-stricken. There's no way to predict how a panicked person will react. They sometimes do and say things that are so completely out of character that they don't even recognize themselves when they later ponder their behavior during the crisis. The adrenaline surge can strengthen parents' arms to the point that they accomplish feats they never could have accomplished under normal circumstances, such as lifting the front end of a car to extricate a trapped child from beneath a tire.

Some acquire a steely calm. All emotion disappears and, like a robot, they go on automatic pilot. Later, they are astounded to realize they ended up doing exactly what needed to be done. Others are overcome by emotion. Logic and reason disappear; their mind freezes; and they cannot recall the most basic information. When tapes of parents talking to 911 dispatchers are replayed on TV, conversations frequently go like this:

How old is your child?
I don't know! Please hurry! He's bleeding!

Even if parents are sure their mind wouldn't fail in a crisis, a panicked babysitter could certainly experience a mental lapse. The solution is to create an emergency list, duplicate it, and post a copy by each telephone in the home. Be sure to include phone numbers for:

- Emergencies in your community (such as 911)
- The emergency room of the local hospital
- Poison control: 800-722-7112 (within area code 215: 215-386-2100)
- Police and fire stations
- Your child's pediatrician
- A neighbor

Police dispatchers and other emergency personnel should be able to help callers focus so they can describe the crisis and the victim's current condition. But be sure to post the following critical information by the phone so the caller can simply read it aloud: Your address with detailed directions to your house, including the names of major intersections, readily visible landmarks, and a brief description of your dwelling (e.g., brown brick house with a red shingle roof and two-car garage facing the street).

Create a subheading for each child, and list the following information:

- Name
- Age
- Sex
- Height and weight
- Medical problems
- Allergies
- Names and doses of prescription medications
- Names and doses of over-the-counter medications

Basic Lifesaving Skills

Basic lifesaving skills are familiar to many people, but used by few. This is the time to refresh those skills—with hope they'll never be used.

CPR

Every parent should take a basic course in CPR, cardiopulmonary resuscitation. The Red Cross and American Heart Association offer courses in communities across the country. In them, students learn to administer artificial respiration to people who have stopped breathing, chest compressions if someone's heart has stopped beating, abdominal thrusts for choking, and basic first aid. The cost of these courses is minimal; they are readily available in most communities. Not all include the specific techniques for reviving infants and toddlers, which are different from those used for adults. Check to be sure that what you need to learn will be taught.

FACT

To find a CPR course near you, check the American Heart Association's web page at *www.cpr-ecc.org* or call (800) AHA-USA1. Or go to the Red Cross website at *www.redcross.org/services/hss/courses*. You can also contact your local parks and recreations department, hospital, chamber of commerce, school district, fire department, ambulance service, or YMCA for course descriptions and locations.

Artificial Respiration

Five minutes without oxygen is enough to cause permanent brain damage; a few more minutes and death is probable. The exception is if the body is very cold, it needs less oxygen, sometimes enabling youngsters to survive for longer periods. If a child has stopped breathing due to swelling of the air passages caused by a medical problem such as asthma, an allergic reaction, or a respiratory infection, artificial respiration should be started immediately. However, if the child has stopped breathing due to an object stuck in his windpipe, artificial respiration might force it further into the child's windpipe or even the lungs. Before attempting artificial respiration, a rescuer should follow the instructions for choking (see the section "Treating a Choking Victim"). For artificial respiration, follow these steps:

1. Place the youngster face up on the ground, lift the chin up and tilt the head back to keep the tongue from blocking the air passages. Examine the mouth and remove any visible obstructions with a curled finger.
2. Cover the child's nose and mouth tightly with your mouth and give two gentle breaths lasting one to one and a half seconds each. Be careful not to blow too much or too hard; this will cause the child's lungs to hemorrhage. When properly done, you should be able to see the child's chest rise. The child's head must remain tilted up throughout to keep the wind passages open.
3. If the child does not resume breathing on his own, administer additional breaths at the rate of about twenty per minute until a medical team arrives.
4. If vomiting occurs, as is often the case, turn the child's head to the side to prevent choking. Then quickly clear the mouth cavity before resuming assisted breathing.

Chest Compressions

The heart delivers oxygen-enriched blood to the brain. If the child has collapsed and is nonresponsive—that is, he doesn't moan, cough, or move even when his shoulder is tapped and his name is called—check for a pulse at the carotid artery. Compressions can damage the heart if it is already beating, so it's important to be sure there is no pulse before beginning. Here is the procedure for carrying out chest compressions:

1. Place a flat hand on the child's chest on the lower half of the breastbone, which is located between the nipples, and push down with the heel of your hand.
2. The child's chest should depress one-third to one-half the depth of the child's chest, far less than is needed for an adult.
3. Repeat this action at the rate of 100 compressions per minute.

When you combine mouth-to-mouth breathing and chest compressions, deliver five chest compressions for each breath until help arrives, and check occasionally to see if the heart has begun beating on its own.

Treating a Choking Victim

If a child is eating or playing with a small toy and begins to choke, his air passage may be partially or completely blocked. Signs of a partially blocked air passage include choking or coughing that starts very suddenly, gagging, or breathing that is noisy and high pitched.

If a child can manage to breathe a little bit, call 911 or get her to an emergency room immediately. Trying to dislodge the object could end up making matters worse by cutting off the child's air completely. If a child's ability to breathe is almost completely cut off or if breathing has stopped altogether, the situation is desperate and the child must have immediate assistance to keep her alive until an emergency medical team arrives.

Symptoms of desperate trouble include:

- The ribs and chest are sucked in when the toddler tries to breathe
- The toddler can't get enough air to cough
- The toddler can only wheeze softly or make soft high-pitched sounds
- The toddler can't make any sound at all
- The lips and skin are bluish

If the toddler is unconscious, look in the child's throat and try to remove the blockage. If that doesn't work, administer two rescue breaths. If the child doesn't start breathing on her own, start chest compressions. Sometimes the compressions will eject the object from the windpipe.

If a toddler can't breathe but is still conscious, the goal is to force her to cough; something she can't do on her own because she is unable to take in enough air. Begin by explaining that you will help her. Quickly position her in front of you, reach around her with both arms, make a fist, and place it so that your thumb rests just above the navel and below the breastbone. Grasp your fist with your other hand. Give five quick thrusts, pressing upward and in. The object may be expelled. If not, give five more abdominal thrusts. Keep trying until the object is ejected.

If the child loses consciousness, lay the child down, lift her chin, open her mouth to look for the object, remove it if you can, and help her breathe with artificial respiration. If her heart stops, start chest compressions until medical help arrives. Toddlers' tongues, throats, and facial muscles aren't well developed. That, combined with the fact that they lack a full set of teeth, increases the risk of choking. Keep pieces of food small and soft, and no hard candies!

Keep small toy pieces out of reach, too, and watch out for loose buttons and snaps on clothing that could fall off and be swallowed. Coins present another hazard. Children swallow more than 3,000 coins per year, according to the American Association of Poison Control Centers. Most pass through toddlers' systems without doing any harm, although some get stuck in the esophagus (warning signs are wheezing, gagging, and excessive drooling) or at the point where the small intestine connects to the bowel.

First-Aid Kit

Whether you make your own or buy one in the store, every home should have a first-aid kit, stored where toddlers' prying hands can't reach it. It's a good idea to keep one in the trunk of the car, too. The American Red Cross recommends stocking the following items:

- Activated charcoal*
- Adhesive tape
- Antiseptic ointment
- Band-Aids (assorted sizes)
- Blanket
- Cold pack
- Disposable gloves
- Gauze pads and roller gauze (assorted sizes)
- Hand cleaner
- Plastic bags
- Scissors and tweezers
- Small flashlight and extra batteries
- Syrup of ipecac*
- Triangular bandage

Use only if instructed by the Poison Control Center

In addition, parents might want to add a bulb aspirator, useful for removing mucus and foreign objects from the nose. For the kit stowed in the car, consider adding an old credit card for scraping out stingers and splinters, sunscreen, and insect repellant.

In one recent year, an astounding 70,242 children under age six were treated in health care facilities after accidentally ingesting medication, ranging from acetaminophen to nitroglycerin. That included more than 6,000 youngsters who ingested diaper products. When it comes to toddlers and medication, you can't be "too careful." Keep prescription and over-the-counter medications locked up and out of reach at all times!

Medication Safety

While it might be tempting to refer to medicine as "candy" when you're trying to get some down a reluctant toddler's throat, don't! Just think what will happen if he gets into a bottle or a box when you're not around. Many parents don't realize that overdoses of vitamins can be dangerous, too. Follow these basic safety strategies:

- Call medicine by its real name.
- Use products with child-resistant packaging.
- Don't confuse "child-resistant" with "childproof." (The name changed when it was discovered how quickly toddlers could get the covers off. Very few items are toddler-proof!)
- Keep medications in their original containers to avoid confusion at a later time.
- Avoid storing liquid medicines in cups or soft-drink containers that might tempt a thirsty toddler.
- Install childproof locks on cabinets, drawers, and closets where medications are stored. (Don't depend solely on locks! Little fingers can sometimes work them open.)

- Keep track of how much medicine has been used. (If you discover his hand in the bottle and pink syrup ringing his mouth, or his hand in the pills and white powder on his tongue, you'll have an idea how much has been ingested.)
- Treat vitamins containing iron like the medicine it is; an overdose can be fatal.
- Check the dosages and use a proper spoon or vial for measuring before each administration.

Don't take your own medication around a toddler—you don't want her to mimic you. Children need to learn that when it comes to prescriptions and over-the-counter medications, they are to take only what a caretaker administers. That includes vitamins! Even when you think a toddler understands, she probably doesn't! Also, it's wise to throw out old medicine, down the toilet.

CHAPTER 9

Techno-Tots

Parents of today's toddlers are sometimes in uncharted waters when it comes to the digital world and raising a child within it. Do you realize that you are the first generation that completely grew up on electronics and now can breezily pass that on to your youngsters? Every generation of parents before you went through a process of learning about computers and cell phones. You have most likely been surrounded by these things your entire life. This comfort with technology means new, conscious decisions can be made regarding your child.

Television

According to Arlene Eisenberg, author of *What to Expect: The Toddler Years*, television for toddlers does have its faults, but there are some positive elements as well. Time in front of the tube can give your tot a view into the far corners of the world with the possibility of exposure to a vast array of everyday and exotic life. By around age two, an hour of television watching will do no harm, especially if there is bad weather that prevents the usual outdoors play and if you can watch a children's program with your toddler.

You might want to investigate public television to see what it offers for a toddler, or enjoy episodes of SpongeBob SquarePants or Phineas and Ferb, which include enough sophisticated humor to entertain you, as well. Each public television station has a website that you might like to explore (some are listed in Appendix B).

ALERT

Informative kids' shows, such as those found on PBS, are okay. But add *Barney and Friends* to *Sesame Street,* and your child is already up to one hour of TV per day. Resist the allure of the electronic babysitter. Your child can learn more from interacting with you.

Once a time limit is set for the amount of TV, stick to it. Otherwise by the time the child reaches school age, you will have a problem on your hands, a TV-addicted child. Your limit needs to be consistently enforced, with, of course, sensible exceptions. For example, if the child is sick, then more television could be allowed, as long as the child understands why the rule has changed.

Boob Tube, Babysitter, or Bribe

Avoid plunking the child in front of the television as if the TV is a babysitter. This is what brings on the hypnotic stare. It is better if you watch with your child, interacting with questions and responses about what the television is showing. You can follow up with art or dramatic activities to further enhance the program.

It is best not to offer TV as a bribe, reward, or to take away privileges as a punishment. This unnecessarily glorifies the attractiveness of the tube, and the child becomes conditioned in an unnatural way. If you are a responsible role model for healthy TV watching, it will be easier for your child to follow accordingly.

Violence and Commercials

Be very careful about what your toddler watches. Ban shows that are violent, even cartoons. Some commercials are unnecessarily garish. Many parents of toddlers stick to public television in order to bypass the commercials. You might want to TiVo programs in order to determine if the quality is what you want for your toddler. You can also fast forward through the commercials if the desired show is recorded.

A steady diet of commercials produces little people who are at the mercy of the ads, the trends, and what is cool. Many advertisers specifically target young children, training them to ask their parents for certain toys, foods, or restaurants. Do you want your child to be your shopping guide? Toddlers are unable to distinguish between want and need. They may think they need an item with the image of a hyped-up action hero, but you have to be adult enough to distinguish that as a want.

Be aware that advertising influences your choices for your child, perhaps in your unconscious motivation to be a cool parent. Does a two-year-old boy have a need for camouflage military gear or a little girl a five-layered tulle dress and a sparkly tiara? Maybe once a year at Halloween. Otherwise let your sense of discerning moderation keep you aware of how advertising attempts to control your choices for your child.

If you allow your toddler to watch TV, make a point of countering the negative influences with positive, both in terms of time and content. In other words, if an hour is spent in front of the TV, spend another hour playing with the toddler or going out to an interesting museum or story time at the library. If something questionable is shown on TV, spend an equal amount of time discussing it with your tot. For example, the shooting of the doe in an otherwise beautiful, peaceful story can be counteracted by commenting, "It was a bad thing for Bambi's mommy to be shot and killed."

Little Zombies

An early educational director of *Sesame Street* noticed that some children move into a trance-like state while watching TV. You may see that yourself, as your toddler watches television for any length of time. Researchers who have studied how babies and children respond to light and stimuli say that youngsters reach a shutdown point and become utterly passive. They are hooked.

According to Marie Winn, whose book *The Plug-In Drug: Television, Computers, and Family Life* cautions against too much TV in the home, about half of parents use television as a reward and TV deprivation as a punishment. Does this place TV as something too enticing? This could be a problematic relationship, similar to developing food problems by rewarding with a cookie. Along the same lines of reasoning, it is wise not to associate TV with toilet training. It is unnatural to reward accurate use of the potty with television shows. Such conditioning places the reward in a category that it does not really deserve. TV-addicted children truly go through the agonies of withdrawal when the plug is pulled, and this is not a pretty sight.

Brains Off

Winn says that the state of mind of a toddler watching TV is like meditation. The cognitive processes are turned off. Television is like a pacifier, a relaxant and sedative for tired people of all ages. It takes the child to a nonverbal state. Many families notice, however, that toddlers act out more after watching TV—perhaps a bodily backlash to being so quieted down by the boob tube.

In extreme cases where young children grow up with hardly any family conversation, children come to preschool almost mute. They were babysat by television but learned no language.

TV Awareness

In your media-saturated home, be aware that your toddler imitates you. One study showed that more than half of infants and toddlers can turn on the TV by themselves, and three-year-olds can put in a DVD by themselves. When offered a toy telephone, some toddlers will put it down and reach for your cell phone. At a very young age, they know the difference between toys and the real thing.

What are some reasons parents give for having a television in a baby or toddler's bedroom? The family may want to watch a different program, and the toddler is shown a DVD or television program in the bedroom. Except in exceptional circumstances, don't overdo this practice. It is better for your child if you view whatever she is viewing with her. Yes, you do need a break from time to time. Try to have your down time when the toddler is asleep.

ESSENTIAL

One study showed that a television going in the home makes it somewhat difficult for toddlers to concentrate on their play. You might tune out the tube, but to your child it is a constant noise that takes effort to ignore. You could consider turning off the electronic hearth and playing some nice music instead. Even better—you and your toddler can create some music together!

The American Academy of Pediatrics recommends that children younger than two not be allowed to watch television and that older children be limited to only two hours per day. One study showed that in many families, toddlers younger than two are glued to the TV. In our present society, interest in media is very high, even for very young children.

Intelligent Internet Use

You will probably want to monitor an older toddler's access to the Internet. Your little techno-tot may be able to negotiate his way around the Internet by age three, but he doesn't have any kind of method of discernment. Of course, you will install blocks and securities to protect your toddler from pornography, violent films, and the family bank accounts and records.

What if some of the websites for children are not so safe and appropriate for toddlers? There are sites with images of an "Evil Barney" decapitating another character with a chainsaw! Needless to say, nightmares and anxieties can result from the monster-ish cartoon. The moral of the story is that you need to explore children's websites *with* your toddler. The computer site cannot be a nanny while you catch up on the dishes or phone calls to your friends. It's human to want a little respite from the relentless work of parenting, but that comes when the child is asleep, or even better when he goes off to college!

The National Association for the Education of Young Children recommends that electronics and other media be thought of as supplementary items for your children. The best activities and learning come from basic, traditional toys and household items, such as blocks, dolls, child-sized furniture, books, kitchen items, sand, water, and art materials. Think of the technological stuff as dessert, not the main course.

Plus or Minus?

Educator Larry Cuban calls computers a "benign addition" to the educational world of a toddler and preschooler. He finds that research shows that such exposure gives young children a slight advantage if the first grade teacher uses programs that are taught with computer software. That's a big "if." Most likely your child's preschool, kindergarten, and first grade will use a predominantly hands-on learning environment, with computer learning added as a supplement. Keep in mind, too, that young children learn very quickly. Even if they have not had access to screens during the toddler years, they will quickly learn when they become available.

ESSENTIAL

If you decide to indulge your child in digital activities, make an effort to balance his playtime with real-world, hands-on activities, as well. He needs large-muscle play and direct sensory experiences in order to develop as a whole person. Too much screen time creates a narrow existence.

The jury is still out on the pros and cons of exploring computers with toddlers. Some experts definitely believe that being comfortable with screens and technology gives them an advantage. Others believe just as strongly that social skills suffer when young children interact too much with computers. As an informed parent, you will have some decisions to make.

Cuban suggests that parents try to find a sensible middle ground. At first, hold the toddler on your lap, as you would when reading a story. Talk about exactly what is happening with the mouse, the cursor, and the screen. Discuss with the child what is happening. In order to benefit from anything on the computer, the child has to understand cause and effect. "When I touch here, I see something different or hear a sound."

ESSENTIAL

Information overload can affect people of all ages. The constant use of digital devices, whether child or adult, creates stress and strain on relationships. It doesn't hurt to detach from the brave new world of everything digital. Signs of information overload can be irritability, inability to make a decision, and difficulty turning off digital devices.

It's Not a Nanny

Resist the temptation to use the computer as a babysitter. Stay with the child. After the lap stage, let the child sit with you while you enjoy the computer together.

Observe honestly before you begin any computer fun with your toddler whether or not he is truly interested. Give him an old keyboard or pick up one at a flea market and let him bang around on it. Is he really engaged, or will it be a passing fancy like any other new toy?

Technological Devices

Some parents feel that iTouch, iPhones, and the iPad are a real boon for those times when you have to wait somewhere and need a way to occupy your toddler. The parent is in control of the applications available for the child, and the child learns great eye-hand coordination. Even portable DVD players can be managed by an older toddler in the back seat of a car or on a plane, making family travel somewhat serene.

ABC News recently reported that Dr. Vic Strasburger of the American Association of Pediatrics (and a professor of pediatrics from the University of New Mexico School of Medicine) said that several studies showed that too much screen viewing before the age of two actually delays language. It does nothing to further language development.

iPods

Journalist Susan Wagner reported that iPods made available in a local preschool were very popular among three-year-olds for the first few days, and then became more or less as attractive as other toys in the playroom. As with a lot of things, novelty adds to the appeal. At the day school, children seemed to especially like apps with animal noises or other funny sounds that rewarded correct choices. The experiment of making iPods available to three-year-olds came about because the principal of the school noticed a child in a supermarket line quite skillfully using a parent's iPhone. He wondered if the device might be helpful for teaching colors, shapes, numbers, and other simple concepts for older toddlers.

ALERT

Parents need to be aware that computer sites for very young children may have ads on them. Notice what the ads are and whether it is something you would desire for your toddler. Young minds are quite impressionable. You don't want to set up a dynamic where your child is begging for something.

Matt Richtel, electronics reviewer for *The New York Times*, notes the availability of a couple of interesting devices listed on Amazon.com—the Easy Link Internet Launch Pad offered by Fisher-Price and the Smart Cycle, a bike that hooks up to a video game. The Launch Pad helps children find sites that are appropriate. You might want to investigate this yourself before teaching it to your older toddler.

iPads

Apple's iPad has numerous attractive, interactive applications that can keep a child's attention for a long period of time. There are simple Mac programs, too, that allow a toddler to hit the keyboard and a new song will play. The main appeal of these devices is the chance to imitate the parents.

Some experts believe that the touchtone devices are in a separate category from television and computer screens. They think that if a child touches a screen on the smart phone or iPad and a response occurs, this is learning about the environment, similar to exploring with paint, blocks, or water. Overall, most people agree that real-world, hands-on experiences are best for the child; screen devices can supplement as another aspect of learning.

ESSENTIAL

Emerging possibilities for using an iPad with your toddler could include videos, short clips from YouTube, toddler-scale games, playlists of music especially selected for your tot, family photos to point to and name, your child's favorite DVDs, and favorite stories with audio. Monitor the audio levels so that they are appropriate for your child.

If you or your spouse are talented with technical gadgetry, you might enjoy customizing particular apps for your toddler—read favorite stories, make groups of photos for vocabulary development—constantly modifying and updating along with your child's development and changing interests. Basically the sky's the limit in the flexibility of the iPad, and it's completely portable, a boon for those times when the child has to wait. Tote it along to the salon or doctor's appointment, and your child will be occupied.

Too Much of a Good Thing?

A psychologist in Austin, Texas, Mike Brooks, sees both sides of the question of whether technology is good for toddlers, and how much. He says that the brains of children are rapidly developing, and doing interesting things helps them to develop cognitive skills. On the other hand, being saturated in media might wire the child to expect a constant diet of intense stimuli. Too much of a good thing, and down the road you may have a teenager with no social skills who will not join the family for dinner.

Software and Games for Toddlers

It will take you a long time to investigate everything that is available for toddlers. Undoubtedly your little one will settle on some favorites and enjoy repetition and mastery. Inger Fountain offers useful suggestions in her article, "Which Early Learning Software Is Best for Your Toddler?" Most early-learning software teaches the use of the mouse, keyboard, and screen. Not a lot of content will be involved. Your child will learn that touching the screen creates a visual change or a voice speaking to her. This is the main point of the simplest programs.

FACT

Many of the blogs concerning apps for toddlers are written by computer programmers who are parents of young children themselves. In desperation for quality apps, they created some and began writing about them. Just Google "apps for toddlers," and you will find a slew of interesting things to read.

Jumpstart and the Learning Company offer Jumpstart Toddler and Reader Rabbit. These companies are trustworthy and their programs are generally frustration free for the toddler. Fountain also recommends software games such as Dora the Explorer, Thomas the Tank Engine, Finding Nemo, Winnie the Pooh, and Bob the Builder. These games have been around since 2007 and are fun and reliable.

Nicole Twohig recommends various applications for your iPhone to keep your toddler entertained while you are in the car or in line at the supermarket. Fish School from Duck Duck Moose is an entertaining program for children as young as two and a half. Probably your smart phone has become an integral part of your life, and your toddler will want his piece of the action. The Apple website offers a wide selection of apps for the youngest children, and various parents' magazines regularly review the newest twenty-five each month. At the time of this printing, Angry Fish is a very popular program for children. Montessorium offers early applications for learning numbers.

The National Association for the Education of Young Children recommends Julia's Rainbow Corner, Starfall, and StoryPlace. StoryPlace offers stories in both English and Spanish, a boon if you'd like your tot to be exposed to Spanish quite early.

Free Shareware

Some free software programs (shareware) include CyberStart for Children, StudyDog, Sebran's ABCs, and TuxPaint. All of these are recommended by the National Association for the Education of Young Children. Sebran's programs are offered in a wide array of foreign languages. Other offerings are Minesebran and Pick a Picture.

When people look at one object and can imagine other uses for it, they engage in the kind of creative thought that leads to innovations. Innovations have brought human beings from campfires to microwaves, from horses to jet planes. To help youngsters develop intellectually, parents should target their toddler's use of digital devices in ways that encourage divergent thinking.

More Pros and Cons

Representatives from the Association of Early Childhood Education say that today's young children are not actually more savvy than children in previous generations. They may use more screen items, but they do not necessarily understand them. They are apt to give up easily and not fully explore each web page, including scrolling down. This seems to indicate that, again, it is always wise for the parent to play the games and activities with the child, when at all possible.

Use your best parental judgment when you select software. Childrens software.com and Superkids.com both do reviews of programs for children. Educator Larry Cuban recommends these reviews and recommendations, even if there is a small charge to access the information.

Microsoft offers PixelWhimsy, a program created by a Microsoft employee who wanted a program that allows toddlers to bang on the keys of a regular computer, without hurting it, creating sounds, colors, and shapes.

Toddlers seem to like PixelWhimsy better than toy computers. Little ones are hard to fool, even at two years old. They like to imitate adults.

Sesamestreet.org offers "The Wheels on the Bus," a simple game in which the toddler touches the keyboard and the wheels go around. Benedetti, a reviewer of games for children, also recommends the sites PBSkids.org, Kneebouncers.com, Noggin.com, and NickJr.com.

Following are some iPhone apps that you might want to investigate:

- Bubble Popper is a fun game in which your toddler touches the rounded shape of the bubble, as in bubble wrap, and the screen emits a popping sound. Much safer than actual Bubble Wrap! There's even a score for how many bubbles are popped.
- Scoops encourages your little one to tilt the screen right and left in order to prevent a tower of ice cream from falling over. She also has a chance to choose scoops of different colors and group them together.
- Doodle Buddy is a little more artsy. This iPhone app lets the tot work with all kinds of backgrounds, shapes, lines, and colors. There is even a way to use a picture of yourself or the child! Of course, older children will draw mustaches on each other, the ultimate revenge.
- Giraffe's Matching Zoo provides a good exercise in matching pictures of animals. It is more portable than the conventional games of Concentration or Lotto, making it one that you might want to take in the car or the supermarket shopping cart.
- Monkey Preschool LunchBox gives you six games, each encouraging several different skills, with a reward of a virtual sticker at the end of the game.
- ShapeBuilder lets your little one drag puzzle pieces into place, making various pictures, numbers, and letters. The game tells the player when the correct shape is made.
- As well as being available on the computer from Sesame Street, Wheels on the Bus can be played on your iPhone. The player can open and close the bus doors, move the wipers, and turn the wheels.
- Alphabet Sonnets is an app that teaches the ABCs with poems and songs.

- First Word Animals teaches kids how to spell the names of animals. You pull the letter to the place in the word, and the phone says the name of the letter and the word. Your older toddler might enjoy this game.
- Tozzle is popular with many parents and children. The player pulls the puzzle shapes into matching silhouettes. The app includes twenty different puzzle shapes.
- iTunes offers Hippo Hooray Colors, which teaches your toddler color recognition and names. He might also enjoy Hippo Hooray Letters and Hippo Hooray Shapes. These games are played merely with a light touch of the phone screen. A voice prompt leads the child through the sequence.

CHAPTER 10

Discipline

Many people think of discipline as punishment, and this is unfortunate. Literally, discipline means to teach or to learn. Disciplining toddlers involves helping them learn how to behave so that they become comfortable in their life and in the company of other people. Parents are the most important teachers in this goal. Ultimately, you want your child to attain self-discipline, and during the toddler years, you start to build a foundation for inner self-control.

Box Parenting

Your toddler becomes quite mobile during the time between eighteen months and three years, and with such mobility comes the necessity of accepting limits. Dr. Michael Osit, author of *Generation Text: Raising Well-Adjusted Kids in an Age of Instant Everything*, believes that a good parenting style is what he terms "box parenting." Such people are neither too bossy nor too permissive. In order to be a good "box parent," you have rules and boundaries within your house, your activities, and your life. Not hitting each other is a rule. This rule applies at home, in the playgroup, and at the birthday party.

Your toddler has to learn about ownership of objects. It is fine to baby-proof a house for the child's safety, but at some point she has to understand that some things are off limits. Firmly say "No, that's Daddy's laptop." "Here's your toy." The toddler will test the limit over and over again. Don't allow yourself to get angry during this testing process. It's not personal, and the child is not defying you. It's up to you to shape your toddler's behavior so she is comfortable in a world that has very real limits about what is okay and what is not.

FACT

Developmental psychologists agree that a nurturing parent-child relationship is critical for toddlers. This single relationship influences youngsters' relationships with other authority figures from today's teachers to tomorrow's bosses. It also impacts how they get along with siblings, peers, friends, and future mates.

Consistency of rules and consequences for not following them are the hallmark of workable discipline. If you waffle and allow your toddler to watch TV or listen to iTunes before breakfast one day and then not the next, you will develop a confused, frustrated child. Keep in mind that you often will have to withstand and overlook the discomforts of the toddler's learning because you are aiming for the child's ability to live comfortably through the later stages of childhood and of life in the long run.

Little Learners

Teaching toddlers rules and self-control is a long, slow process. They have little experience on which to build, and their language skills prevent them from understanding much of what is said to them. In addition, their memory skills are so poor that they forget much of what they've been taught from moment to moment and from day to day. Finally, they lack the intellectual skills to use what they learn in one situation to guide their behavior in another.

FACT

The solution to many problems becomes obvious once parents understand what is driving toddlers to act as they do. Don't assume that troublesome behavior stems from naughtiness, contrariness, or mindless negativity. Look at what toddlers are trying to achieve. Be flexible as you help them achieve their goals in an acceptable manner.

Teaching about No

When you say "no," it is clear in your mind exactly what you want the toddler to stop doing or to stay away from. But what is obvious to you may not be at all clear to the toddler. How do you teach what "no" means? Here are a few ideas:

- Change your tone of voice when you say it. Use a firm, low tone of voice, and maintain direct eye contact.
- Accompany your words with a frown and shake of the head.
- Try to get your child to repeat your words, or at least your gestures.
- If your child mimics your words or gestures, smile and gush, "That's right!"

Toddlers may still not associate the phrase and gesture with an expected behavior, but at least they are being helped to focus on those two important words.

Don't Just Say No

The problem with "just saying no" is that toddlers don't learn what they can do. A child may not be trying to create chaos and ill will as she goes from one forbidden activity to the next. She doesn't know what is off limits and what is permissible. And unfortunately, if your toddler hears "no" too often, especially without a clear consequence to follow up, she will learn to tune you out. Instead of so many "nos" try redirecting your child to another behavior or activity. Offering alternatives may not prevent toddlers from becoming upset if they're very involved with something, but offering alternatives provides an important lesson: When the road she wants to go down is blocked, she needs to find another road.

Too Many Nos

The easiest way for parents to reduce the number of "no-nos" and "don't touches" is to childproof the home by putting away and securing as many dangerous and fragile objects as possible, and to provide lots of objects for your toddler to use and enjoy. On the other hand, if you leave a few things that are untouchable, you have an opportunity to teach, "No, that is Mommy's" or "No, that is Daddy's." In this way, when you visit other homes, you have a way of speaking to the child so she understands that it is not possible to touch everything.

ESSENTIAL

Instead of saying "no-no," some parents prefer "That's not okay." Either way, it takes many repetitions for youngsters to decipher the meaning and longer still to relate the words to their behavior. Keep in mind that your toddler will be hearing "no" from sitters, day care teachers, and relatives. It is helpful if they understand what it means.

Ultimately, the goal is for toddlers to learn to control themselves instead of relying on adults to control them. But developing self-control won't be accomplished in a matter of days, weeks, or even months or years. Until then, you may be better off putting more energy into controlling the environment. That way, you can spend less time struggling to control your youngsters and more time enjoying them.

The Trouble with "No"

As anyone who has studied a foreign language knows, learning to understand and use negative words is no small task. In English, things get particularly confusing. Even adults aren't always sure what answering "yes" to a question means; for example, "You're not going to touch the stove, are you?" When addressing toddlers, keep things very direct and simple!

Since negatives like "don't" occur at the beginning of sentences, toddlers often don't hear them. Especially in a noisy environment, they may not even realize they're being spoken to until you have made it halfway through the sentence. So when you say, "Don't touch the stove," the toddler may only hear ". . . touch the stove" or ". . . the stove." It's no wonder toddlers so often do exactly the opposite of what their parents are telling them! This is not willful disobedience. They are struggling to attend to what they've heard.

Make it a habit to tell toddlers what to do rather than what not to do. Instead of "Don't touch the stove," you might say instead, "Keep your hands at your sides!" or "Come over here right now."

Accentuate the Positive

Instead of nagging your toddler about what not to do, use these sentences:

- "Stay on the grass."
- "Use your soft voice." Model it for him.
- "Ask your sister for the truck. Can you say 'truck, please'?"
- "Put your hands behind your back and put your nose up close to the flowers so you can smell them—like this."
- "Put your cup down on the table. Then I'll give you a drink."

Why Not?

Try to be prudent about giving explanations to your toddler about why she cannot have something or do something. She may not understand your reasoning and will learn to ignore you when you are speaking in a long, involved way. As your child gets used to the idea that some things and situations are forbidden, you may approach some categories of why not. For example, some things belong to other people, and it's not okay to bother other people's things.

QUESTION

Do parents ever need a time-out?
Absolutely! If you find yourself rising to a boiling point, give your toddler a timer and take her to a childproofed room. Make sure she has something engrossing to do. Set the timer for about twenty minutes (a three-year-old can probably handle thirty minutes), and tell her that when the timer says "ding" you'll do something together.

Some things will hurt them. A toddler has fallen down enough and run into enough objects to understand what it means to hurt. And some things are just because you say so. You are the protector of the child, and both of you have to understand that. If you see the child across the lawn in imminent danger, you have to be secure enough to make the child stop, even from a distance.

Redirection

Often you can reshape the situation so it becomes a "yes" instead of a "no," making life much more pleasant for both of you. Redirection of the child's attention and modifications to the environment lessen confrontation. Here are some examples:

- Jumping on the furniture. You may have a house rule of no jumping on the furniture, but your toddler forgets. Put a pile of pillows on the floor and say that is a good place to jump. Clear away coffee tables with sharp corners and other hazardous furniture and let her jump as much as she wants.

- Throwing toys. It's hard to live with projectiles flying through the air, so create some soft, harmless objects that cannot hurt anything. Roll a couple of socks together and let her throw them around the house. A Nerf ball is also safe to throw.
- Playing in the toilet. It's just water in a container, but somehow it seems unsavory to let your child play in the toilet. Instead, lay down some towels and place a plastic dishpan of water on the pad. Give your tot some water play containers, and let him play.

Offering Choices

When simple redirection fails, try a different approach. Let's say that Jenny wants to paint. Her mother declines and offers her an alternative, "How about playing in your sandbox?" Jenny loves the sandbox, but her upset over her mother's refusal to let her paint quickly escalates into loud wails and roars. What's going on? It could be that she wants an indoor activity, so the sandbox fails to appeal. It could be that she is working on autonomy issues and needs to have a hand in deciding what she does next instead of always being told what to do.

ESSENTIAL

Distraction works especially well before youngsters have achieved what child psychologist Jean Piaget called object constancy. This means that objects still exist even if you can't see them. To young toddlers, out of sight really does mean out of mind. This is one reason toddlers cry so hard when you leave them. To them it genuinely seems you've ceased to exist!

Offering choices gives toddlers an opportunity to practice making decisions and to have more control over their life. However, make sure what you offer is a real choice. "Would you like to come with Mommy now?" is not a real choice. "How about trying some of these carrots?" is not a real choice either, unless you consider that the toddler can say "no" to what you are suggesting. A choice implies at least two alternatives.

Jenny's mother could say, "Painting is messy, and we have company coming over soon. You can play in your sandbox or read a book. Which would you prefer?" Jenny may need to finish wailing her disappointment over not being allowed to paint before she'll be ready to move on, in which case her mother can say calmly, "When you decide whether you want the sandbox or a story, let me know."

When offering choices:

- **Keep them limited.** Toddlers can become confused and overwhelmed when considering too many options. Until age three, they may have trouble with more than two.
- **Don't insist on an immediate decision.** Crying is a toddler's way of expressing disappointment. The victory comes when they're able to recover and forge ahead.
- **Hold firm.** This can be difficult in the face of intense toddler opposition. Remember, you are the adult, and your toddler needs your consistent, calm strength.

In Case of Danger

You must step out of the teaching role when your toddler is approaching danger. That way, you can stage an immediate rescue.

For instance, sooner or later most youngsters will want to explore electrical cords. When a young toddler reaches for one and suddenly hears his parent's loud voice, he is likely to pause, smile, and reach for the cord again. The parent may believe the child's pause means he understood the "No, don't touch!" warning. From the child's ensuing smile and renewed attempt to reach for the cord, adults may assume the kind of defiance that makes them want to tear their hair out by the roots.

However, the pause may simply be a response to your voice; it doesn't mean that he understood the warning. Even if he does surmise from your tone that he is being warned about something, he may not realize he is being warned away from the cord. How can toddlers comprehend that a cord is dangerous when they don't know about either cords or danger, and haven't even touched one yet? They don't have the knowledge of electricity that you have.

When a toddler is approaching danger, follow these steps:

1. Say, "No! Don't touch!" or "Stop!" in a firm, authoritative tone.
2. If the child pauses, be sure to smile, nod, and provide positive reinforcement by saying, "Thank you" to let him know he responded correctly: he paused.
3. Don't wait to see what will happen next; grab him fast.
4. Explain, "That's dangerous, honey. It will hurt you."
5. Say "No-no," shake your head, and frown to convey your message nonverbally.
6. Try to get him to say "No-no" and shake his head.
7. Physically move him away from the danger.

If the child toddles back to the cord, you will need to either repeat the process as often as needed, distract him by providing something different to do, or offer him choices for alternate toys or activities.

ESSENTIAL

To make sure your toddler listens to you and not her own motivation to touch anything and everything, it is imperative to establish and maintain a good relationship. To this end, pick your battles, focusing on only one or two issues at a time; praise more often than you chastise; and spend more time enjoying each other's company than you spend praising or chastising.

If you physically move him away from the cord, he may conclude that you are playing a wonderful chasing game. He may head back in that direction the moment he is released, hoping for more. Once again, you may see his actions as defiant. It's important to consider that by this point the cord may be the farthest thing from his mind.

Would it be easier just to issue a warning and then slap the child to drive home the message that he must stay away from a dangerous object?

Although it might seem easier in the short run, there are a number of problems with slapping a toddler to convey the no-no message:

- Toddlers may become frightened of the parent. Slaps that are delivered "out of the blue" can make youngsters chronically tense and uncomfortable around anyone they have learned may hit them unexpectedly. If a child thinks he and his parent were playing a chasing game and didn't realize touching the cord was the issue, the slap will certainly take him by surprise. This can seriously undermine the parent-child relationship.
- Toddlers may learn that when their parent uses that particular tone of voice, they had better run fast to avoid being hit. This is not a lesson that will serve them well when the danger is approaching a busy street, hot stove, swimming pool, or a big dog! This is the opposite of what you are trying to teach.
- Toddlers may learn that they must not do certain things when their parent is around. The sooner children can move from needing parental control to controlling themselves, the better for everyone.

Even after toddlers understand that they're not supposed to touch particular items, they may still be driven to engage in forbidden activities, because they have two voices inside of them issuing very different directives. Mother Nature pushes them to explore and become independent. Their parents insist that many interesting activities and objects are off limits and oppose their desire to make up their own mind.

Too Much Praise

Resist the impulse to constantly praise simple, ordinary acts. It has the effect of making your toddler unnecessarily dependent on your opinion, when becoming a full, separate person involves making up one's own mind and doing things, simply because it's the thing to do. Too much praise creates an individual who is insecure in the world.

Children with good self-esteem feel pleased with themselves. When evaluating their own behavior, they feel they measure up to their personal expectations. But praise can actually serve to undermine self-esteem.

First-born children, whose parents are apt to applaud each small gurgle and goo and record each new accomplishment in their bulging baby book, tend to be the least emotionally secure and suffer more problems with self-esteem than the rest of the brood, whose successes receive far less attention. Meanwhile, the middle child, typically lost in a no-man's land between the accomplished older sibling and the darling baby, has a harder time finding ways to impress. Yet youngsters sandwiched in the middle of the pack tend to be more self-confident.

ALERT

There's nothing wrong with saying "Good" to teach a child to do things in a certain way. Certainly there are "right" and "wrong" ways to do many things. However, giving positive feedback in situations that are meant to be pure fun can cause toddlers to turn play sessions into grim tests of their competence.

The following parent comments point out some of the pitfalls of praise:

- "I like the bright colors in your drawing" suggests to the child that to please the parent, she should use bright colors. Expressing interest and asking a neutral question such as "Tell me about your picture" enables the child to share her drawing and her feelings about it without having her choice of crayons judged.
- If the parent exclaims, "Good catch!" when the ball lands in their toddler's arms, it's understandable why she becomes upset when it lands on the floor on subsequent tries; the youngster assumes they are "bad" catches.
- "Good girl!" the parent says when the toddler uses the potty by herself. This kind of evaluation—"You're good because you did what I wanted"—can cause toddlers who are in the throes of a struggle over independence to respond by refusing to use the potty thereafter. Instead, try, "You should be proud of yourself." Although that still conveys your opinion, it encourages the child to evaluate herself in a positive light rather than to focus exclusively on your opinion.

Praising Self-Control

After an hour or so has gone by without a repetition of a particular behavior problem, parents should make it a point to praise their child's accomplishment. Because toddlers get into so many things and break so many rules, it's easy to spend more time focusing on what they do wrong than on what they do right.

If, when you say, "I'm so glad you didn't touch Daddy's laptop," the child runs toward it, hurry on over but try to give him the benefit of the doubt. There's a good chance he'll look at the laptop without touching it and announce that it's a no-no, or wait for you to frown and shake your head and discuss this no-no with him once again. If so, he's making fabulous progress! Going the direction of the forbidden item is his way of indicating that he understands what you're talking about. Give him a hug and try to let him know you share the delight in his accomplishment. It's important for toddlers to realize that they really are capable of learning self-control and pleasing their parents. And parents will feel much better knowing that the child is making strides in learning to keep himself safe.

Time-Out

Providing time-outs is an excellent teaching device to help toddlers learn to adhere to important rules and regain control when they are unable to contain themselves. Simply tell your toddler to sit down until she can settle down and observe the limit you have set or behave in accordance with the rules you have established.

The rule of thumb is to assign one minute of time-out per year of age, so a two-year-old should be required to sit for two minutes at most. Some mature toddlers will be able to sit longer. If toddlers weren't upset to begin with, they may become very angry about being prevented from engaging in the activity they have chosen. You may wish to start the clock only after the child has settled down.

When the child has regained control, discuss the event that precipitated the time-out to help her learn from the experience so she knows what to do if the same situation arises in the future. It helps to begin the discussion by praising the toddler for having regained control. Besides starting the discussion on a positive note, praise helps little ones focus on their important accomplishment, and keeps both the parent and child from being overly focused on the misdeeds.

FACT

Many parents send toddlers to their room for time-out, but some youngsters need to be constantly watched. Also, some toddlers can feel rejected. The point of time-out is to teach, not to punish, although until children learn the advantages of being contained, they may feel punished. You'll have to judge the situation for yourself, keeping in mind your child's temperament.

Reviewing what transpired and figuring out what to do differently is beyond younger toddlers and will be too hard for older toddlers until they are familiar with the process. In the beginning, you may have to do most or all of the talking for your toddler:

Do you know why I sent you to time-out? Blank stare
Because you turned on the TV after I told you not to. Blank stare
You can't watch any more TV today. Too much TV watching isn't good for kids, remember? Blank stare
The TV needs to stay off, okay? Nods

There's still no guarantee that the toddler understood the question. If she turns on the TV again, the parent will need to assign another minute or two in time-out. The point of time-out is to teach several important lessons children can use throughout their lives:

1. Important rules must be followed.
2. If people disregard rules, there are consequences, which may be unpleasant.
3. If people don't control themselves, someone else will control them.
4. When people are upset and out of control, taking a brief time-out can help them calm down.

Most children learn the value of time-outs in short order. In fact, once they have become accustomed to the procedure, toddlers will begin sitting down or running off to their room when they are upset over a parental demand or prohibition. During their self-imposed time-out, they will finish crying and re-emerge, settled, a few minutes later.

Disciplined Sleep

Having a toddler on a sane sleep schedule makes for a calmer household, but it may take some time and cooperation among all the family members. Whether parents put balky toddlers down for the night and let the tantrums run their course or let them stay up until they collapse from exhaustion, it works best to get the toddler up at the same time each morning and prevent long naps that compensate for missed sleep. Studies on insomnia demonstrate that establishing a schedule is helpful. Being extra tired ups the odds that children will be ready to sleep at the next nap or bedtime.

The invariable routine of a set bedtime and nap schedule goes a long way toward regulating toddlers' sleep patterns. The human body operates in circadian rhythms—a predictable cycle that causes people to fall asleep at night and awaken in the morning at about the same time each day. These rhythms change over the life span. If left to their own devices, teenagers would stay up half the night and sleep half the day; on the other hand, senior citizens naturally fall asleep early and awaken shortly after dawn. In general, toddlers will be happier with themselves if sleep is regular and orderly.

When a toddler's negativity sets in and he feels driven to disagree with every other thing the parent does or says, he may resist going to bed just because he's been told that's what he must do. Again, parents need to resist taking this personally and remain focused on the child's innate struggle for autonomy and independence.

Letting toddlers be in charge of some bedtime decisions can help satisfy their need to be in control. Let them pick which story is read, which pajamas are worn, which stuffed animals go into the crib, whether the night-light is on or off, and which music you play.

Sometimes a little reverse psychology can help. When older toddlers refuse to stay in bed, some parents have successfully bored them to sleep. They refuse to provide any attention, announce that they themselves are going to bed, proceed with their normal bedtime preparations, and climb into bed, feigning sleep. Ideally, children become bored enough from the lack of attention and ask to be taken to bed, or they wind down and fall asleep on their own. Then the parent can climb out from under the covers, carry the youngster to his bed, and enjoy the rest of their evening undisturbed. Obviously this trick is only workable if it is safe for the toddler to be up and about the house by himself.

Spanking

While spankings may more quickly control a child who is repeatedly engaging in forbidden behavior, the fatal flaw is that the parent is controlling the child's behavior. Children need to learn to control their own behavior. Corporal punishment is controversial, but even some social worker champions of abused youngsters consider spanking to be a reasonable course of action in situations involving imminent danger, such as running into the street, reaching for a hot stove, provoking an animal, or running around a swimming pool. They recommend an on-the-spot administration of three swats on the bottom with the open hand (never an object) accompanied by an explanation such as, "Running into the street is a no-no! It's dangerous!" Like hitting a puppy with a newspaper, the goal is for the sound of the swat and the parent's angry voice (not pain) to evoke the correct response to danger—fear.

ESSENTIAL

You will have to make up your own mind about the place of spanking in disciplining your toddler, and seek consensus with your spouse, relatives, and caretakers. Some parents believe that the only way to create a nonviolent world is to engage in no violence in the home. Sometimes your disapproval and consistent caring is enough to shape your child's behavior.

Discipline with Snacks and Meals

Many parents find that eliminating unscheduled snacking is easier said than done. Children's refusal to eat dinner means that they will be hungry soon after. If parents hold firm on their policy of allowing nothing to eat until the next regularly scheduled meal or snack, they soon have a very cranky youngster on their hands. If they hold firm through the crankiness, they have a truly hungry child on their hands, and the "I hungry" wails can be wrenching enough to thaw the firmest parental resolve.

Children will not die of hunger from being put to bed without their dinner. Unless they are suffering from diabetes or another disorder, they won't end up nutritionally deficient, either. So if parents don't back down, the problem will be solved when the child sits down to breakfast with bona fide hunger pangs. In general, limiting snacks with empty calories cuts down on behavior problems around food.

CHAPTER 11

Everybody Eats

As your baby moves into the toddler years, you have an opportunity to set in place some good eating habits that will be healthy for later years. If your baby has eaten a wide range of healthy foods, it is likely that the shift to foods from the family menu will not be difficult, although some toddlers go through a phase of being a little picky. It's not unusual for a toddler to want to eat one food for breakfast, lunch, and dinner!

When to Wean?

Cultures vary tremendously in the area of weaning a baby or toddler from nursing. Western societies tend to frown on nursing "too long," although that is changing in recent decades. Generally it is up to you and your toddler to wean when you decide to wean. Your toddler may become bored with it and gradually taper off. You may go back to work and need to taper off because of new lifestyle commitments. However and whenever it occurs, it is your own business.

If you continue to nurse past age two or three, you will need to teach your toddler some specific ways of asking to nurse. He will need to learn that there are situations where it will be comfortable for you and others where he will have to wait for a while. It still is the mother's body, even though shared, and you may need to assert some boundaries so you're not embarrassed in a playgroup or social situation.

Mother's milk contains nutrition that is unsurpassed anyplace else in nature or on the shelves of a supermarket. The child gets immunities and antibodies that are unavailable elsewhere, and children who nurse longer tend to be less inclined toward obesity later in childhood.

FACT

The American Association of Pediatrics now recommends that breast-feeding continue for at least twelve months, and "thereafter for as long as mutually desired." The World Health Organization recommends "two years of age or beyond." Weaning at eighteen to twenty-four months is associated with higher IQ; virtually no research is available on youngsters weaned at older ages.

In societies where nature is allowed to take its course, self-weaning occurs between ages three and four; the minimum age is two and a half. When they are ready to stop nursing, they simply taper off and lose interest. If you want to wean a toddler before he is becoming bored on his own, it may be a bit of a challenge. Your little one receives great emotional comfort from nursing, and it is a big change in the dynamic between mother and child to move toward weaning. You can soften the blow in the following ways:

- Choose a time when the youngster isn't coping with other major stresses.
- Tell your child you are going to wean him.
- Provide milk in a cup with meals.
- Nurse after meals, when the child has less of an appetite.
- Eliminate one bottle or nursing session at a time, beginning with the one the child is least attached to—typically in the middle of the day.
- Avoid the cues that trigger the desire to be nursed by staying busy and sitting in a different chair.
- Spend the time you would have devoted to nursing reading a story, reciting nursery rhymes, or playing together.
- Offer bottle-fed babies a bottle of water.
- Wait five days before eliminating a second bottle or nursing session.
- Eliminate bedtime feedings last. (Provide other kinds of comfort until the child learns to fall asleep without being nursed. If possible, have Dad handle bedtime.)

High Chairs and Booster Seats

When your child is ready to eat solid foods it becomes necessary to find her a place to sit and eat. Choose a high chair with a wide base, since that adds stability. To keep toddlers safe:

- Position high chairs away from hazards, such as stoves, windows, and drapery cords.
- Don't allow the child to stand in the chair unsupervised. (If the chair tips or the child loses his balance and falls, it's a long way to the floor.)
- Use the safety belt rather than relying on the tray to hold the child in.
- Be sure the tray is properly latched on both sides, as babies tend to push against the tray when seated.
- Periodically check for loose screws and a wobbly base.

Magazines or old telephone books wrapped in contact paper make adequate booster seats, although their lack of a safety belt makes them useless for youngsters who refuse to remain seated. Buying one for everyday use so that older toddlers can sit at the table has some advantages. Tending to toddlers can be easier when they are sitting at the same level, then adults can eat with fewer distractions.

Applesauce, milk, and tomatoes dribbling down your toddler's legs will eventually land on your floor. Until her aim improves to the point where most of the food ends up in her mouth, spread a few newspapers or a drop cloth under her high chair to cut down on cleanup.

Putting the child's plate and cup on a tray can help contain the mess, and being on the same level with everyone else makes her feel more like part of the family. Dishes with a suction cup help keep them in place when the toddler is in the stage of playing with everything that can be picked up. As she mimics those around her, her behavior, manners, and even food choices may improve.

If you place your toddler in her high chair while you're finishing the cooking and meal preparation, give her a finger food, such as crackers to keep her occupied for a few more minutes. Young toddlers tend to do gravity experiments, dropping peas and other bits of food onto the floor. You can decide for yourself whether it's worth making an issue. Generally, if your child is hungry, she will eat the food.

Solid Foods

By now your toddler is well into solid foods, eating softer, plain versions of your family fare. Whether you are still nursing him or introducing milk from a cup, your toddler needs solid food. You will want to introduce new foods gradually, at least two to three days apart, so you can assess your toddler's allergies, if any. Common symptoms of food allergy include itchy, watery eyes; repeated sneezing attacks; itchy skin; clear mucus running from the nose; rash; hives; very red cheeks; or behavioral changes.

Five Squares a Day

Toddlers have a reputation for being finicky eaters, but the truth is that their growth rate is slowing down at this stage. They are developmentally becoming quite skilled in various aspects of their being, but they are not adding very many pounds between eighteen months and three years. Don't be tempted to push quantities of food on little ones, but do encourage a wide range of healthy tastes. Because toddler tummies are small, offer them five small meals a day rather than three big ones, emphasizing finger foods.

Go Organic

As much as possible, steer your toddler away from overly processed junk foods. Organic foods from your natural food store or farmer's market are much healthier for everyone in your family, including your little one. Read labels in the supermarket. If the ingredients include substances that your grandmother probably could not pronounce, then your toddler does not need to eat them!

ESSENTIAL

When you're cooking, especially if it's a shared time with your toddler, turn off the phone, television, music, and computer. It's not necessary to be instant messaging or texting while preparing lunch. One thing at a time, and easy does it, makes for better cooking and a higher-quality time of interaction with your assistant chef.

If you do your own cooking, you can be assured of the quality of the result. You know what's in the food that you prepare. You never have to worry about salt, sugar, or any other mysterious ingredients that might go into your child's delicate stomach. You have complete control over what you feed your child when making your own food, and you can tailor your recipes to your baby's developing preferences.

Limit Sugar and Caffeine

Many already prepared foods include large amounts of sugar or high-fructose corn syrup, and too much of it alters your child's taste preferences, setting up a dynamic for later eating difficulties. Colas contain caffeine, which causes jitteriness in people of all ages, and that's the last thing you need in a toddler who is already climbing everything in sight.

Back to the Earth

Growing your own vegetables is wonderful for your family, including the toddler. There is nothing like firsthand knowledge of digging the hole, putting in the seed, watering it, watching for the first leafy shoots, and then pulling up the carrot and eating it! Children who participate in gardening truly understand that food comes from the earth, not just from the store.

Homegrown tomatoes, carrots, and lettuce are so much more flavorful, it's much easier to get kids hooked on the taste. Families don't need a garden; many vegetables have been developed that do well in patio pots. Herbs, of course, can be grown at any time of year; all they require is a sunny window. Help little ones pinch off chives, basil, parsley, cilantro, oregano, or other favorites to sprinkle on their salad or cooked vegetables.

Kitchen Helpers

Include your toddler in the decision making. For instance, "Do you want to put green or black olives on the salads?" and let her dip her (washed) fingers into the jar to add some to the plates. At mealtime, be sure you praise your little chef! It may take an eighteen-month-old ten minutes to extricate a slice of cheese from its cellophane wrapper, and it may be pretty mangled by that point. Still, the parent can place a piece of bread on the child's plate, hand her the remaining cheese, and tell her to put it on her bread to finish making her sandwich.

It only takes a few minutes spent together in the kitchen each day—by the time youngsters are three, they will be able to make a substantial contribution. In the long run, parents will be paid back with interest for the time and extra work kiddie "help" costs them now. In the short term, the benefits include:

- The entertainment value of a fun activity
- The boosts to self-esteem that come from actively participating in family life

- The time spent interacting with parents and other family members
- Increased interest in eating what they've prepared
- A sense of accomplishment
- Increased autonomy
- A recognition of their worth as a contributing family member

One-Hit Wonders

The predictability of an unvarying menu can help anxious youngsters feel more secure. Refusing to eat anything except a few special dishes can also be a way of establishing personal control. There are two distinctly opposite, but equally valid, ways of approaching this problem.

ESSENTIAL

Lots of books for toddlers deal with the issue of food. *The Very Hungry Caterpillar* by Eric Carle is an award-winning book they'll love. *Cloudy with a Chance of Meatballs* by Judi Barrett will tickle their funny bones.

Finicky Eaters

The first way is to eliminate all food struggles by serving what your child wants. If a war for control is driving the resistance, catering to toddler demands eliminates the toddler's need to battle over food. Supplement his diet with vitamin tablets, milk, and fruit juice to maintain nutrition. Continue to make other foods available by placing them on his plate if he'll allow them to be there, or place them on a separate plate nearby. If both of those create upset, simply follow your normal serving procedures for the rest of the family.

If your toddler does request something additional, dish out a serving. Studiously avoid questions about whether he likes it and comments about being glad that he's eaten something besides the usual. The goal is to not draw attention to his eating or make an issue of it, thereby preventing a basis for renewed resistance.

The second way is to ignore the child's demands, serve what you will, and wait until hunger motivates him to eat. The refusal to eat a well-balanced meal often stems from snacking. Some toddlers constrict theirdiets to the point that it seems that if it were up to them, they'd only eat one or two things—such as grilled cheese sandwiches, fish crackers, hamburgers, or a particular type of cereal—three meals a day, every day. "If I don't fix what he wants, he won't eat anything," their parents claim. But how true is that, really? Limit snacks and your child will eat well at meals.

FACT

Toddlers, like adults, will eat out of boredom. If the parent responds to requests for a snack by offering several healthy alternatives but the child refuses anything but a cookie, she's probably not hungry. An appealing activity or nap may do a better job of eliminating the crankiness.

Further, toddlers must be simultaneously nurtured (by being fed) and given firm limits (by restraining them in a high chair and keeping them from throwing food). Balancing the two is a heady emotional experience, and research shows that parents who had highly conflicted relationships with their own parents have a harder time filling both roles.

All the emphasis on food can make the toddler years particularly trying for adults with eating disorders. This is a good time to enter counseling, begin therapy, or join an Overeaters Anonymous support group to get some real insight. There are meetings available by conference call over the phone, so you will not even need to get a sitter.

Calorie Counting

Toddlers need about 1,100 to 1,300 calories per day, proportionately from the various food groups. Large, active children will need to have a little more, and smaller, sedentary toddlers will need fewer. If you're an avid label reader, you can avoid foods that have a high level of calories from sugar, as they don't offer much nourishment.

When it comes to menu planning, variety is important for more than making toddler taste buds tingle. No single food is perfect, so children need to eat many different foods for optimal nutrition. For instance, oranges are rich in vitamin C but lack vitamin B$_{12}$. Apricots are high in beta-carotene. Scientists have only just begun to unravel the exact components of plants and animals that are good for humankind, and they continue to add to the list.

FACT

Calorie counting gets tricky, especially when half of everything that goes onto toddlers' plates ends up on their clothes or on the floor. Parents may find it easier to think in terms of the number of servings. In general, if you're offering a wide array of nutritious foods, and the cantankerous two's are not intruding on mealtimes, your toddler is doing fine.

Only a few generalities are certain: fresh foods are better than processed; pesticide-free food is healthier. So take up cooking and go organic! The typical American diet consists of so much poor-quality food; parents need to learn to separate the wheat from the chaff so they can identify the good stuff. Fortunately, labeling has improved, which makes it easier to figure out which packaged goods are healthy choices.

The first thing chefs need to know is that besides supplying vitamins, minerals, and other ingredients needed for good health (such as fiber), foods provide energy. Energy is measured in calories. Calories, which are measured in grams, come from three sources: proteins, fats, and sugars. Children need all three kinds. Parents need to keep track of the kinds of calories their youngsters consume to be sure they are serving enough of each. However, you do not need to be a scientist. Common sense goes a long way toward serving your toddler (and your family) nutritious meals. You might make it a point, though, to become very aware of food advertising and inform yourself about what is actually good for your toddler and what is good for the food manufacturers' profit margin.

Food Essentials

The United States Department of Agriculture creates educational information for the public about nutrition and food groups. The most recent version is called a food pyramid, with the quantities within each section varying according to the age and needs of the person. The food groups are as follows:

- Grains
- Vegetables
- Fruits
- Milk
- Meat and beans

An extra category includes snacks, oil, beverages, salt, and sugar.

The site at *www.mypyramid.gov* offers an interactive page for parents of young children. You can enter your toddler's age, level of exercise, and special needs and receive information about nutrition.

You don't have to be a scientist to nourish your toddler in a healthy way. However, it is important to become informed and turn your gaze away from overzealous advertisers who might tease you into thinking that their overly processed wonder is the best thing for your child. It's probably not.

Protein

Protein, which is essential for good nutrition, comes from meats, poultry, fish, eggs, nuts, and beans. It's the extras—the skin and fat or addition of oil for frying, butter for baking, and cream sauces for smothering—that quickly add to the calories from fat. Milk, cheese, and yogurt are also high in protein and are rich sources of another essential nutrient, calcium. Low-fat products are preferable for children over age two because they have fewer calories from fat. Provide two to four toddler servings of meat and high-protein alternatives daily, and three to four servings of milk, yogurt, and cheese. One toddler serving equals:

- 1 whole egg or 2 whites
- ¼ cup baked beans
- ¾ cup milk

- 3 slices turkey luncheon meat
- ¼ cup nonfat dry milk
- ¾ ounce hard cheese
- ½ cup yogurt
- ¾ ounce poultry, meat, or fish
- 3 tablespoons cottage cheese
- 1½ tablespoons peanut butter

ALERT

Contrary to what people often think, grains are healthy foods and are not fattening. It's when you add butter, cheese, whole milk, and assorted fat-rich sauces that the calories from fat quickly add up.

Grains

Bread, rice, cereal, and pasta, which are made primarily or wholly from grains, provide energy from complex carbohydrates. Parents should provide six to eleven servings per day. One toddler serving equals:

- ½ slice whole-grain bread
- ⅓ cup cold cereal
- ¼ English muffin
- ¼ cup cooked pasta or rice (brown or wild is best)
- ¼ whole-grain bagel
- 2 to 3 whole-wheat crackers
- ¼ cup hot cereal

Unrefined grains are healthier than highly refined grains, even if the manufacturer says that nutrients are put back into the product. Keep in mind that all that processing is done to lengthen the shelf life of the product. You have to keep in the forefront of your mind, that the closer to nature the food, the healthier it is for your toddler.

Fat

When it comes to calories from fat, the problem is usually keeping children from getting too much, especially after age two—processed foods tend to be loaded with it. But don't let round tummies and folds of baby fat fool you. Toddlers don't need low-fat diets unless there's a special reason! Parents should provide five to eight servings per day from ages twelve to twenty-four months, and add a half serving to each end of the range from ages twenty-four to thirty-six months. One toddler serving equals:

- ¾ cup whole milk or yogurt
- 9 French fries
- 1½ cups 2% milk
- 2 chicken nuggets
- 1 tablespoon peanut butter
- 1½ ounces beef, lamb, or pork
- 1 egg
- ½ tablespoon oil, butter, margarine, or mayonnaise
- 2½ ounces poultry
- ½ cup ice cream

ESSENTIAL

All calories are not created equal! A calorie from a substantial grain or vegetable genuinely nourishes a child. A calorie from a sugary food or drink is empty. It does nothing to contribute to a child's health. Too many extra calories from fat and sugar sources, and the result is a weight problem.

Vegetables

Vegetables contain protein. Also, what makes vegetables so important are the vitamins and fiber they contain. Most of the vitamins are lost in the canning process, so fresh is always better. The recommended daily allowance (RDA) charts on packaged foods list how much of needed vitamins and other nutrients foods contain. If you're using a lot of preprocessed foods, learn to read the labels! Keep these points in mind:

1. Frozen vegetables are better than canned, since fewer vitamins are lost in processing. Vegetables lightly steamed in cookware with a tight-fitting lid are better still. Raw vegetables are best of all.
2. Starchy vegetables like potatoes and yams are especially rich in nutrients, but they become a less-than-great choice when fat—butter, cheese, gravy, sour cream, or oil—is added.
3. Beans, which are rich in vitamins and fiber as well as protein, can meet vegetable or protein requirements.

Fruit

Fruit—including fresh, dried, frozen, and home-squeezed into juice—is rich in vitamins, especially vitamin C. Beware of fruit canned in sugary syrup, and juices that contain mostly sugar and only a squirt of real fruit juice. A few drops can result in a label that proclaims in large letters, "Contains real juice!" The question is how much juice, and you must read the label to find out. Aim to be an alert, intelligent shopper!

Offer two or more servings of fruit per day. One serving equals approximately one tablespoon per year of life, so two-year-olds need at least four tablespoons per day. The equivalent is:

- ½ cup (4 ounces) of juice
- 3 to 4 tablespoons of fruit

Don't Forget Fiber!

Fiber is important for proper functioning of the bowels. Hefty portions serve as an antidote for chronic constipation. Offer three or more servings of vegetables per day. One serving equals approximately one tablespoon per year of life, so two-year-olds need at least six tablespoons per day. Besides raw vegetables, other high-fiber foods include whole-grain breads and cereals, beans and peas, and fruit.

Calcium Counts

Calcium is required for bone growth, so to ensure your child gets enough calcium, you will need to provide daily doses from another source. Good choices include broccoli, calcium-fortified orange juice, calcium-fortified soy milk, canned sardines or salmon (with the bones), goat's milk, kale, tofu, and turnip greens.

FACT

Toddlers need four to six cups of liquids daily under normal circumstances—more in hot weather or if they are ill with fever, vomiting, or diarrhea. Besides water (from the tap or bottled, plain or carbonated), good sources of liquids include soup, fruit or vegetable juices, and milk.

Vitamins

If your toddler is eating a wide variety of foods, you probably do not need to fret about specific levels of specific vitamins. Nature tends to take care of itself if you are offering (and your child is eating) many foods that are in natural forms. If you want more detailed information about recommended daily allowances for young children, check *Smart Medicine for a Healthier Child* by Janet Zand, Rachel Walton, and Bob Rountree.

In general, your toddler should eat a food rich in vitamin A and a food rich in vitamin C every day.

Foods rich in vitamin A include: apricots, broccoli, Brussels sprouts, cantaloupe, carrots, green leafy vegetables, mangos, papayas, and sweet potatoes. Foods rich in vitamin C include: bell peppers, broccoli, cantaloupe, citrus, kiwi, mangos, papayas, peaches, potatoes (with skin), strawberries, sweet potatoes, and tomatoes. As you can see, there are several foods that supply both vitamins.

Leisurely Meals

If toddlers take a long time to finish a meal, why rush them? Nowhere is it written that food must be consumed within fifteen minutes. The modern trend to rush does not have to be followed at mealtime. Toddlers need a long time to eat for several reasons. It is challenging for them to get food onto a spoon or fork and into their mouth. Furthermore, they don't have many teeth to chew with, and their poor ability to coordinate the muscles of their face and mouth makes chewing and swallowing difficult.

And of course, they must pause to enjoy the sensation of eggs sliding through their fingers and the sound of pickles being banged on a plate. Given that all that fingering and mouthing is good for their motor skills and cognitive development, they derive lots of benefit from the assorted activities they indulge in while satisfying their bird-sized appetites. Let them take their time. Otherwise, they may have difficulty consuming enough to keep them well nourished.

To end a marathon meal but still ensure she's had enough to eat, try the following tactics:

- Announce that since she's not eating, the meal is ending, and you're going to take away her plate.
- If she doesn't begin aiming the food toward her mouth on cue, she may not have understood. Demonstrate by removing the plate.
- If she fusses, assume she is still hungry and return her plate to her.
- If she resumes playing instead of eating, offer to feed her. (Until their fine motor skills develop, toddlers have trouble getting food into their mouth.)
- If she eats or allows herself to be fed, wait to remove the plate until the next time she begins playing. Then remove it for keeps.
- Offer water if she cries, and reassure her that she will be served again at snack time or the next meal.

Given a natural, relaxed environment around meals and food, most toddlers will choose well. In order to help them along, keep yourself on the high road. Stay away from junk foods. Allow plenty of time for eating, even offering to help, if your toddler needs it. Offer healthy foods when your child is hungry, even if they've been refused previously. Don't force your child to eat anything. This will set up difficulties that could result in an eating disorder later in life. Give your little one small amounts of food and let her know she can ask for more. Allow your toddler to eat as little or as much as she wants (from healthy foods, not processed and sugary snacks).

Make Food Interesting

To entice kids to eat good foods, be creative! Here are a few ideas you can try:

- Cut bread with cookie cutters to create interesting shapes before topping with cheese or vegetables. The leftover bread can be frozen and eventually used to stuff chicken or turkey.
- Slice a banana lengthwise to make a boat; stand a piece of sliced cheese inside to make a sail; and float it in a pool of blueberry yogurt. You can even infest the water with shark fins made from salami slices. (If that combination doesn't sound appealing to you, remember that your child probably won't mind, and it all ends up in the same place, anyway!)
- Spread strips of toast with cream cheese or peanut butter and top with a row of raisins for an enticing dish of "ants on a log."
- Make pancakes topped with fruit placed like facial features.

The first few times tots taste peas, broccoli, and any number of other foods parents consider healthy, it is common for them to turn up their nose and vigorously shake their head, or even spit out the food. After trying again and again, the best recourse, nutritionists say, is for parents to try yet again and again. It can take eight to ten exposures before a youngster develops a taste for a new food. Remember the first time you tried an unusual delicacy from another culture?

Many toddlers turn out to dislike certain foods. That's only natural. Just as many adults don't like liver or escargot, your toddler will evolve certain definite preferences. When your toddler is in a growth spurt, he may be more receptive to new foods. Offer them early in the meal, when he's more likely to be hungry.

Restaurant Survival

Toddlers can make very unpleasant dining companions in restaurants because dining out requires two skills they haven't yet mastered: sitting and waiting. Taking them to places designed for adults is apt to be a miserable experience for the parents, the child, and other patrons as well. The rule of thumb is not to look to restaurants for a place to relax and enjoy yourself.

ALERT

> Be careful to keep your voice down when chastising your toddler. Parental nagging is often louder and more incessant than an occasional whine from a toddler, and hence more disruptive to other patrons. Keep the edge out of your voice. It will be unpleasant for fellow diners, worse than your toddler's natural childish sounds.

You can minimize upsets, however, by arriving prepared. In general, the more upscale the restaurant, the longer the wait; so if the cupboard in your diaper bag is bare, don't even wait for the waiter—as you're being seated, ask the host to bring bread or crackers immediately. It's a good idea to arrive with entertainment, too. Try to bring something new and different; otherwise, the novelty of items on the table will hold much more appeal. This might be the time to introduce a new app on your iPad. Rather than beginning the litany of no-nos the minute a small hand gravitates toward a coffee cup, scan the table for items your toddler can safely play with. Trying to prevent youngsters from touching anything guarantees a series of noisy scenes. Toddlers simply must have something to do, so be realistic. Allow them to shred a napkin or to bang a spoon if there's a tablecloth to dampen the sound.

CHAPTER 12

Is It Bedtime Yet?

Minding a toddler is a demanding full-time job. It's no wonder that caregivers look forward to toddlers' sleep time like thirsty desert wanderers crawling toward an oasis. For many parents, the child's time asleep is the only time they can have a few quiet moments alone, work on a hobby, return phone calls, take care of mail, or have an adult conversation. Like everything else about toddlers, the need for sleep varies dramatically from child to child, from nine hours to thirteen hours or more.

How Much Sleep?

How are parents to decide how much sleep their toddler needs? If a child is relaxed and content, it's doubtful that she's sleep deprived, no matter that parents have deep circles under their eyes from entertaining her eighteen hours a day. But since fussier toddlers tend to have more difficulties sleeping, it can be hard to sort out whether the fussiness is caused by a lack of sleep or if their high-strung personality keeps them from getting concentrated, restful sleep.

FACT

The journal *Sleep* reported that nine- to twelve-month-olds averaged two naps per day. At fifteen to twenty-five months, the average dropped to one afternoon nap. Most children continue afternoon naps until age four.

To facilitate getting a toddler to sleep, try getting her into bed when she's sleepy. This means she's physically more relaxed. It's harder when she's physically and emotionally tense from being tired.

Reading the Signals

A common reason that children of all ages don't want to sleep is that they don't want to miss out on something. They want to live every moment to the fullest. They don't want to be shut up alone in a room while other family members are out in the living room having fun. Even if everyone else is in bed, some youngsters would rather be out in the living room having fun all by themselves than lying awake in a darkened room.

Not all toddlers run on the same clock, however, and it is difficult when theirs doesn't adhere to the rest of the family. Some night owls have a hard time sleeping at night no matter how early they get up; early birds may awaken long before the rest of the family despite having gone to bed late the night before. Instead of their biological clock being reset by a consistent schedule that conforms to the rest of the family, they lie awake in bed and are chronically sleep deprived.

Just as toddlers need to tune in to the internal signals that let them know when and how much they need to eat, it is essential that toddlers learn to interpret the internal cues that indicate a need for sleep so that one day they can take care of themselves.

The Battle of the Bed

If you have a struggle getting your toddler to take naps and go to bed at night, you are not alone. Sleep problems routinely appear near the top of the list of the child-rearing problems across America. It is interesting to know, however, that in cultures where families bed down together—sleep problems are uncommon.

Monster Patrol

Certainly the continuing after-lights-out attention seeking from toddlers, and the ongoing worries about monsters and burglars among older children suggest that fear and loneliness are exactly what they experience. In many cultures, parents get toddlers ready for bed and then allow them to rejoin the family until they express an interest in sleeping. If they don't ask to go to bed, parents wait until they fall asleep on the couch or wherever, then carry them into a shared sleep area.

If fears of the dark are keeping your toddler awake, try dousing monsters and assorted goblins in beams from a night-light. It can stop them in their tracks. Often a fear of a nighttime visit from a wild animal or cartoon character can be overcome by outfitting the child with a special repellant guaranteed to render a beastie harmless. The repellant can be anything from a flashlight to a small magic stone (make sure it's too big to fit in the mouth!) to a designated stick they can wave like a magic wand. Since sound can banish monsters, keeping a rattle under their pillow to shake at the shadows in their closet and the branches outside their window can also hold imaginary beasts at bay. Placing a protective object in the room, such as an oversized teddy bear to stand watch, can be reassuring.

The Family Bed

American taboos are quickly falling by the wayside as more parents find that the age-old solution of letting toddlers sleep with them virtually eliminates bedtime scenes and helps everyone get better rest. Although this practice appears more kid-friendly on the surface, there's no guarantee that it will enhance a toddler's life. The loss of the parent's alone time can make it harder to remain patient with the youngster during the day, which is clearly not in a toddler's best interest. Additionally, the loss of private time with the spouse can jeopardize marital relationships, which, given the stress of rearing a toddler, may already be strained.

Big Bed Safety

Toddlers are probably in greater jeopardy from sleeping alone in a crib than from bunking with parents, given the risk that they'll climb over the bars and fall to the floor, become trapped between the mattress and the bars, or that another emergency will arise that a parent asleep in another room won't hear. Still, accidents in big beds do occur, and parents should take commonsense precautions before deciding to sleep with their little one.

Bad Bedfellows

Many parents find that having the family snuggled up together in the same bed produces some of their warmest moments. Others find it far from pleasant. Some toddlers thrash, toss, elbow, wiggle, wet, and generally make difficult sleeping companions. Early risers may chatter, hum, poke, and play.

If parents don't want to share their bed, moving the crib or toddler bed into the parent's bedroom can eliminate the loneliness and enhance children's sense of safety and security. This usually translates into less resistance at bedtime. Some children can tolerate being on the opposite side of the room with a curtain or room divider to provide some privacy for the parents.

If parents decide to move a small bedfellow, the best time to initiate the project is when separation and attachment issues are less of a factor—typically around age three. Otherwise, aim for a period when the child isn't going through a lot of other difficult adjustments, separation anxiety isn't a major issue, the child wants to grow up rather than regress to baby days, and independence conflicts aren't paramount.

From Crib to Toddler Bed

Cribs are recalled due to safety defects and hazards from time to time, so check with the manufacturer before making your purchase. When conducting your own inspection, watch for the two common problems. First, the slats shouldn't be more than 2 ⅜ inches apart so children can't get their head caught between them. Second, make sure older models weren't painted with a lead-based paint.

Sleepy Climbers

Cribs are not for climbers! Be careful about putting toys into a toddler's crib; if he steps on top of them, it may give him just the boost he needs to make it up the side and over the bars. A fall from such a great height poses the risk of injury. Some little monkeys surprise their parents by managing to climb out not long after their first birthday. Put some padding on the floor beneath the crib to soften it in the event of a fall. As soon as your little one begins scaling the bars, it's time to move up to a toddler bed.

Toddler beds are a great next step because they have raised sides to keep youngsters from falling out—and from feeling afraid they might fall out. They are also lower to the floor and pose less danger in case a child finds it fun to climb over the side.

ESSENTIAL

Many children are in love with their toddler bed initially because they're so easy to climb out of! Parents must decide whether it's better to lower the bars, which makes climbing less dangerous or to keep the bars up to prevent a fall while sleeping. Another option is to have the child sleep on the mattress on the floor.

Since many toddler beds use the same size mattress as a crib, it's best to stick with the old one if at all possible. The familiar feel and smell of the old mattress can help smooth the transition from the crib. The quality of toddler bed frames varies dramatically from brand to brand. If you plan to lie down with your child to read stories or sleep, be sure to get a model sturdy enough to support both of you.

Making the Transition

How will your toddler handle the transition from crib to toddler bed? There's simply no way to predict it. It's smooth as silk for some, decidedly difficult for others. If a child is very resistant to change, slow to adapt to new situations, or a sentimentalist, leaving the safety and security of the crib can be trying. Given a toddler's love of predictability and routine, it's a bad idea to let him step into his room to find his beloved crib gone. He may not find his parent's idea of a great surprise to be so wonderful. Perhaps he didn't like his crib at all. Nevertheless, it was the steady friend that kept him safe night after night for as long as he can remember. If possible, provide a gradual transition. The secret to getting youngsters to give up their crib more willingly, many parents say, is to have them participate in the process from the very beginning.

Staying Put

The toddler who won't stay put in a toddler bed poses a real dilemma for parents: What to do with a little one who scurries out of bed the minute parents have finished tucking him in? What to do with the little insomniac who rises in the middle of the night and forays into the living room when everyone is asleep? The first step to getting a child to stay in bed is to discuss it.

ESSENTIAL

As with anything you are trying to teach your toddler, bedtime procedures are established with baby steps. Be patient and consistent as you train your child to stay in bed for the night.

Explain that it is dangerous for him to be up by himself, that he must stay in bed unless it's an emergency, and that he is to call Mommy or Daddy from his bedroom if he needs something. After that explanation, which a child may or may not understand, make it a policy to studiously avoid further conversation. Limit verbal exchanges to repeating in a firm tone of voice, "You're supposed to stay in bed unless it's an emergency. Go back to bed and call if you need something." (This assumes the parent has a baby monitor or is close enough to his room to hear him call.)

Walk him back to his room, help him into bed, issue another reminder to call if he needs something, and leave. Toddlers in this situation are apt to cry or call before you make it through the bedroom door. If that happens, turn around and go right back to his bedside to check on him, just as you promised.

In getting across any new idea to a toddler, you need to go one step at a time and show him how things are supposed to go. Stepping out of the room and turning right back around to go back in demonstrates what is to happen: He calls; you respond. That can provide reassurance that having to be a big boy sleeping in a big bed doesn't mean he is expected to be independent. If a toddler doesn't start climbing back out of bed the moment the parent turns to leave, that should be considered a victory.

ALERT

It may seem inhumane to install a door protector and close the door to contain a toddler who keeps popping out of a toddler bed after everyone else is asleep. But given the danger youngsters can get into roaming the house, it may be the only recourse. Be sure to completely childproof the bedroom first!

Remain calm and matter-of-fact as you approach your child's bed, and say, "I heard you calling. Is everything all right? What do you want?" Provide a drink of water if a child says he's thirsty; do the monster check again if he's scared; then give him a pat and tell him he's doing fine, that it will take a while to get used to the new bed. Repeat the procedure several times, trying to avoid all conversation except:

I heard you call. What do you want?
You're fine now. It's time to get some sleep.
Good night.

Begin extending the time between visits to the child's room. Difficulty with the transition to a strange bed is understandable, too. Many adults have a hard time sleeping when they're away from home for the very same reason.

Winding Down

Insisting that toddlers nap or go to bed when they aren't sleepy can provoke power struggles. Instead, have them observe quiet time. A noisy environment can certainly interfere with a child's ability to fall asleep. After entering dreamland, some can tolerate a lot of hullabaloo; others remain susceptible to being awakened by sounds, especially during lighter phases of sleep. If you can't produce a quiet environment on cue, classical music can help to mask telltale sounds that suggest interesting happenings are going on elsewhere in the house.

To create a quiet and relaxing transition, help them unwind by providing soothing entertainment such as listening to music or looking at books. Bath time routines help, too. Discourage continued requests to get up by putting a kitchen timer in their bedroom. Tell them that, unless it's an emergency, they must wait until the alarm sounds before getting up or calling to you.

Once they do relax, sleep may not be far behind. Even if sleep doesn't follow immediately, children need to learn to relax and spend time entertaining themselves. Common strategies parents use to help their toddler fall asleep include rocking them to sleep, singing lullabies, telling stories, giving back rubs, holding their hand, and taking the child into their bed.

ALERT

Nursing and giving children a bottle to help them fall asleep is not a good idea, dentists say, because the milk pools in their mouth, rotting their teeth. The same problem applies to juice and other sweet beverages. Remember: only water!

Meanwhile, some desperate parents have gone so far as to childproof their little night owl's bedroom, leaving no outlet uncovered, no hard edge exposed. They empty it of all toys except board books, stuffed animals, and other toys that can be safely enjoyed without supervision, and remove all furniture but the bed. They install a gate across the doorway to contain their toddler, and allow them to play until they're ready to sleep, instructing them to call Mommy and Daddy if they need anything. Then they head off to dreamland, and let their night owl entertain herself.

Exercise

Exercise relieves pent-up energy born of stress, tension, and the basic need to be on the go. Be sure your child gets lots of chances to run and jump and engage in active physical play during the day. A child's exercise class may encourage more sedentary types to move more and sit less. Then, spend more time engaging in quiet, pleasurable activities before naps and bedtime to soothe frazzled nerves. Try an extra-long bath, a second storybook, or a third chorus of a lullaby. Remember, however, that although stress can make it harder to relax enough to sleep, this too is something children need to learn to do. Anytime they are able to recover from an upset during the day, point it out. This skill will serve them well at night.

Sleep Time Rituals

Rituals that induce relaxation can help toddlers make the transition from a busy, active day to sleep. Going through an invariable progression from taking a bath, hearing a story, listening to a lullaby, and saying prayers helps toddler insomniacs, just like their adult counterparts. As people come to associate the ritual with sleep, their bodies automatically begin to relax.

Many parents don't consider instituting naptime rituals, but they can make a real difference. It's good to communicate with your babysitters or child care workers, if possible, so that the routine never varies. Rituals should be designed to soothe, so avoid stimulating activities like roughhousing, tickling, and exciting or scary stories.

Some children engage in troublesome rituals such as repetitive rocking, which can escalate into head banging, as a way to soothe themselves. It usually stops by eighteen months. You can help by not overreacting, by padding the sides of the crib, and by beefing up other bedtime rituals to provide a more gradual transition.

Sleep Skills

The downside of all that rocking and singing and back rubbing and music playing to quiet fretful children and help them fall asleep is that they come to depend on someone or something outside of themselves—a real problem if they wake up in the middle of the night. Children need to learn eventually to handle the task of falling asleep—and of falling back asleep—unassisted.

ESSENTIAL

To help toddlers wind down at bedtime, check out books like *Goodnight Moon* by Margaret Wise Brown, *Dr. Seuss's Sleep Book*, *Time for Bed* by Mem Fox, and *The Going to Bed Book* by Sandra Boynton.

Many parents dedicate themselves to learning how to put their child to sleep, when the goal should be for toddlers to learn to put themselves to sleep and to put themselves back to asleep after awakening. Sleep experts point out that children need to acquire a specific set of sleep skills. Surprisingly, they don't come naturally to many. Children must learn how to fall asleep, fall back asleep, and sleep through the night.

Learning to Be Alone

The first step is for children to learn to spend time alone. Being comfortable spending time alone in a crib or toddler bed is a prerequisite for falling asleep and for falling back asleep. By handing toddlers a stuffed animal after they awaken in the morning or from a nap, leaving the room, and waiting five to fifteen minutes to rescue them, parents can give them time to practice being by themselves. Some experts say this can serve them well at night.

Sleep Cycles

Children cycle in and out of different sleep phases throughout the night, entering a light sleep phase six to eight times. It is during these light sleep periods they are most likely to awaken. Adults typically awaken three to four times per night, although they may not be alert enough to remember. If toddlers awaken fully during each and every cycle, and must depend on a parent's help to get back to sleep . . . that becomes never-ending. Sometimes parents can alter the sleep cycles by breaking into them. Try awakening the toddler just before you go to bed. Spend a few minutes smiling and chatting. Then help her fall back asleep.

Holding Firm

In two-parent homes, it may be best to have the adult who is less intensely connected to the child be the one to manage bedtime complaints and middle-of-the-night pleas for attention. Since bedtime brings up separation issues for adults as well as for children, the more connected parent may experience some anxiety that the child picks up on. This can intensify the distress and separation anxiety of both. The parent in charge of putting the child to bed should be firm and matter-of-fact.

Handling Hysteria

What if two weeks later the child still manages to scream for an hour? With toddlers, there's no way to predict what will happen. Sometimes the parent's attitude plays a role. If the parent is distressed about the child's intense crying, the youngster will sense it. The timed parental visits to the nursery meant to reassure may have the opposite effect.

What happens when parents refrain from running into their wailing toddler's bedroom to help him fall asleep, and he is so upset he vomits? Or he cries so hard, he can't catch his breath and begins gasping for air? This is the point at which many parents decide the "give him time to learn to settle himself down" approach is doing more harm than good. Check with your pediatrician to see whether it's okay to hold firm under these circumstances. If so, be as sympathetic as you would toward any little person who is having such a hard time mastering something difficult. Then change the sheets, clean him up, tuck him in, give him a pat, and tell him he'll be okay. Tell him it's time to sleep, wish him sweet dreams, and leave. Return a few minutes later to check on him to be sure he's not ill.

Sleep Strategies

If a child awakens crying and parents determine that he isn't ill, they can verbally reassure him that he is fine or offer a stuffed animal or other favored toy for comfort. What happens next is up to each family. Philosophies of what's best for toddlers differ. Sleep problems are among the toughest, and what is acceptable to parents in one household is definitely not workable in another. You can:

- Leave and stay away no matter how hard the child cries, so that he can eventually learn to fall asleep by himself. (Be sure the hard crying doesn't signal illness or injury.)
- Remain physically present to provide some reassurance and moral support, moving a chair a few inches farther from the crib each night until you are out the door, thereby helping the child to feel more secure while he learns to fall asleep on his own.
- Hold, rock, sing, carry, and otherwise soothe the child to help him fall asleep.
- Invite the child into your bed.

Whether you sleep together or apart, or whether you respond to each call from the bedroom, only go in when your child is hysterical, or resolutely stay away, don't judge others negatively for doing it their way—and don't let them judge you.

Nightmares

The brain waves of tiny babies suggest that even the youngest members of our species dream. Similarly, many toddlers have nightmares. Because children in this age group have such a poor ability to distinguish reality from fantasy, it can be impossible to convince them that the monsters and big bad bears aren't real. Nevertheless, provide lots of reassurance that "it was just a dream." When they're old enough, they'll understand the difference.

There are no proven ways to eliminate nightmares, but you can encourage your child to share the bad dreams, since this helps many toddlers feel better. If her vocabulary is limited, try to help her tell it. If she says, "Bear," ask, "Was it a scary bear?" Avoid questions like, "Was the bear trying to eat somebody?" so as not to implant more fear!

Sleep Terrors

These sudden, unexplained bouts of screaming and wild thrashing within the first few hours of going to sleep can be terrifying to parents who find themselves unable to comfort their youngster. Although children appear to be awake, they are actually asleep during these episodes and have no memory of them on awakening. Sleep terrors are believed to occur at the transition from one phase of sleep to another. The only reported dangers are sleep walking, which can lead to injury, and some very upset parents.

Cut Back on Caffeine

Some toddlers are affected more than others, but anything containing caffeine is on the list of before bedtime no-nos—exactly how long before depends on the toddler. Likewise, it's a good idea to keep anything with caffeine off the list of toddler foods and beverages if getting them down for naps is a problem.

FACT

"Good night, sleep tight, don't let the bedbugs bite" can conjure up frightening images that are later replayed in dreams. Instead, try the far gentler Spanish saying: "*Duérmate con los angelitos*" (pronounced d'where-mah-tay cone lows ahn-hay-lee-toes) or the English equivalent: "May you sleep with the little angels."

Cane sugar and artificial colorings have also been known to turn some youngsters into whirling dervishes. So do some food allergies. Exercise greater-than-normal caution about bedtime snacks for toddlers who have a hard time winding down and dozing off.

CHAPTER 13

Very Special Toddlers

Some toddlers will be toward the ends of the continuum of various abilities and development. You may find that you have a little Einstein, and the typical how-to toddler books just don't seem to apply. Every parent believes that their child is special, but you know in your heart that your child is really special. Or you may discover that your toddler has medical difficulties or significant developmental lags. In either case, there is a wealth of information to help you.

The Gifted Toddler

Gifted children can show incredible emotional and social sensitivity, such as wanting to share a bounty of birthday or Christmas gifts with families who are not as fortunate. Some are physically sensitive, becoming irritated over socks that don't feel right, clothing tags that scratch their skin, or fabric that is too rough. Some sensitive toddlers will take off their shoes whenever they can, preferring direct contact with the floor, carpet, or grass.

They're Intense

Very young gifted children can feel strong passion about their interests, such as being able to identify various models of cars and even wanting their own subscription to a car magazine. Your toddler may be passionate about sharks and beg to go to a museum to see displays about sharks.

FACT

If your gifted child insists on the same story repeatedly, remember that hearing words in context is the best way to build vocabulary. The more words kids understand at age two, the better they read in first grade. When toddlers know a story by heart, it is easier for them to match the written words to the sounds as you run your finger along the text.

Why Do They Do That?

Gifted tots develop skills in the same sequence as everyone else, but they do it faster. When the backgrounds of geniuses were examined, one study found that they had begun talking at an average age of nine months! And since that's an average, many began much earlier! Still, many were far less precocious, so even exceptionally late talkers aren't out of the running for a Nobel Prize.

Your gifted toddler may turn on lights all over the house, change the language of the TV or DVD program (French is nice for a change), play with control knobs in the car, and try to use all the kitchen appliances. You will have to be very quick to stay ahead of her! Keep in mind her safety as well as opportunities to investigate.

According to a quotation from writer Pearl S. Buck, "The truly creative mind in any field is no more than this: A human creature born abnormally, inhumanly sensitive. To him a touch is a blow, a sound is a noise, a misfortune is a tragedy, a joy is an ecstasy, a friend is a lover, a lover is a god, and failure is death."

There's Types of Smarts

Currently, it is not possible to assess intelligence in toddlers reliably. For older children and adults, genius means performing at an exceptional level in one or more of the following areas identified by Howard Gardner, winner of the MacArthur Award:

- **Linguistic intelligence.** Exceptional abilities at speaking or writing characterize a genius orator or writer.
- **Logical-mathematical intelligence.** Gifted scientists have special abilities to think and reason abstractly.
- **Spatial intelligence.** Talented architects, choreographers, and engineers are able to visualize forms and shapes and comprehend spatial relationships.
- **Interpersonal intelligence.** The hallmark of great leaders and therapists is their capability to understand and influence people.
- **Intrapersonal intelligence.** The uncanny ability of some special people to plummet the depths of their own mind has transformed the world. Metaphysicists like Carl Jung and Jean-Paul Sartre are in this group.
- **Kinesthetic intelligence.** Outstanding athletes and dancers possess special physical abilities.
- **Musical intelligence.** The special talent of musical geniuses is the ability to tune into subtle nuances of sound and rhythm.

In one study on children aged two and a half with IQs at the top of the chart, parents reported the following personality characteristics:

- 90 percent were described as "sensitive"
- 83 percent liked to concentrate on one activity at a time
- 79 percent had high energy or activity levels
- 50 percent needed less sleep than other children
- 44 percent were sensitive to clothing tags and other tactile sensations

Gifted Challenges

Some studies have found that gifted children appear to have short attention spans because they become bored so easily. Others have found them to be overly excitable and unusually intense, with greater emotional extremes, including more compassion, sadness, and depression.

More intelligent toddlers are likely to have more frustrations to contend with than other youngsters. Their minds can concoct projects, problems, and solutions, but they are blocked by their physical limitations. For example, they can figure out how to solve a puzzle but lack the motor coordination needed to fit its pieces into their proper places. Or they may have complex ideas to express, but don't have the verbal skills to communicate them.

A gifted toddler who can speak very well may be puzzled by other children who do not answer her questions or talk in fluent, complete sentences. It seems quite odd to her. Gentle adult intervention can quiet the child's perplexity.

The exquisite sensitivity that enables them to note subtle differences in texture, movement, color, and shape means that what others perceive as a blank wall can appear to them as a vibrant palette. Because they are constantly bombarded with sensory stimuli, they are more stressed. The extreme interpersonal sensitivity causes some tots to tune into other people's feelings. They are aware of hints of criticism and displeasure that other toddlers don't notice. Ironically, the combination of extreme sensitivity, high energy level, and reduced need for sleep are characteristics of children often diagnosed as "hyperactive." There may be a lot of very misunderstood toddlers out there!

Gearing Up for Greatness

Programs designed to nurture toddler genius, ranging from the Institute for the Achievement of Human Potential headquartered in Pennsylvania to the Yew Chung International Schools in China are firm that at this stage, the following should occur:

- Focus on the whole child, including emotional, behavioral, and social development.
- Toddlers should be free to follow their own inclinations by having a range of materials available for them to explore.
- Toddlers should not be pressed to pursue structured learning activities.
- Use a loving and nurturing approach when working with toddlers.
- Participate actively; your role in learning is central.

It is not necessary to directly teach a gifted child. It is better to provide the situation, set the stage so that the child can discover and form conclusions on her own. In-depth, complex, high-power thinking takes place as children struggle to figure things out for themselves. Anyone who says, "She's just playing" doesn't understand how toddlers learn!

Genius Troubles

If your toddler is exceptionally difficult to manage, it could be because she's literally too smart for her britches! An estimated 20–25 percent of gifted children have social and emotional problems—twice the normal rate, according to Ellen Winner, PhD, who has studied gifted children and prodigies. Meanwhile, for moderately gifted children, the rates of maladjustment were the same as for average children. Similar problems with hyperactivity and attention have been found among highly gifted (IQ from 140 to 154) and learning-disabled boys.

Early Achievement

In this same study, reported characteristics of genius toddlers included:

- 94 percent were very alert as infants
- 94 percent had a long attention span as an infant or toddler
- 91 percent showed early language development
- 60 percent showed early motor skill development
- 48.9 percent were ambidextrous at some period of their development
- 37 percent had imaginary playmates

It's also interesting to note that the age at which mothers of gifted children gave birth was older than average—30.8 years. Is that because older moms tend to be more patient and tolerant than younger ones and work with them more? There are no proven theories.

ALERT

Teaching strategies appropriate for older children actually inhibit toddler learning. Toddlers seem to have an innate sense of what they need to learn next; structured learning activities imposed by adults distract them from the work they know they need to do!

Special Gifts

Regardless of whether parents suspect giftedness, they should provide a wide range of learning experiences to stimulate brain development. They also need to respect toddlers' choices about how to spend their time. Pushing and pressuring can propel toddlers down the path of rebellion, burnout, or the trap of molding themselves to fulfill someone else's dreams.

Children's abilities differ. Some are intellectually superior; most are average; and some are clearly slow. When intelligence is very limited, the challenge for parents may be learning to appreciate their youngster's other special gifts.

Rest assured—each child has them. For instance, the typically loving natures and sunny dispositions of children with Down syndrome remind the rest of us about the importance of pausing in our self-absorbed, busy lives to share a heartfelt smile with a stranger and grace an acquaintance with an affectionate hug. Look for your child's strengths, and cherish them!

Little Question Box

Gifted toddlers ask a lot of questions. Some you may be able to answer and some you cannot. It is good for your toddler to see how you find out answers to questions. You might reach for a book off your shelf, find out from the Internet, or go to the library to find some different resources. If you come up with zero and have to say, "That seems to be a very hard question where the answer is difficult to find," that's okay, too.

As your toddler matures and interests start to become apparent, you may want to seek out mentors for your child who have particular talents to share and discuss with the little one. Perhaps the neighbor has a beautiful flower garden and would be happy to spend time with your little horticulturist. You might have a scientist friend who would take your child (and you) to a planetarium for an exciting look at the stars. You might know a musician who wouldn't mind having the child present at an orchestra rehearsal. Usually gifted adults rather like gifted people of all ages. They have enormous respect for the unbridled curiosity of fellow gifted folks.

Your example as a curious adult is wonderful for the gifted child, as curiosity is a consistent trait among gifted people of all ages.

Hazards Ahead!

Watch out for perfectionism! It can be deadly for the child. Gifted toddlers will likely be emotionally sensitive and easy to blunt with too much prodding or pushing. It's a good idea to remember that the process of the quest of learning is what engages the mind, not the result. The result may be momentarily interesting, but the joy is in careening down the path to get there.

The child needs to understand that he is loved for who he is, not for what he does. The best prevention for the harms of perfectionism is to give the child plenty of unconditional love and affection. It also is sensible to let the child fail from time to time. Failure is definitely a part of life, and even a very young child can learn that he's okay, even if things don't turn out quite as expected.

Social Relationships

According to James Alvino, an editor for *Gifted Children Monthly*, a gifted toddler may have particular challenges in social relationships. The parent can watch for signs. Does your child:

- Argue incessantly?
- Act as if what others say is not important?
- Want to always prove a point?
- Insist on describing things or people in detail?
- Dominate conversations?
- Act impatient if someone else is getting attention?

Such behavior can harm social relations for the child, and some gentle reminding and guidance will rub off some of the rough edges. You can acknowledge that the child has a right to his point of view, but so do the other children.

Alvino goes on to say that sometimes gifted children will withdraw in discouragement. Does your child:

- Prefer to be alone?
- Scorn silliness?
- Seem nervous around other people?
- Seem completely absorbed in his own interests?
- Refuse to be interested in others' projects?
- Show intolerance?
- Resist involvement with others?

While it is typical for even toddlers of a young age to have a longer than usual attention span, the parent can become alert if the child seems to genuinely not like people or want to be around them to any degree. In extreme cases, professional help might be needed to build the child's confidence.

You're in Charge

Parents of gifted children can sometimes become seduced into manipulations and conversations in which the child senses the parent's insecurity. You have to know when to put your foot down and stick with something, just because you said so. In other words, pick your battles and realize that you, as the older person, are in charge, even if your toddler is very bright and has initiated a lengthy debate over something that is annoying to you. Don't become intimidated. A child who learns that he can manipulate his parents becomes an unhappy, insecure child in the long run.

Future UN Interpreter

If you are bilingual, can you teach your gifted toddler both languages? Definitely yes! Some theorists believe that it is easier for the child if each person in the family speaks primarily in a single language. For example, Grandma may speak in Spanish but Aunt Susie in English. A gifted child, however, can sort out the languages, even if one person speaks in both tongues.

Katherine Knox, who teaches English as a second language at Colorado State University, believes that children go through several stages of becoming bilingual. First, they will mix the two languages, sometimes choosing the word that is easier to pronounce. Then at a later stage, they will speak in one language or the other, one at a time. It is typical that children from bilingual families speak fluently a little later than children from homes where only one language is spoken.

Gifted Play Activities

Activities for gifted toddlers may seem at first glance similar to activities for all toddlers, and they are. But if you add a bit of the quality of investigation, they will be even more engaging for the young, inquiring mind. Think of the gifted toddler as a very young scientist or artist and set the stage, materials, and atmosphere. The child will take it from there.

Boxes

Cardboard boxes are great for gifted kids of all ages, providing entertainment that can last for hours. Keep a supply of various sizes and shapes on hand, including empty shoeboxes, Band-Aid boxes, tea boxes, tissue boxes, gift boxes, packing boxes, and cereal boxes.

Make a Playhouse

The most wondrous of all, of course, is an appliance box. If you haven't bought a refrigerator or big-screen TV lately, you're bound to find a giant box at your local recycling center or at stores that sell large appliances. Cut a door, windows, even a small escape hatch, and your toddler has a castle, fort, spaceship, cave, or anything else she can imagine.

ESSENTIAL

Give your child some ideas for creative play, but let his creative imagination do most of the work. You'll be surprised to realize how much he has learned from you already, and you'll have a better understanding of how his mind works. If you can, step aside a bit and encourage rather than direct.

You can go all-out with paint on the exterior, contact paper, wallpaper, and fabric scrap curtains. Outfit the playhouse with a small pillow and blanket to make a little bed. Better yet, let your gifted child decide how she wants it decorated. But don't go too far. Even the best packing boxes don't last forever.

Make a Fort

Use boxes to make a pint-sized kitchen. Cut a square in the side of a box for an oven door and draw or paint burners for a stovetop, a refrigerator, and a freezer door so they'll open, just like on your kitchen appliance. Cut a small hole in the top of a box and insert a plastic whipped topping container for a sink; then cut cabinet doors in the front. Stock the kitchenette with cottage-cheese-container bowls, pots, yogurt-container cups, and a few plastic spoons. Show toddlers how plastic coffee-can lids can be platters and plates. Engage your gifted toddler in detailed conversation about what is needed to outfit the kitchen.

FACT

Although structured play activities and games have value, the best activities are open ended. Allow time for your child to choose and create her own play scenarios. She will benefit the most when she has the opportunity to explore the themes and ideas that are most important and relevant to her.

Literacy Activities for Your Gifted Toddler

Literacy is the ability to interpret and use written forms of communication. Gifted children often love books and anything having to do with language and ideas. There are many skills that your child will need to learn how to read and write—however, the most valuable thing you can teach your child might be an attitude. Children who develop a love of reading at a young age are more successful readers in school. Take the time now to share books and stories with your child. Even a young gifted toddler will thrive on stories and books. Take the time to play lots of literacy games with your child, such as these:

Captions

This is a fantastic way to show your child that words are talk written down. This is a major abstract concept that relates to reading. Your child will be particularly motivated to "read" her own words. For this activity you will need:

- Bond paper
- Crayons or markers
- Picture book (optional)

1. Whenever your child draws or paints a picture, ask her to tell you about what she created. Write down her words, and create a caption for the art work. Be sure to read it back to her.

2. As an alternative, you can show your child photos or pictures in a book. Invite her to supply a caption by asking her to tell a story about the picture. Again, be sure to write down and review her words.

Does Not Belong

This activity teaches visual discrimination in the same way as the well-known *Sesame Street* song, "One of These Things Is Not Like the Other." You can make many game pieces in varying degrees of complication. For this activity you will need:

- Ruler
- Light-colored construction or bond paper
- Markers or crayons

1. Using the ruler, draw lines to divide each sheet of paper into four equal sections.
2. Draw or color identical shapes or pictures in three of the sections. Choose a different square on each sheet to leave blank.
3. Draw an item that is different from the others in the fourth square. For example, you may have three squares and one triangle, three red dots and one blue dot, or three dogs and a cat.
4. Ask your child to identify the object that is different.

Using Books

A love for books and reading is a gift that will last your child a lifetime. Remember books are not meant to be decorations to be gazed at from afar. If you are worried that your toddler will rip or chew a book, buy her books that are made to be extra durable. Let your child have the opportunity to look at books and peruse the pictures. These activities are a great way to use books as a springboard for further literacy development. The love of books will create a lifetime of happiness for your gifted little one! Here are some ideas that could be fun:

- **Reading to stuffed animals.** Encourage your little philosopher to read to her animals. You might be pleased to hear the true concern and sophisticated inflections in her voice as she shares bedtime stories or anytime stories with her furry friends.
- **Handmade books.** Take some of your child's paintings, and ask her to tell you what it's about. Hand print those words, exactly as she states them and arrange them close to the paintings. Staple several pictures together and read it to her as any other book. She will love it because it's her own words.

Story Songs

Enjoy long involved songs together, such as "Froggy Went a-Courting" and "I Know an Old Lady Who Swallowed a Fly." If you don't know these songs, ask your parents or grandparents. They probably learned them when they were young.

Storytelling

Long before the invention of the printing press, fables, myths, and tales were being shared with young children. Each time the tale was told, it was shaped by the teller's interpretation and expression. Today there are literally thousands of wonderful books available for children. But you shouldn't be afraid, once in a while, to put down a book and spin a yarn for your young child. You have the opportunity to bring a story to life. Use different voices and facial expressions to add interest. Encouraging children to make up stories is a great way to facilitate imagination as well as promote both early verbal and written literacy skills. Get started by involving children as you develop a tale. Seek out skilled storytellers among your family, friends, and acquaintances, and ask them to tell stories to your tot. Be sure to take pictures of her enraptured expression!

- Flannel boards are a great way to tell stories and encourage a gifted child to rearrange the characters and parts of the story. You can buy a ready-made flannel board at a school supply store or make your own with felt scraps and Velcro.

- Make scrapbooks of your toddler's favorite topics or experiences. You might make separate books on themes, such as interesting jobs, things to eat, places to go.
- Make a texture scrapbook using scraps of such things as sandpaper, corduroy, silk, fake fur, aluminum foil, and burlap. Encourage your child to talk about the feeling of each texture.

Special-Needs Toddlers

If you have a knowing sense that your toddler is not developing normally, have her tested for hearing, vision, and diagnosis of development. You are entitled to screening through the Individuals with Disabilities Education Act (IDEA), as well as education, care, and assistance for your toddler and yourself.

ALERT

If a child can't learn some colors, parents should consider the possibility of blue-green color blindness. If he can't learn any, he may be completely colorblind. See a professional. Color blindness is an inconvenient handicap, but most color blind adults easily compensate with other abilities.

You have many decisions to make in regard to your special-needs toddler. It will be easiest to manage if both parents unite as a team, consulting physicians and other specialists together. Keep careful records of tests and consultations, so that time-consuming testing does not have to be repeated. Write everything down in a notebook or digital file. Become as informed as you can about the diagnosis. There are helpful organizations listed in Appendix B, and you can find online support groups to guide you through the rough times.

Respite

Plan respite for yourself if you take care of your special-needs toddler at home. If the disability is severe, residential care may be viable, especially if you are the head of a single-parent family. As with regular day care, choose a home that feels warm and caring, and inquire about taking your child home for weekends or special events. Form friendships with other parents of toddlers with challenges.

Stages of Growth

Special-needs kids will go through some of the same stages of growth as other toddlers—learning to feed themselves, going to the bathroom, and wanting to assert themselves independently. You may have tantrums and scenes on your hands, and many of the same techniques are in order for your special-needs child—consistency, remaining calm yourself, rewarding positive behavior.

Don't forget to have fun with your disabled toddler! Play with toys, enjoy outings, meet people for lunch or some fun in the park.

Siblings

The brothers and sisters of your special little one also need support and assistance. Make time for them, occasionally without the challenged sibling. Watch for signs of stress, such as being withdrawn or acting out. Having a special-needs child affects every family member, and your alertness and strength as a role model will help everyone navigate a healthy way. If you are honest and factual with your other children, they will form a positive, accepting attitude. Watch out for any tendency you may have to pressure your other children to compensate for the disability of your special-needs child.

Attention Deficit Disorder

According to John Roth, a pediatrician at the University of Louisville, children of all levels of intelligence and age can be affected by attention deficit disorder, commonly called ADD, or ADHD including the element of hyperactivity. Such children cannot harness their talents or energy.

Symptoms of ADD or ADHD

The major symptoms of attention deficit problems are inattention, impulsivity, and hyperactivity. Such a toddler can wear out the family! Emotional support for the child is crucial, building self-esteem, as much as possible.

You can structure activities in shorter increments of time to allow for briefer periods of concentration.

ESSENTIAL

Sometimes an adjustment in diet will calm down the child. Aim toward diets that are free of additives, sugar, and preservatives. Be on the special lookout for caffeine, a stimulant that contributes nothing to a toddler who is already in high gear. Chocolate and carbonated drinks generally include caffeine.

Most children with ADHD outgrow the symptoms once their nervous system matures, usually about at the age of puberty. Many experts consider these symptoms not a disorder, but simply a variation along a continuum, with some children being very calm and others especially active. ADHD is not related to level of intelligence. They may seem to be less intelligent, but that is because they have trouble focusing on one thing for any length of time.

Observe with Peers

Being very active sometimes can be attributed to higher intelligence. If you wonder if your toddler is truly ADHD, it can help to observe him in relation to his peers. For example, does he seem to have a shorter attention span than the other children? Does he have difficulty following simple instructions? Is he demanding and overly emotional, having frequent outbursts and temper tantrums? Does he have more trouble sitting still than the other children? Does he behave more recklessly—run into the street, grab a cup of hot coffee, or hit a strange dog? Does he resist authority and require constant attention? If many of the answers to these questions are "yes," then you may wish to consult your pediatrician.

Other Disabilities

Some of the other chronic challenges that can occur in young children include autism, asthma, AIDS, severe allergies, cancer, cerebral palsy, cystic fibrosis, diabetes, Down syndrome, epilepsy, hearing impairment, muscular dystrophy, sickle-cell disease, and visual impairment. Also, children who had a low birth weight due to their mother's abuse of substances during pregnancy may have developmental challenges during the toddler years. Each of these particular difficulties requires specialized treatment for the child and ongoing support for you. Your physician can recommend local and national organizations associated with each situation.

Caring for Yourself

As a parent of a child with challenges, you require special attention yourself. It can be exhausting to try to keep up with the energy level of such a child. Get assistance from other family members so you have down time. Treat yourself to a spa session, a revitalizing yoga class, or simply a walk by yourself in a beautiful, wooded park. Time-outs are for parents, too!

Assistive Devices

Disabled toddlers can learn to operate switches of all kinds. Specialized equipment exists that creates music or other rewards when the child moves his head a particular direction. Your special-needs toddler can learn to touch a screen for the reward of shapes and colors.

Children with severe communication delays can receive help with devices that expand their language efforts. Your little one can indicate, "I want to eat," or "I want to go outside," by selecting a button on a screen or touching a picture. If your special-needs child starts early, communication will develop more rapidly, allowing more social interaction with people of all ages. Such devices may be paid for through the IDEA law, and some libraries and community centers have switch toys and other things you can try out before committing to them. Some cerebral palsy organizations offer a program called Tech Tots.

IDEA offers other services, such as customization of items for special-needs toddlers, including training for the parents in how to use special equipment.

Team Effort

Often a team comes together to help you map out a program that best supports the development of your disabled little one. Each person communicates with every other member of the team so that the child has continuity going from home to the various locations that provide care.

As the parent of a special-needs toddler, keep in mind that it is the law that your child receives as much assistance as is required for him to live at the maximum level of development. It may take some diligence on your part to search out the various agencies and state programs that carry out the IDEA requirements.

CHAPTER 14

Families Plus

At this time in the twenty-first century there is no one-size-fits-all family. People live alone or in various couplings and groups that were not obvious in past generations. How ever you find yourself on this shifting social map, the important thing is that you are happy with your life, so you can relate happily with your toddler. The quality of your home life and personal life is important to raising your toddler, as all that occurs with your little one occurs in the context of the relationships at home and outside the home.

And Baby Makes Three

You may be the primary caretaker of your toddler, but your primary relationship is your marriage. How can this be? Is this new math? It may seem confusing, as your little one is absolutely dependent on you for survival. Moment by moment, each decision and action has an immediate bearing on the well-being of your toddler. You may feel that you have a lot to juggle with work, significant others, and being an informed parent. At times you feel like a master performer with several balls in the air! Your life is one of sometimes dramatically shifting priorities. Flexibility is always the name of the game.

ALERT

If you can't expand the quantity of time you spend with your child, improve the quality by carving out a twenty-minute slot to spend with your little one during which you studiously avoid teaching, disciplining, reprimanding, and controlling. Stick to singing, reading, tickling, and laughing!

However, the best way you can be a good parent is to have a good relationship with your spouse. It is actually unhealthy for a child to be the whole focus of a family. Real life isn't like that, and such a child can grow up to be a very self-centered, unpleasant, maladjusted individual. The healthy atmosphere of your home comes about from a healthy, well-balanced loving relationship between the primary adults in the home.

How can you nurture your relationship while you are so busy raising a toddler?

- Schedule dates on your calendar, and make sure your spouse does the same.
- Arrange for a sitter, so you can go out, or trade babysitting with another family. You have to have adult time and adult conversation in order to be a happy, fulfilled person.
- Set up a date night for at home on the sofa. Order out your favorite food and cuddle up with an adults-only DVD with your spouse after the toddler is tucked in for the night.

- Check in daily with your sweetie by text or phone to exchange caring words. This is not the time to ask for someone to pick up milk or dry cleaning.
- Resist the temptation to bring home work or to continue it with instant messaging and texting while sharing family time. Remind each other that everyone needs attention, free of digital devices!

ALERT

Families that are extremely child centered create children who are never satisfied, and ultimately miserable. Indulgence creates a person who is unhappy and difficult for others to be around. A toddler needs to develop some delayed gratification muscle, and it is up to the parent to teach that skill. Your child is immensely wonderful but not the center of the world.

Schedule regular talks with your significant other to iron out difficulties that are sure to arise in the care of yourselves, your home, and your children. Are the responsibilities fairly shared? Brainstorm some ways to rearrange the tasks to add variety and alleviate boredom and frustration. If necessary, seek out therapy or counseling to ease the two of you over the rough spots.

Be sure to keep up your magazine subscriptions concerning topics you really enjoy, apart from being a parent. Follow current event news, if it interests you, in order to remain capable of having an adult conversation. Keep up friendships with people who do not have children and invite them over for dinner from time to time. Or indulge in an entire weekend away with your spouse while the grandparents care for the little one. Such private time will rekindle the warmth that sometimes gets set aside from the demands of caring for a toddler. Research shows that parenting a toddler is a stressor on marriages, but you can counteract that with intelligent action to keep your relationship alive and strong.

Divorce

Toddlers find it unnerving when family routines change, and divorce is a big change. If it seems that ongoing arguments are tearing apart the family, ultimately it is best for the child to have a peaceful, loving home, even if with only one parent. It's not necessary to go into a lengthy explanation to a toddler. It would be upsetting and confusing to try. Simply say that Mommy and Daddy are going to live in separate houses. "Mommy is still your Mommy, and Daddy is still your Daddy. That will never change." Keep as much of the child's routine the same as you possibly can. It might work best if the visiting parent takes the little one out for some daytime or evening hours together but bring her back home to sleep. It is a large adjustment for a person of any age to learn to sleep at a different location.

Remain as civilized and cooperative as possible with your ex in connection with arrangements for the care of your toddler, especially when talking in front of her. Continuing respect for the other as a parent ultimately best serves your child.

Do not be surprised if your toddler regresses in language or toilet training during a divorce and the aftermath. Even if tantrums had begun to diminish, they may start up again. Realistically, adults have their difficult moments, too, as the family structure changes, so give the little one extra patience and tolerance as she finds a new comfort zone. Do your best not to scold.

QUESTION

How many children in the United States live with a grandparent?
Washington Post staff writer Carol Morello says that the recent census figures indicate that at least 2.4 million children in this country live with at least one grandparent. Factors are the recession and changing career patterns of young parents.

If you are the custodial parent, do your best to keep the child's schedule consistent, with the same rules and discipline as before the separation or divorce, and continue to spend loving, affectionate time with your toddler. Seek out books at the library or bookstore that explain in simple terms what happens when parents decide to go their separate ways. Your toddler will gradually grasp that she is not alone in this new phase of life. Seek out support groups of single parents with small children, so your little one will see that others may have similar families.

Expect a bit of confusion after the spouse moves out. Toddlers may not grasp what is occurring until *after* it has occurred. Constantly reiterate to your child that she is loved by both parents, even if the other parent is not in the house every day. Resist the impulse to emotionally lean on the child. Don't talk about your problems with your toddler. Such a dynamic frightens and confuses a toddler. If you are distressed (which is entirely normal in such a dramatic situation), seek out a professional to help you over the rough spots.

Remember that toddlers have a different sense of time, compared to adults. Try to arrange for the noncustodial parent to see the child very frequently. Your toddler cannot comprehend "Daddy is coming on Saturday."

Single Parenting and Dating

If you are a single parent, it is likely that you will be interested in dating after you have adjusted to the ending of the previous relationship. Spare your child the revolving door effect of too many people coming and going. While you are exploring the dating scene and seeing a variety of people, meet them elsewhere, not at home.

If you use Internet dating sites, note if your prospects show photographs of themselves with children. If the kids are their own kids, they might be indicating that parenting is a priority for them. Watch out for people who are photographed with other people's children as a come-on, just to portray an image of one who likes kids.

When you have connected with someone who seems like a good prospect for an ongoing presence in your life, only then introduce them to your child. Keep it light. And don't introduce a new person as a "new daddy." If you are certain that your new significant other will be a continuing presence in your life, slowly and cautiously include the toddler in outings. Let the new relationships evolve naturally. A heavy-handed approach will end up disappointing all concerned.

Parents of the Same Sex

Families come in all sizes and shapes. There are millions of homosexual family units in the United States, with many of them raising children. Many such families are relatively anonymous and invisible to the neighbors and community. Often one person in the couple had a heterosexual relationship before coming out as gay, taking the child into the new relationship. A toddler has no context for evaluating straight or gay. The only thing that is important is having a loving, stable home.

As a homosexual couple, you may choose to adopt a child and form a loving family unit in that way. Some couples choose to go the artificial insemination route or have a surrogate mother to gestate the child. If you explore any of these alternative routes, seek out support and social connections or join kindred online chat groups, as there will be those who do not really understand what you are doing.

FACT

There is no evidence that having homosexual parents causes children to be inclined toward homosexuality themselves. Children who are raised by homosexual parents, in general, have no more psychological or emotional difficulty than any other children. Teens and preteens may experience teasing from their peers, but this is changing as U.S. society becomes more tolerant of diversity.

As with any marriage, the most important thing is to create a loving, safe, stable framework for the growth of the child. Two warm, interested parents who are present for the child are always better than one.

A friend of the opposite sex may be able to provide your toddler with a model for that gender. Such an individual, as a regular presence in the child's life, can round out his understanding of gender and his place in the scheme of things.

Grandparents

Grandparents can be a real boon to raising a toddler, as they have been through it and know the ropes. They are somewhat detached from the anxieties of child rearing and can give both you and your toddler a break from the usual routine. What are some possible outings and activities that grandparents might enjoy with the little one?

Eating Out

Given the challenge of coping with toddlers in standard establishments, it's better to stick to kid-friendly restaurants. Many places have been specially designed for families with tots. Unfortunately, they often come up short in the nutrition department, but areas for climbing and crawling offer some compensation by offering opportunities to practice their physical skills. Grandparents shouldn't expect to relax while toddlers entertain themselves, however. Most structures are overly challenging for tots, and if bigger kids are roughhousing, play areas can be outright dangerous. Close monitoring is imperative. If a sign forbids children under a certain height from entering an area, believe it! On the other hand, ignore the signs prohibiting big people from entering if your toddler is in a potentially dangerous situation. Climb on in and stage a rescue!

Trek to the Toy Store

Grandparents are usually known for bringing toys when they come for their visits. A little grandchild spoiling is okay every now and then, but it helps if you can provide guidelines for grandparents to avoid toys that don't meet with your approval. What can you recommend for the grandparents' shopping when gift-giving occasions roll around? They might enjoy getting some of the more traditional toys:

- The old-fashioned, low-tech "classics," like teddy bears, rubber balls, baby dolls, and toy cars.
- Outdoor toys such as retro classic Big Wheels and Flyer wagons. Choose a wagon that is relatively low and well built, with no sharp edges. The pampered grandchild will be happy for long periods of time, loading the wagon and hauling things around. It is also a way for

you to transport her during a neighborhood walk, a change of pace from a stroller.

- Old-fashioned blocks. Blocks are a popular standard toy for toddlers. Grandparents may find themselves wanting to join in with block play, as the larger sets are quite appealing. A standard set of sixty shapes (including cones and cylinders) offers infinite possibilities for houses, stores, or whatever your tot's imagination might dictate. Combine with small cars, and the toddler will be happily occupied for quite some time.

- Dollhouse. By three years old, the little one might enjoy a dollhouse, complete with furniture, dishes, linens, and people. These miniature environments provide another opportunity for dramatic play, but on a smaller scale. Toddlers can have many happy moments arranging the pieces, especially when shared with an attentive adult. Many accessories that are a part of miniature environments are too small for toddlers, so don't be tempted to get into the collectible realm, at least at this age.

- Musical instruments. The sky's the limit in the realm of budding rock stars. The grandparents may want to get a beginner piano, drum set, guitar, or a set of percussion instruments. The main focus for instruments for toddlers would be free exploration and expression with sound. It might be fun to include strange and interesting sounds like animal sounds, train whistles, and other odd things.

FACT

Building with blocks develops a foundation for more advanced science comprehension including gravity, stability, weight, and balance. These concepts help the toddler understand the physical world around her. This kind of orientation makes her feel more secure and grounded.

Grandparents may also be handy at making things. Your toddler might want to join in or the grandparent can surprise the little one with some great handmade goodies. Some possibilities might include:

- Workbench. The first set of plastic tools will be fun for introducing your toddler to the names and purposes of the tools, but an older toddler can graduate to actual tools and scraps of wood (check the pieces for slivers that could become splinters, and take them off). On a low, sturdy table, set up a workbench play station on the patio or in the basement. Make available several pieces of wood, a small hammer, some sandpaper, and glue. The little carpenter will be happy hammering, even without nails, which could be too tempting to put into the mouth. Woodworking is a marvelous sensory experience, and remember that girls will find it just as appealing as boys. As your toddler matures, gradually add real tools, always staying nearby yourself to demonstrate how they are used and to prevent injury.
- Sewing cards. Grandparents can make sewing cards to help your toddler learn eye-hand coordination. Mount a picture with a clear outline onto firm cardboard, perhaps an image from a coloring book. At regular intervals punch holes along the outline of the picture. The child can "sew" along the line with a shoestring or piece of sturdy yarn with a piece of masking tape rolled around the end to make a firm tip. Try the stitching yourself first to see if the holes are large enough.
- Homemade musical instruments. Grandparents may remember from their youth such goodies as a tissue paper kazoo, cigar box banjo, and drums made from oatmeal boxes.

Babysitters

Part of taking care of yourself as a parent is getting out and enjoying yourself, doing things that make you happy apart from being the person of greatest importance in your child's life. You might want to maintain a career outside the home, take classes, do volunteer work, or socialize with friends. Even a nice lunch and movie can make you feel really good.

How do you choose someone to sit with your toddler? Think first about qualities of maturity and good judgment. If you decide on a reliable teenager, it's best if you already know the person quite well or at least have excellent references. An older person, neighbor, or the child's grandparent could be a possibility. Before setting up the arrangement, it would be wise to have the person come to your house and get acquainted with your toddler in her natural setting.

ALERT

> You may want to stipulate that anyone caring for your toddler has to know how to perform CPR, chest compressions, and other emergency first-aid procedures correctly. You can search online or inquire at your local Y or Red Cross for low-cost courses. Having all members of your family and caregivers certified provides you peace of mind.

Toddlers can be skittish about new people, so give it some time. If she's willing, let her show the visitor her room and her favorite toys. You all three can sit down and get comfortable together. Follow your intuitive feeling about the person. If something doesn't feel right, look for a different person. Be clear about ground rules, whether or not the sitter can be on the phone or computer while taking care of your toddler. A firm rule of no visitors has to be established. It should be emphasized that there will be no smoking or alcohol use while caring for your little one.

Some teenaged sitters attend babysitting training programs that prepare them for emergencies and what to expect from children of different ages. If the sitter knows CPR and first aid, that's even better. Make sure the sitter has information about poison control, fire, and police handy. On the day and time that you're going out, give yourself plenty of time to prepare everything—a meal for your child and the sitter, phone numbers for the sitter to call, if needed, and information about which neighbors could be helpful in a pinch. Leave enough time to go over a detailed schedule with the sitter. If your toddler will be doing the same things she normally does, the time will go more smoothly. Let your sitter know when you might call and check in to see that all is well.

Try not to be rushed with these arrangements, or your toddler will pick up on your anxiety. Give a warm hug and goodbye and go on out the door. If there are blood-curdling shrieks coming through the door as you leave, keep on going. The crying will stop fairly soon, and if you go back, the situation is worsened. It is typical for toddlers to experience separation as life threatening. They have not yet learned that people and things continue to exist, even when they are temporarily out of sight.

When you come back home, resist the impulse to awaken your toddler. Undoubtedly, she will be peacefully slumbering after a fun time with a new personality.

According to Burton White, director of the Center for Parent Education in Newton, Massachusetts, it is best for the child if the parent is the primary caretaker for the first five or six months of life. It is during the earliest months that the infant forms her sense of relationship to the environment, especially that most important significant figure.

As loving as nannies, grandparents, or other substitutes might be, they simply do not give the child as much attention as a parent. However, by the toddler years, a warm, attentive environment will be fine for the child, as long as the parent selects the place carefully. White notes that children who are not responded to and spoken to often enough tend to fall back intellectually. It is unknown whether or not such constraints can be made up for later in the child's life.

One option for those delicate in-between years is a parents' co-op. The atmosphere in this type of arrangement is likely to be warm and flexible, with parents taking turns caring for a small group of toddlers. It is crucial that the adults of small children are responsive to the child's needs and inquiries.

Caregivers' Home Safety

Follow every precaution and be sure that any home your child stays in is as toddler-proofed as your own. Before you allow your toddler to stay with a sitter or grandparents, carefully go through the house, looking for the following safety situations:

All caregivers and sitters simply must avoid the following:

- Keeping a gun at home to which a toddler could have access (Guns and ammunition must be stored separately, locked up, and out of reach.)
- Driving under the influence of alcohol or any illicit drug
- Giving alcohol to a toddler
- Leaving drugs—illicit or otherwise—within reach of a toddler

- Putting toddlers under forty pounds in a car without a safety seat
- Putting children over forty pounds in a car without a safety belt
- Exposing youngsters to domestic violence
- Injuring a child in any way, including hitting hard enough to leave a bruise or welt
- Shaking an infant or toddler (which can cause brain damage serious enough to result in death)
- Dragging a youngster by the arm (the combination of a pull and a twist causes spiral fractures)

Special care needs to be taken to avoid hazardous or unhealthy situations. The best introduction to creating a safe and healthy environment for children throughout their lives is the process of childproofing. Once your toddler has become mobile, you have to look at your home and any other home your child visits in a different way. (For more on what to do to childproof a home see Chapter 8).

Day Care Environments

If you want your toddler to be in day care, what should you look for?

1. Does the physical space offer some choice for the child in terms of being with others or being alone? Is there a good balance of materials for structured activities (puzzles, pegs) and unstructured activities (clay, paint)?
2. Does the instructional setting seem to lend itself to real learning? Does the teacher ask open-ended questions? Is the adult-to-child ratio reasonably intimate? Do the children reflect diverse backgrounds? How do the teachers respond to questions from the parents?
3. Is there a structured curriculum and daily schedule? Are deviations permitted when the children need to shift gears, such as when it has rained for days and then a sunny day appears? Are the children allowed to finish what they have started?
4. What is the social-emotional climate of the day care center? Is there a relaxed mix of solitary play and groups? Are there quiet times and times of exuberance? Do the teachers force the children into groups, or does the child have a choice about what to pursue?

Young children like to have a place for their own belongings. Do you find storage cubbies for each child's things, clearly labeled with names in large, readable letters?

In the program for toddlers do you find evidence of a schedule each day? The eighteen-month- to three-year-old child finds comfort in the steadiness of a routine. Some day care centers make a visual schedule, including pictures of children in the group doing what is supposed to be done at that time. In that way the teacher can say, "See the picture of Lucy lying down? It's nap time now."

You might like to choose a day care center that offers real-time streaming video, so that you may see what your tot is doing while you are at work. A company called Micro-steps.com offers such a service. Some up-to-date centers have an active web presence, where you can check out recent photos of the children, upcoming events, and helpful tips for parents.

FACT

This time of becoming an individual includes separation and can be difficult. However, it will be easier if your toddler feels securely attached to you. When she knows that she can rely on you for love, comfort, and reassurance, she will be emboldened to take those first tentative steps away from you. She will stop crying soon after you leave the center.

Your toddler deserves to be in a trustworthy environment that allows him to test limits and take risks, with the support of loving, consistent adults. Does the center include helpful information for parents? Sometimes parents can assist in the classes for a discount on the fee. You might want to investigate religious-affiliated centers, as they are generally less expensive than other private programs. Depending on the family circumstances, public programs are offered that are sometimes free or offered on a sliding-fee basis.

CHAPTER 15

Potpourri of Toddler Activities

With a few months of experience you will be able to think of a typical toddler day in bite-sized chunks of fifteen to twenty minutes, just enough time for something interesting to do. It will become second nature for you to carry along interesting items when you go out for errands such as having the car serviced so the little one will be occupied. And your mind will plan ahead for those moments of down time, when it seems imperative that you and your toddler shift gears.

Brainy Language Fun

Basically, language arises from the desire to experience and talk about life. It stands to reason, then, that in order to have things to talk about, there has to be stuff going on! Interesting activities give your toddler food for thought and food for speaking, when the time is right.

Sensory Experiences

Language development is related to a lively approach to the world through the senses. What can you do to enrich your toddler's sensory experience?

- Go to an art museum and look at the large paintings and sculptures. Talk about color, shape, and size.
- Vary the music you and your child listen to. You don't need to be limited to children's songs. Cover a wide repertoire of classical, blues, world music, rock and roll, jazz, punk, alternative, and country music and have fun describing it with vocabulary connected to sound—fast, slow, loud, soft, smooth, happy, sad—and have fun dancing around the room to express the mood of the music.
- Get out the karaoke machine and ham it up. You may be surprised at how your little one naturally uses a microphone and belts out a pretty good tune.
- Explore the language of touch. Look for things around the house that are furry, soft, hard, smooth, warm, cool, rough. This discussion could include the shapes of items as well and questions such as, "Where is the smooth red ball?" "Can you bring me the cool ice cube?"

Outings

This is a good age to take children out and about, creating even more things to talk about. Go to the zoo and watch all the animals. Reinforce with books about the animals after you are back home. A trip to an ice cream parlor is rich with opportunity (as well as calories). Let your child decide what flavor of ice cream she would like, how many scoops, and whether in a cone or a cup. Will she need a few napkins? How about a spoon? Where should we sit? All these discussions are real to the child. "Oops! The ice cream is melting and dripping. Now Mommy's ice cream is melting and dripping." The repetition makes an impression on the child and very soon you will hear those words being spoken, and almost always in the correct context. The human brain is amazingly sensitive and organized, like a fantastic computer. You will see it in action, as your child adds vocabulary with leaps and bounds.

FACT

Appropriateness is everything when it comes to activities for toddlers. You need to be familiar with what toddlers can and cannot do, what they enjoy, and what may frustrate them. You probably know better than to purchase a chemistry kit for your two-year-old or to ask your three-year-old to join you in a game of Gin Rummy.

Library Story Time

Most public libraries have a toddler story time. This makes a marvelous outing and creates a lot to talk about. It's a chance for you to meet other parents and socialize a bit. With weekly story times you will probably make friends among the others in the book circle. Have some fun selecting just the right chair or pillow to sit on and getting some books to take home afterward. Children's librarians are a good source of information about specific books for particular ages of children. You may find that in your community the bookstores also offer story times for toddlers

Fine-Tuning Listening

Seize opportunities to encourage your toddler to tune in to the world of sound. For example, when you're in the car, point out the shriek of a police siren, the blare of a horn, or the whistle of a train. When you go for a walk around the neighborhood, unplug your earbuds and talk with your toddler about the tweet of a bird, the rustle of leaves, or the whoosh of the wind.

In the house, listen together to the crackle of a fire, the hiss of a kettle, or the ring of a kitchen timer. Use your voice as well; hum, whistle, and sing to your little one. She won't care if you can't carry a tune.

Careful listening helps toddlers to reproduce the sounds needed for speech today, to recognize the subtle differences in sound needed for speaking tomorrow, and to sound out words when they're learning to read in the years to come.

Your Little Sous-Chef

Your toddler will love to cook with you! Everyone loves to eat, and getting food ready to eat is a purposeful kind of play. Involving little ones in food preparation creates the kind of pride of accomplishment that can bring about a willingness to eat their creations. Pull up a chair or step stool so youngsters can join you at the counter. Enlist their help with a variety of food preparation chores by giving very young toddlers directions for one simple task at a time and giving a hands-on demonstration. Toddlers as young as fifteen months should be able to help with a number of chores such as:

- **Setting time on a digital timer.** This is a good chance to practice numbers and counting.
- **Scrubbing fruits and vegetables.** Since a simple rinse in water is all that's required, this is an easy one for toddlers.
- **Pouring water.** Let them pour water a cup at a time into the pot that will be used for boiling pasta, rice, eggs, vegetables, or cooked cereal. Have fun counting. Keep them away from the stove, and let them work with cold to lukewarm water only!
- **Spreading.** Let them use a plastic knife to spread peanut butter or cream cheese on celery sticks.
- **Making omelets.** Let them sprinkle shredded cheese onto the eggs; the eggs and pan must be cool.
- **Cutting cookies.** Put each ingredient for the cookie recipe into a separate bowl. Help toddlers pour them all into one bowl, stir, roll out the dough, and cut it with cookie cutters.
- **Stirring juices.** After you pour the thawed juice into the pitcher of water, have your toddler stir. Teach him to stir gently, but use a big pitcher so there's room to slosh!
- **Cleaning the counter.** Toddlers can wipe down the counter with a damp dishrag or sponge. (Not that you'll end up with a clean counter

for the first year or two or even three. Focus on the participation, not the result.)

- **Setting the table.** Keep the directions simple! First instruct them to put a fork by each plate. When they are finished, they can do the spoons, and then the bread knives. They can also put out the butter, ketchup, salt and pepper, napkins, too, if they're given one item to do at a time.

Holidays, Parties, and Celebrations

A toddler does not have a clear sense of time, particularly in the large sense of a year. It can be fun, however, to add festive touches of decorations, food, and creative activities to a child's party. Invite just a few friends, and keep everything simple. The best way to plan for a successful children's party is to lower your expectations. Toddlers are easily impressed, so you don't need to hire the most popular performer around and a cast of thousands to entertain your guests. Invite only a few of your child's playmates, and keep the party short and simple. Refreshments, gift opening, and two or three simple activities would be plenty.

By about age two, children are old enough to understand and get excited about the prospect of having relatives and friends over, receiving presents, eating cake and ice cream . . . of "Me birthday party!" To help make your child's party a success, keep these tips in mind:

1. Include your toddler in the planning, having her help select the refreshments and the theme.
2. Keep in mind that clowns or mask-wearing magicians would scare a toddler.
3. Keep it short, at around two hours. The anticipation beforehand and the excitement of the party itself are apt to fray your child's nerves—not to mention yours!
4. Ask other parents to stay with their children for the duration of the party. It's hard for one parent to supervise a group and keep everyone safe.
5. Consider having your child open presents after the guests leave so they don't get upset about wanting presents, too.
6. Provide party favors to help everyone feel included.

Holidays

People of all ages enjoy the holidays. The toddler years are a fun time to start to enjoy some special festive themes. Holidays are special times when ordinary routines are broken and there are new foods, visitors, and activities. The excitement can be overwhelming for young children. Although you want a holiday to be fun for your young child, remember that she may need some quiet one-on-one time with you.

Scary Things

The older toddler may enjoy arts and crafts activities associated with Halloween—finding a pumpkin, watching an adult carve a face, cleaning out the seeds and perhaps roasting them in the oven for a fall snack. Your toddler can make a spider out of a paper plate with some glued-on legs. Young children enjoy costumes, but be careful again to not let the child become over-stimulated with trick or treating and too much candy.

New Year

Your child will enjoy making noise and helping to celebrate the New Year without having to stay up until midnight. You might make a noisemaker and wear a funny hat to celebrate the coming of the new year. Explain in a simple way that a new time is beginning. The child will not understand complex descriptions of the calendar and time, and will probably fall asleep before midnight.

Valentine's Day

Love is in the air! Your toddler is just starting to learn about love and relationships. At this stage in her life, your toddler's greatest love is probably you. But soon, her social world will be expanding. Talk about love and caring while you do these projects with her. Here is a great chance to reinforce recognition of the colors pink and red, too.

Valentine's Day is a good time to talk about shapes, sizes, and colors. There is also the emphasis on giving to others. Your toddler will enjoy making valentines and giving them to friends and family.

St. Patrick's Day

It is said that anyone can be Irish on St. Patrick's Day. Focus on the color green and share some of the legends and lore of this holiday with your child. You can enjoy stories about elves, leprechauns, and fairies, and note the fun of everyone wearing green. This is a good time to talk about rainbows and the colors in the rainbow.

Easter

There are many symbols and traditions associated with this holiday. Easter eggs and the Easter Bunny may be the two most familiar to young children. Here are some simple activities that your toddler is sure to enjoy. Your toddler will likely be enthusiastic about making and talking about bunnies and colored eggs. Natural dyes are interesting to try. Onion skins or beets make very nice colors. Brewed black tea makes a warm, delicate brown. When you use natural dyes, you may need to soak the eggs in the dyes overnight, remembering that the longer you dye, the darker and brighter the color.

A toddler is mature enough to hunt for slightly hidden Easter eggs. You can tuck the eggs around the house so that a piece of each one shows, making it easy and fun for the toddler to find the treasures.

Fourth of July

Your toddler is too young to understand the history behind this holiday. Keep it simple, and explain that you are celebrating the country's birthday. Your child will love being a part of the festivities. The fourth of July is a great opportunity to talk about the flag's colors of red, white, and blue. If your neighborhood has a Main Street parade, that can be exciting for a toddler. Who can resist the rhythm of majorettes and marching bands? It can be an opportunity afterward to experiment with marching and imitations of the various band instruments.

Thanksgiving

The history of this holiday is more than your child can understand. Discussions about Pilgrims and Native Americans are not relevant to your child's experience of the world around her. The turkey, on the other hand, is a concrete symbol of the Thanksgiving meal. You may also choose to have a discussion about abundance and thankfulness during this holiday. Your child might enjoy being a part of Thanksgiving shopping and meal preparation, learning about particular foods—cranberries, pumpkin, stuffing, and turkey. The concept of gratitude is a bit abstract, but you can weave it into the preparations for the day.

Your older toddler can help set the table, an important job and a chance to practice naming the utensils, counting them, and talking about positions of items.

Chanukah

Chanukah is a Jewish holiday steeped in traditions. Don't forget to share some of your favorite ways to celebrate with your young child. This holiday lasts for eight days. Your toddler can be a part of the Menorah tradition, a good opportunity for counting to eight.

The important symbol of the Star of David is another chance to talk about geometric shape and color.

Your toddler will enjoy spinning her body like a dreidel. The song can be sung to the traditional dreidel tune or to "Row Row Row Your Boat." Teach your child the following song and then have her spin around while she sings it:

Dreidel, dreidel, dreidel,
I'm spinning all around.
Going slow and going fast
Until I'm on the ground.

Christmas

Even your young toddler will be aware of the hustle and bustle of the Christmas season. It is hard to shelter her from the music, the commercials, the movies, the decorations, and everything else. She does not have to be a passive bystander, though. These activities will encourage her to contribute festive decorations for your home. The shopping and meal preparation make great times for learning new words.

Your toddler can help to decorate the Christmas tree, naming each item as it is placed on a branch. You and she can make colorful items to put on the tree—ornaments or chains. Some families keep these little treasures for years, remembering the toddler's second or third Christmas again and again.

Kwanzaa

Kwanzaa is a relatively new holiday, honoring the heritage and history of African Americans. It could be a simple way to introduce your child to the traditional colors of Kwanzaa.

Activities for a Rainy Day

What do you do when the weather is rainy or cold, and your child is stuck inside all day? Dr. Seuss addressed this problem in one of his best-known stories, *The Cat in the Hat*. The children in this story seemed to be doomed to sit forlornly by the window watching the rain, until the Cat in the Hat comes to entertain. Fortunately you don't need to juggle fish or fly a kite in the kitchen to turn a gray day into a fun day.

Shadow Dancing

Here is a great way to get your child moving. Perhaps you can get the whole family to join in. For this activity you will need:

- A light-colored wall
- A bright lamp
- Favorite music recording

1. Position the lamp in the middle of the room, leaving plenty of space between the lamp and the wall.
2. Turn on the bright lamp and darken the rest of the room. Aim the lamp directly at the wall. Stand your toddler in front of the lamp so that his shadow is cast clearly on the wall.
3. Put on the music and encourage your child to dance so that his shadow dances, too. For a cool-down activity, show your child how to use his hand to create simple shadow puppets.
4. Use your own hands to make shadow animals. With practice, you can make a dog with ears and a barking mouth or a lovely gliding swan. Make up stories about the animal shadows. Your toddler will be enchanted.

Create a Restaurant

Young children love to pretend to cook and eat food. As a bonus, you can reinforce manners and social skills while your child is playing. For this activity you will need:

- Table and chairs
- Paper plates, cups, and napkins
- Plastic tableware
- Poster board
- Crayons
- Notebook
- Plastic or real food

1. Let your child help set up the restaurant. Show him how to set the table.
2. Let your child create a menu on the poster board. You can have him color pictures of the food he wishes to serves. Alternatively, he can paste on magazine pictures.
3. Sit at the table and let your child take your order. Supply him with a small notebook so that he can pretend to write down your order.
4. If desired, let him serve you real or pretend food.
5. Set up a pretend cash register with play money and pretend to pay for the meal, counting out the dollars and cents.

ALERT

During rainy days, your toddler will need more exercise to make up for lost time playing outside. Play marching band, do exercises together, dance to wild music and freeze in place when the music stops. Without enough large muscle activity, you might have a very cranky toddler on your hands.

Play Nurse and Doctor

Many young children are concerned and often fascinated about injury and illness. The subject of doctors and hospitals is something that your child may wish to explore. You can easily change this into a veterinarian theme; simply add a few stuffed animals and a pet carrier. This is a natural way to name parts of the body and describe what hurts. For this activity you will need:

- Doctor's or nurse's hat
- Old adult-sized short-sleeved white shirt
- Fabric marker
- Dolls or action figures (to act as patients)
- Band-Aids
- Gauze or ace bandages
- Rubber gloves
- Plastic syringe

1. Fit the hat onto your child. Make a lab coat by drawing a pocket and adding a name to the shirt.
2. Let your child put Band-Aids on the dolls and pretend to give them shots to make them feel better.
3. Take the stuffed animals to the veterinarian and enjoy questions and answers about what is wrong with the pet.

Play Store

Gather things from around the house and your toddler's room to represent the merchandise for sale. Set the items up on a coffee table for the store display. You can make signs to name the items and list items, or just go with your imagination. Take turns with him, being the customer and being the salesperson. This is a good time to practice questions about price, color, and size. You will be surprised at how fast he picks up your intonation and ways of interacting, as he has heard you do this in all the stores you have visited together. You could create a clothing store, toy store, bookstore, grocery store, or a variety store that has a little of everything.

Cooking

A rainy day is a good time to cook something together with your toddler. You might create a marvelous homemade stew. Let your little one wash the vegetables, place each chunk in the pot with whatever stock you use as a base, and stir. You, of course, do the slicing, and protect your assistant from the hot burner. Cooking is a great way to teach counting, names of the ingredients, colors, and shapes.

FACT

Cooking develops math skills (counting and measuring), nutrition, and science concepts (prediction, cause and effect). Cooking is even more fun if you make a large picture recipe on poster board. Use cutout shapes of cups and spoons showing the number needed in the recipe.

Puppets

Puppets are magical. Not only can they breathe life into any story, but they often seem to have a wonderful effect on young children. Many children who have speech difficulties or are shy often feel more comfortable using puppets for expression. A child can project her own fears, wishes, and dreams through the character of a puppet. Make a puppet with your child and watch her imagination soar.

Rubber Finger Puppets

This a quick and easy way to make finger puppet characters for your child.

For this activity you will need:

- Old rubber dishwashing gloves
- Scissors
- Permanent markers

1. Cut the fingers off the rubber gloves.
2. Let your child use the markers to create a face and other features.

Paper Plate Puppets

Because this project is so simple, you may wish to let your child make a few puppets and then put on a show.

For this activity you will need:

- Dessert-size paper plate
- Crayons
- Wooden craft stick
- White craft glue

1. Let your child decorate the plate with crayons to make a face.
2. Help her glue on the stick to use as a handle.

ESSENTIAL

You can buy a puppet theatre from a toy store or toy catalog, or you can make one from a large packing box. Cut it down to a toddler-sized height, cut an opening for the stage window, and attach a curtain made from a piece of fabric. Velcro would work well for this. You are ready for a fabulous puppet show!

Sock Puppets

Save the stray socks your laundry seems to create and make puppets out of them. Stitch bits of yarn and scraps of fabric to make the facial features. If you stitch on buttons for the eyes, sew them well, as they are choking hazards for small children. Your toddler can embellish the features with fabric markers. If you want to be really creative, make a whole family of puppets using felt ears, red felt tongues, bow ties, or lace collars. Encourage your child to name the parts. Sock puppets are wonderfully malleable and expressive with the movements of the hand inside the fabric. The little creatures really come to life and evolve into surprising personalities. This is a good way to make language development extremely fun.

For this activity you will need:

- Socks
- Needle and thread
- Scrap pieces of yarn and fabric
- Felt
- Buttons
- Fabric markers

Stormy Weather Fun

When bad weather is approaching, you may be facing more of a challenge than entertaining your child. It is common for young children to be frightened of storms. You need to set a good example—if you remain calm and nonchalant, chances are your child will stay calm as well. These activities will keep your child occupied and may even distract him from his anxiety.

Explore the Sensory Aspects

Take your child to a window, porch, or patio and notice in detail what happens with a rainstorm or snowstorm. Talk about the smells, sounds, wind, temperature, and movement. Exciting vocabulary arises out of these times!

Weather Art

Make pictures of a day that is something like the day that is happening. Encourage your toddler to show the elements and someone outside wearing appropriate rain or snow clothing.

Books and Songs

Sort through your child's library and read some stories that have weather as a central theme. *A Snowy Day* by Ezra Jack Keats would be a good choice. You could also sing the following song together:

Rain, rain
Go away
Come again another day.

Rain Sticks

Rain sticks have long been popular as musical instruments in other cultures. Now you don't have to go to a fancy import store at the mall to find them—your child can make one out of materials you have around the house. Many children find the sound of a rain stick to be very soothing.

For this activity you will need:

- 1 cardboard paper towel tube or mailing tube
- Crayons
- 2 squares of tinfoil, large enough to cover the ends of the tube
- Masking tape
- 1 long pipe cleaner twisted into a loose coil
- ¼ cup dry rice

1. Let your child color the tube for decoration.
2. Fasten one tinfoil square on the end of the tube with masking tape. Leave the other end open until the tube is filled.
3. Help your child fit the pipe cleaner into the tube. Assist him in pouring in the rice.
4. Close the other end of the tube with the second square of tinfoil. Show your child how to tilt the stick back and forth to create the rain noise.

Play Phone

Your toddler most likely loves to imitate you talking on a cell phone. If he's willing to use a toy cell phone (many toddlers are too sophisticated, insisting on the real phone), set up two phones and encourage him to call anyone he'd like. You can be the other speaker. Don't be surprised if he carries on full conversations, filling in the other person's words.

QUESTION

What is the difference between art and craft?
Art is open ended. Craft has the aim of making a specific end result. Although you may use craft materials in making art, art as an activity is healthier for toddlers.

Make a Train

There are many dramatic-play props that you can make with a box. This project is just a suggestion to help spark your own ideas. When cutting the rope, be sure that none of the sections is long enough to be a safety hazard.

For this activity you will need:

- Three or more large boxes
- Lightweight rope, cut into three 1-foot sections
- Scissors
- Tempera paint or markers
- Teddy bears, dolls, or action figures (to act as passengers)
- Engineer's hat
- Small suitcase

1. Arrange boxes to form cars of the train. The front car is the engine. You can designate passenger cars, a dining car, and a sleeping car.
2. Cut a small hole in the front and back sides of each box so that holes in all boxes line up.

3. Connect the boxes with the sections of rope. Knot the rope ends on the inside of each box to secure them. A rope in the front can be used to pull the train.
4. Let your child decorate the train with paint or markers. The train is then ready to carry its passengers.

Playing train can spark conversation about where your toddler might want to go. Who would she like to see who lives far away? What should she take along in a suitcase? If possible, follow up with an actual train ride or take the train ride first.

Make Play Dough

Play dough is universally enjoyable, so why not learn how to make your own? For this activity you will need:

- A saucepan
- ½ cup salt
- 1 cup flour
- 2 tablespoons cream of tartar
- 1 cup cold water
- A few drops of food coloring
- 1 tablespoon of vegetable oil

1. In a saucepan, combine ½ cup salt, 1 cup flour, and 2 tablespoons cream of tartar.
2. Then add 1 cup cold water, a few drops of food coloring, and 1 tablespoon of vegetable oil. Your toddler can help with the measuring, counting, and placing the ingredients into the saucepan. Caution him about the heat of the burner, though. Mix until smooth, and cook over medium heat, stirring frequently.
3. When the mixture sticks to the pan, sticks together firmly, and is no longer slimy to the touch, it's finished. Turn it out onto waxed paper, knead it a dozen times, and let it sit.

4. When the dough is cool, store it in a container with a tight-fitting lid or sealed plastic bags to prevent drying.

ESSENTIAL

Remember that toddlers don't care what they make as long as they get to roll, rub, pat, dab, and draw while they're making it. Adults might care about the finished product; little ones prefer just to putter.

Now comes the fun. Sit down with your child and show him how to:

- Roll bits of play dough into a worm or snake
- Roll a bigger piece into a ball
- Flatten the ball into a cookie or pancake
- Pinch off little bits to make peas and put them onto a tiny play-dough plate
- Prick it with a pen or pencil
- Slice it with a cheese slicer
- Cut it with a plastic knife
- Cut it with cookie cutters

Supervise carefully to be sure your toddler doesn't try to make a "meal" of the cookies and pancakes.

Art Box

Decorate a box and fill it with an assortment of nontoxic supplies:

- Bows and pieces of ribbon
- Coloring book
- Construction paper
- Scraps of foil
- Cotton balls
- Crayons or markers (washable)

- Envelopes
- Glue sticks
- Pipe cleaners
- Paper or old newspaper
- Paper bags, cups, and plates
- Pictures from magazines, greeting cards, and postcards
- Stickers
- Watercolor kit
- Wrapping paper odds and ends
- Yarn and string (16 inches or shorter)
- Pieces of sponge

FACT

Older toddlers may enjoy having their very own easel. Some easels have a dry erase surface on one side or a chalkboard. Look for a child-height tray for paint containers and brushes. Easels are also available in tabletop models. Clips, apron, and paper, and you're ready for your small Frida Kahlo!

Pull out the art box on a rainy day! The possibilities are limited only by your imaginations! Younger toddlers can put stickers on paper plates and cups and dab markers onto newspaper. You can cut out the center of a paper plate to make a crown tots can decorate.

Although you often have to curtail your toddler's rainy-day artistic explorations because they are especially messy, try to accommodate his urge to explore. It's important to accept the fact that your house won't be as tidy as it was before your tot became mobile, especially if you're spending more time inside.

Recipes: Cooking for and with Your Toddler

The recipes marked with a chef's hat are suitable for cooking with your toddler.

Steamed Grapes and Squash

Have you ever tried cooking grapes? They add a great taste when paired with butternut squash. Steaming grapes makes them more tender and less of a choking hazard. In addition, you don't need to peel them. You should still supervise your child closely when eating any kind of grapes.

INGREDIENTS | YIELDS 5 SERVINGS

1 medium butternut squash
15–20 large, seedless green grapes

1. Wash squash. Peel, remove seeds, and cut into 1-inch cubes.

2. Place squash in a steamer basket. Place in pot over about 2 inches of water. Bring to a boil and steam for about 6 minutes.

3. Wash the grapes. Cut in half, if desired.

4. Add grapes to steamer basket and steam for another 6 minutes, or until tender when pricked with a fork.

5. Serve in pieces, or mash to desired consistency.

Regular Pasta

Don't rinse pasta before serving to your toddler. The starch in the cooking water will make the pasta a little bit sticky, which is perfect for young fingers.

INGREDIENTS | YIELDS 1 SERVING

4 cups of water
¼ cup boxed spaghetti or other pasta

1. Bring the water to a rapid boil in a large saucepan.

2. Add pasta and stir to separate the noodles or spaghetti. Continue boiling for 10–12 minutes, or according to package directions. Pasta should be soft and completely cooked.

3. Let cool completely; then cut into ½-inch-long pieces for your toddler to pick up and self-feed.

Scrambled Eggs with Cheese

Use a mild cheese in this recipe, especially if your toddler hasn't had a wide variety of cheeses yet. Mozzarella melts particularly well, as does Monterey jack or a mild Cheddar. Avoid sharp cheeses until your toddler is more used to them.

INGREDIENTS | YIELDS 1 SERVING

1 egg

1 tablespoon milk (regular or soy)

2 tablespoons grated cheese

Cooking with Milk

It's safe to cook with milk as long as you're using pasteurized milk. It's safe to scald milk (heat to just below the boiling point), but you don't want to actually boil it—boiling causes a skin-like layer to form on the surface. Always make sure your milk tastes and smells fresh before serving it to your toddler.

1. Crack the egg into a bowl and add milk. Beat thoroughly.

2. Pour the egg into a medium-hot nonstick frying pan, adding a bit of oil or butter if the egg starts to stick.

3. Scramble the egg, adding the cheese about halfway through. Continue scrambling until the egg is cooked and cheese melted.

Cheese Squares

Baked cheese squares are a delicious way to get some extra protein in your child. Be patient while this finger food is baking—it may take longer than you think.

INGREDIENTS | 4 SERVINGS

3 ounces Mozzarella, Cheddar, or Monterey Jack cheese

1 cup all-purpose flour

1 egg

1 cup cottage cheese

1. Preheat the oven to 350°F.

2. Shred the cheese into a medium bowl.

3. Add the egg, flour, and cottage cheese. Stir well.

4. Place into a greased baking dish.

5. Bake for about 45 minutes, or until a toothpick in the middle comes out clean. Cool and cut into squares.

Banana-Grape Yogurt Dessert

While grapes are a choking hazard for the under-one crowd, toddlers can eat grapes as long as they are sliced into halves or quarters. Let your little one self-feed these sorts of fruits, so she can regulate how much she puts in her mouth at a time. As always, supervise!

INGREDIENTS | YIELDS 1 SERVING

½ banana
¼ cup seedless grapes
¼ cup yogurt

1. Peel the banana, removing any brown spots, and cut into thin coins.

2. Wash the grapes and slice into quarters.

3. Combine in a bowl with yogurt on top.

4. Let your toddler self-feed under careful supervision.

Broccoli with Oranges and Almonds

A great way to serve vegetables: mix them with sweet fruit! Even fussy eaters will find something they like in this broccoli dish, which combines fruit with broccoli and nuts.

INGREDIENTS | YIELDS 3 SERVINGS

½ head of broccoli
2 tablespoons butter
¼ cup sliced almonds
4 cups water
½ orange

1. Wash the broccoli and remove the stem. Dice into small florets.

2. Heat butter in a medium saucepan. Toast the almonds for about 5 minutes, or until lightly browned.

3. Bring water to a boil. Add broccoli and cook for about 15 minutes, or until broccoli is tender.

4. Slice the orange in half and remove the fruit with a grapefruit spoon. Cut into small pieces. Toss cooked broccoli, almonds, and oranges together.

5. If the textures are too challenging, omit the almonds and purée the broccoli and orange, adding milk as necessary to thin the mixture.

Baked Apples

For the older children, make a caramel sauce from butter and brown sugar; then pour it inside the apple with raisins or cinnamon candies. Serve with ice cream.

INGREDIENTS | YIELDS 1 SERVING

1 apple
1 teaspoon white sugar
⅛ teaspoon cinnamon
¼ cup water

Make a Dumpling Out of It

A fun trick for toddlers or older children is, instead of baked fruit, to make baked fruit dumplings! Combine 1 cup flour, ½ cup shortening, 2 tablespoons ice water, and a dash of salt to make a dough. Knead for a couple of minutes; then wrap around your fruit and seal with a tight pinch. Bake at a slightly higher temperature, around 400°F.

1. Preheat the oven to 350°F. Wash the apple. Remove the top core, leaving the apple intact.

2. Sprinkle sugar and cinnamon on the inside of the apple. Pour the water into a small baking dish, then place the apple in the center. Bake for about 45 minutes, or until the apple is completely cooked.

3. When cooled, fork-mash to a suitable consistency. If desired, the entire skin can be removed once the apple is cooked.

Melon Bowls with Yogurt

Just about any small melon can be used for this recipe, and it's a fun one for small children to help prepare. Allow your child to scoop out the melon seeds with a spoon or an ice-cream scoop, and encourage her to eat the yogurt directly from the melon. Start her out on a road to healthy eating!

INGREDIENTS | YIELDS 2 SERVINGS

1 small cantaloupe or honeydew melon
½ cup blueberries
1 cup yogurt

1. Slice the melon in half. Slice a small piece of shell off the bottom so that the melon will sit easily on a plate.

2. Scoop out and discard all seeds.

3. Wash the blueberries well, sort out any damaged berries. If using large berries, cut each in half.

4. Fill the hollow in the melon with yogurt. Top with berries.

5. If your toddler has trouble scooping the melon out, assist by removing pieces using a melon baller or grapefruit spoon.

Baked Zucchini

Baking zucchini with tomato sauce and cheese is almost like giving your toddler pizza—but a healthier one that's also lower in fat. Add salt and pepper for older kids.

INGREDIENTS | YIELDS 2 SERVINGS

1 medium zucchini
½ cup tomato sauce
½ cup shredded Mozzarella
1 tablespoon oil

1. Preheat the oven to 350°F. Scrub the zucchini and trim both ends. Slice into rings.

2. Place zucchini in a baking dish. Smother with tomato sauce and Mozzarella and oil, then cover the dish.

3. Bake for 45 minutes, or until zucchini is very soft and cheese is melted. Serve as is or fork-mash if desired.

Leafy Greens with Almonds

This is a fun recipe that uses lots of spinach. Leafy green vegetables are some of the most beneficial ones out there. Most toddlers need little encouragement if they've been offered such vegetables from a young age. Almonds add a pleasant crunch, but don't substitute walnuts or peanuts; those nuts are larger and chunkier, and not safe for young children.

INGREDIENTS | YIELDS 1 SERVING

1 cup fresh leafy greens
2 cups water
2 tablespoons butter or margarine
2 tablespoons sliced almonds

1. Wash the green leaves thoroughly, removing any damaged parts.

2. Steam in a small amount of water for about 10 minutes, or until the vegetables turn a bright green color.

3. Melt the butter in a small frying pan. Toast the almonds for about 5 minutes, stirring constantly to prevent burning.

4. When the almonds are toasted, mix with the spinach. Fork-mash if desired.

Baked Sweet Potatoes

There are a variety of different kinds of sweet potatoes. Yams have a bright orange interior and a sweet taste and soft texture. True sweet potatoes are lighter and firmer.

INGREDIENTS | YIELDS 2 SERVINGS

1 medium sweet potato or yam

Too Dry

If your baked potatoes come out too dry, it's probably due to a combination of factors, starting with temperature. Cooking potatoes at 400°F makes the outside cook faster than the inside, leaving you with a burned skin and a hard, dry, undercooked middle. Also, look at the type of potato; yellow-fleshed potatoes tend to be dryer than their white-fleshed cousins.

1. Scrub the sweet potato thoroughly with a vegetable brush. Cut out any bad spots. Poke 8–10 holes into the potato, using a fork or other sharp implement.

2. Bake at 350°F for 1 hour, or until the potato skin is crispy.

3. When cooled, cut the potato in half. Scoop out the potato from the skin, and fork-mash if desired.

Simple French Toast

French toast is not really a French food. By most accounts, it originated in the United States hundreds of years ago. Some think the original French toast was made by soaking toasted French bread in a mixture of wine and orange juice. Tasty, perhaps, but definitely not for your toddler!

INGREDIENTS | YIELDS 3 SERVINGS

1 egg
1 tablespoon milk or water
1 teaspoon white sugar
Pinch of cinnamon
1 tablespoon oil
3 slices whole wheat bread

Dress It Up!

Once your little one has mastered simple French toast, try adding fruit to make it a bit more appealing to the rest of the family. Mix a few mashed blueberries or strawberries into the egg mixture, for example. Or, if you want to try a creamier French toast, add a little applesauce to the egg mixture. You can also add a little vanilla or almond extract.

1. Combine the egg, milk, sugar, and cinnamon in a medium bowl. Beat thoroughly.

2. Heat oil in a large frying pan. One at a time, dip the bread slices into the egg mixture and soak for about 10 seconds. Flip the bread over and soak on the other side.

3. Place each of the bread slices into the heated pan.

4. Fry on each side until lightly browned, usually 1–3 minutes per side.

5. Let cool completely before cutting into pieces and serving as finger food.

Noodles with Cheese

Pasta comes in many different shapes, so it's perfectly acceptable to veer from the traditional macaroni! Experiment with conchiglie (shells), farfalle (bow ties), fusilli (twists), rotelle (wagon wheels), or any other fun shape your child might like.

INGREDIENTS | YIELDS 3 SERVINGS

4 cups water

¾ cup elbow macaroni (or other shape)

2 tablespoons butter

2 tablespoons all-purpose flour

1½ cups milk

¾ cup grated cheese

Choosing a Cheese

For basic macaroni and cheese, try using Cheddar, Colby, or Monterey jack cheese. Mozzarella melts very well on pizza, but isn't great for cooking into a toddler's meal because it tends to congeal rapidly. Experiment with different kinds of cheeses to see which kind your child likes the best!

1. Bring the water to a rapid boil in a large saucepan.

2. Add the macaroni, stirring to break up the pasta. Cook for 12–15 minutes, or until noodles are completely tender. Drain.

3. In a small saucepan, melt the butter over low heat. Stir in the flour, whisking constantly until it's dissolved. Add milk and cheese, stirring constantly, until it thickens into a sauce.

4. Pour the cheese sauce into the noodles, tossing to mix.

5. Allow to cool before serving to your toddler.

Dried Bean Stew

A variation on Indian dhal recipes, bean stew allows for more variety. If your family is partial to split peas, for example, feel free to use those instead. Any sort of meat can be substituted for the ham, and of course the meat can be omitted entirely for vegetarian families.

INGREDIENTS | YIELDS 4 SERVINGS

¼ cup dried lima beans

¼ cup dried black beans

4 cups water

1 small potato

½ cup tomato sauce

½ cup ham, diced

1. Wash the dried beans. Place in a large saucepan with enough water to cover them. Soak overnight in the refrigerator

2. In the morning, drain the soaking water and refill with fresh water, about 3 inches over the top of the beans. Bring to a boil; then simmer for about 1 hour.

3. Wash and peel the potato. Dice into small pieces; then add to the cooking pot.

4. Add in the tomato sauce and ham. Continue simmering until potatoes are cooked, about another 45 minutes.

5. Allow to cool; then fork-mash before serving.

Cottage Cheese with Fruit

Summer fruit with cottage cheese is a great combination for young eaters. This simple meal provides protein along with healthy fruit. To make the dish a little soupier, slice the fruit on a saucer; pour any juice that comes out right on top of the cottage cheese.

INGREDIENTS | YIELDS 1 SERVING

½ peach
1 plum
1 apricot
½ cup cottage cheese

Beyond Purées

Once your child is 18–24 months old, almost none of her food will need to be puréed. While she may still enjoy thinner textures, it's also a good idea to challenge her with more chewing foods. Most recipes for this age group can be fork-mashed or simply served as is.

1. Wash and peel the peach, remove the pit, and cut into thin slices.

2. Wash the plum, remove the pit and cut into thin slices.

3. Wash and peel apricot, remove the pit, and cut into pieces.

4. Place a scoop of cottage cheese into a toddler dish. Spoon the fruit on top.

5. Fork-mash if desired.

Cheesy Twice-Baked Potatoes

Twice-baked potatoes are a popular dish for the entire family, and a great way to use up leftover baked potatoes. When cooking for the rest of the family, you might incorporate bacon crumbles and diced green onion to the potato before rebaking, and also add a dash of salt and pepper.

INGREDIENTS | YIELDS 2 SERVINGS

1 russet potato
1 ounce shredded Cheddar
1 tablespoon cream cheese
½ tablespoon butter

1. Scrub the potato thoroughly with a vegetable brush. Cut out any bad spots.

2. Pat the potato dry with a paper towel; then poke 8–10 holes into the potato, using a fork or other sharp implement. Bake at 400°F for 1 hour.

3. Once the potato has cooled, slice it open and carefully remove the potato flesh.

4. Mix the potato with the Cheddar, cream cheese, and butter. Stir well, then put it back inside the potato shell. Bake at 350°F for another 15–20 minutes.

5. Slice into strips before serving, or remove the potato skin entirely. Fork-mash if desired.

Yogurt Fruit Drink

Here is a healthy summer drink. It could even be made into a winter drink! Simply substitute whatever fruit is in season—it's hard to go wrong with puréed fruit and yogurt. If you're out of fruit, use fruit juice instead.

INGREDIENTS | YIELDS 2 SERVINGS

2 strawberries
1 peach
½ banana
1 cup vanilla yogurt

1. Hull and clean the strawberries. Cut in half.

2. Wash and peel the peach. Remove the pit; cut into pieces.

3. Peel the banana and remove any damaged spots. Cut into chunks.

4. Place strawberries, peach, banana, and yogurt in the blender. Mix until a thin drink results.

5. Add water as needed, 1 tablespoon at a time, if too thick.

Fresh Fruit Salad

Fruit salad is one of the true joys of summer. And the best part: you can substitute any of the ingredients with whatever is in season. It's nice to provide a combination of flavors, colors, and textures; just make sure the pieces are the right size for your child to pick up with his fingers.

INGREDIENTS | YIELDS 3 SERVINGS

1 kiwi
¼ cup strawberries
¼ cup blueberries
¼ cup raspberries
½ small mango
½ cup seedless grapes

1. Wash the kiwi well and trim off both ends. Slide a tablespoon between the fleshy fruit and the peel. Run the spoon around the entire edge and the fruit should slide out intact. Cut into small pieces.

2. Wash the berries and remove any stems. Cut the strawberries into quarters. Blueberries and raspberries can either be served whole or, if they're large, cut in half.

3. Remove skin and pit from mango. Slice into small pieces.

4. Wash the grapes and slice each in half.

5. Combine all fruits in a small bowl, and refrigerate until ready to use. Fork-mash if desired.

Creamy Chicken and Potatoes

This simple creamy dish combines cubes of chicken and potatoes with a creamy, cheesy sauce. Just the thing for your child to practice using his new fork on!

INGREDIENTS | YIELDS 4 SERVINGS

1 small potato, cubed

1 cup water

4 teaspoons butter or margarine

2 teaspoons all-purpose flour

½ cup milk

½ cup cooked chicken, cubed

2 tablespoons grated cheese

1. Peel the potato and cut into cubes. Place the potato in a pot with water. Bring to boil, reduce heat, and simmer until tender, about 10–15 minutes. Remove from pot and drain.

2. In a small pan, melt butter over low heat. When melted, stir in flour until well mixed. Add milk and whisk until smooth.

3. Cook over low heat, stirring often, until sauce begins to thicken.

4. Add potato and chicken. Stir for about 3 minutes until all ingredients are heated through.

5. Remove pot from heat. Add cheese and stir until melted. Cool to lukewarm and serve.

Chicken with Apricots

One way to save time with this recipe is to use canned apricots instead of fresh. Since canned apricots already have a fair amount of juice, you can also omit the preserves. Simply take 3–4 apricot halves and about a tablespoon of juice, dice into small pieces, and pour on top of the chicken before baking.

INGREDIENTS | YIELDS 2 SERVINGS

1 small boneless, skinless chicken breast (about 6 ounces)

1 apricot

1 tablespoon apricot preserves

½ tablespoon butter

1. Wash the chicken breast and remove any skin or fat. Place in the bottom of a greased baking dish.

2. Dice the apricot into small pieces. Mix with the apricot preserves; then spread over the chicken.

3. Dot the top of the chicken with butter; then bake at 350°F for 30 minutes, or until the chicken's internal temperatures reaches 170°F. The juice from the chicken should run clear when pricked with a fork, and the chicken meat should not be pink when sliced.

4. Allow to cool; then dice into small pieces for your toddler to self-feed. You can also fork-mash if desired.

Chickpea and Tomato Salad

Chickpeas, are a great staple for toddlers because they're mild in flavor and high in protein. Cooking the chickpeas won't make them much softer, so be sure to fork-mash thoroughly. Cooking the tomatoes will soften them, so feel free to cook them for 10–15 minutes before using.

INGREDIENTS | YIELDS 2 SERVINGS

½ cup canned chickpeas
½ cup tomato
1 teaspoon olive oil
1 teaspoon red wine vinegar
½ teaspoon sugar
¼ teaspoon lemon juice
1 tablespoon parsley

1. Drain the chickpeas and rinse well.

2. Wash the tomato and remove the stem and any tough white flesh. Dice into small pieces.

3. In a small bowl, mix together the oil, vinegar, sugar, and lemon juice.

4. Toss the dressing with the chickpeas, tomatoes, and parsley. Fork-mash before serving. If your toddler seems averse to the sourness of the vinegar, either omit it or skip the dressing entirely.

Simple Hummus

Hummus is a classic Middle Eastern dish that can be served in a variety of ways. While serving it on pita bread is traditional, be flexible! Spread it on toast, or have your toddler dip a cracker (or even a finger) into a dish of hummus.

INGREDIENTS | YIELDS 2 SERVINGS

1 clove garlic, optional
1 cup canned chickpeas
1 teaspoon olive oil
1 tablespoon tahini
1 teaspoon cumin
1 teaspoon lemon juice
1 tablespoon water

1. If using garlic, peel it.

2. Rinse the precooked chickpeas. Place in food processor or blender and purée completely. Add the garlic and purée until well chopped and smooth.

3. Add the olive oil, tahini, cumin, and lemon juice. Continue puréeing for about 1 minute, scraping down the sides of the bowl as necessary.

4. Add enough water to make a smooth paste. Purée until smooth.

Creamed Tuna on Toast

Creamed tuna is a quick, easy meal suitable for children of all chewing abilities. If toast doesn't tickle your child's fancy, try serving with crackers or breadsticks.

INGREDIENTS | YIELDS 1 SERVING

1 tablespoon butter
1 tablespoon all-purpose flour
½ cup milk (regular or soy)
¼ cup chunk light tuna
1 piece whole-grain bread

A Sweet Touch

Having trouble getting your toddler to eat tuna? Creamed fish recipes can be made a little sweeter by adding a touch of sugar to the white sauce. On the other hand, some prefer a dash of salt with their tuna. You can also make this meal more visually appealing by adding a handful of peas for color. Again, be careful about serving tuna too often because of the amount of mercury in it.

1. Melt the butter in a small saucepan.

2. Add the flour, stirring constantly until dissolved. Add the milk and continue stirring until it forms a thick sauce.

3. Turn off the heat and add the tuna. Stir until mixed and creamy.

4. Serve on top of a piece of whole-grain toast.

Strawberry Ice Pops

If you don't have plastic molds, try using disposable paper cups to make this summertime treat. Insert a popsicle stick once the pop is partially frozen; then simply peel off the cup when it's time to eat.

INGREDIENTS | YIELDS 4 SERVINGS

4 large strawberries
1½ cups water
½ cup orange juice

1. Purée the strawberries in a food processor or blender.

2. Add water and orange juice to the food processor and mix until completely combined.

3. Pour into a rack of 4 ice-pop molds. Freeze for at least 5 hours before serving.

Creamy Fruit Popsicles

Not sure you want your child having all the additives commonly found in creamy popsicles? Make your own! While you can substitute soy milk for cream in this recipe, it doesn't freeze as well, so the end result will be a little icier than a dairy popsicle.

INGREDIENTS | YIELDS 4 SERVINGS

1 peach, diced
1 cup water
½ cup heavy whipping cream

Substituting with Canned

While canned peaches don't cut it for every recipe, they actually work just fine when making creamy popsicles. If you use the kind that are canned in syrup, the popsicles will come out a bit sweeter. You can even use the canning syrup instead of some of the water in this recipe.

1. Place the peach in a food processor or blender. Purée completely.

2. Add in the water and cream. Continue puréeing until the mixture is smooth.

3. Pour into a rack of 4 ice-pop molds. Freeze for at least 5 hours before serving.

Berry Smoothie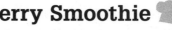

Feel good about serving your child a super-healthy beverage. The yogurt has acidophilus and other live cultures to aid a happy tummy, and berries (particularly blueberries) are known for their potential cancer-fighting abilities.

INGREDIENTS | YIELDS 2 SERVINGS

½ ripe banana
2 large strawberries
¼ cup raspberries or blueberries
¼ cup apple juice
½ cup yogurt (regular or soy)

Why Banana?

Bananas are in most smoothie recipes because they help with the texture—they make a smoothie thicker and creamier than it would be with only yogurt. Without banana, a smoothie would be more of a slushie, or an iced fruit drink.

1. Peel the banana and remove any damaged spots. Cut into slices and place in a blender or food processor.

2. Wash the berries and remove all stems. Cut in half and place in the food processor. You can use either frozen or fresh berries.

3. Add the juice and yogurt.

4. Blend until the drink is completely smooth.

5. Refrigerate any leftover drink immediately.

Best Baked Potatoes

If you don't have an hour to bake a potato in the oven, don't despair. They can also be cooked in the microwave with little sacrifice in flavor. Follow the same washing and pricking instructions; then cook on high for 5 minutes. Turn the potato over and cook for another 4–5 minutes. If the potato middle isn't soft, cook for another 1–2 minutes and recheck.

INGREDIENTS | YIELDS 2 SERVINGS

1 medium russet potato
½ tablespoon oil

Good Potatoes for Baking

The russet is the quintessential type of potato used for making baked potatoes and potato skins. There are several types of russet potatoes: Burbank, Norgold, Frontier, and Ranger are just a few varieties. Yellow and red potatoes also bake well, though with their thinner skins, they may fare better in the microwave.

1. Preheat the oven to 350°F.

2. Scrub the potato thoroughly with a vegetable brush. Cut out any bad spots.

3. Pat the potato dry with a paper towel; then poke 8–10 holes into the potato, using a fork or other sharp implement.

4. Pour the oil into a paper towel and rub it around the potato. Place on a baking sheet and bake for 1 hour, or until the potato skin is crispy.

5. When cooled, cut the potato in half. Scoop out the potato from the skin, and fork-mash if desired.

Spinach with Apples

Depending on how readily available fresh spinach is in your area, frozen spinach may or may not be a time-saver. In the bagged-salad section of most grocery stores, you can find spinach year-round, and it actually takes less time to cook than it does to thaw frozen spinach. Also, if you only need a small amount, using fresh spinach ensures little waste.

INGREDIENTS | YIELDS 1 SERVING

2 cups fresh leafy greens or ½ cup cooked spinach
½ apple
3 cups water

The Salad Version

When making a grown-up dish using the same recipe, how about a spinach and apple salad? Chop fresh spinach leaves and apples, and throw in ½ cup raisins and walnuts. Serve with a light dressing of olive oil, balsamic vinegar, and a dash of salt, sugar, pepper, and dry mustard.

1. Wash the spinach leaves thoroughly, removing any damaged parts.

2. Wash and peel the apple, removing the core and seeds. Dice into small chunks.

3. Place the apple in a medium saucepan and cover with water. Bring to a boil and cook for 15–20 minutes, or until apples are starting to soften.

4. Add the spinach and more water, if necessary. Return to a boil; then cook for 10–15 minutes, or until spinach is thoroughly cooked.

5. Fork-mash if desired.

Vegetable Soup

Vegetable soup is one of the most flexible recipes out there. Use chicken, vegetable, or beef stock for added flavor—black beans or chickpeas instead of kidney beans are acceptable substitutes as well. Clean out your vegetable drawer while creating several healthy meals for your toddler!

INGREDIENTS | YIELDS 3 SERVINGS

½ cup green beans
1 tablespoon butter or margarine
½ small onion, diced
1 medium red potato, diced
1 medium carrot, diced
½ cup kidney beans, cooked
Dash of salt and pepper
4 cups chicken stock or water

1. Snap the ends off the green beans, and then cut into 1-inch segments.

2. Melt the butter in a large saucepan. Add the onion, and sauté until it becomes translucent.

3. Add potato, carrot, green beans, kidney beans, salt, pepper, and chicken stock. Bring to a boil, and simmer for at least 1 hour. Longer cooking will make the vegetables more tender and enhance the flavors, but 1 hour is the minimum cooking time.

4. If desired, fork-mash the vegetables before serving.

Cauliflower with Cheese

Cauliflower may not be everyone's favorite vegetable, but don't let that prejudice prevent you from serving it to your toddler. Serving it up with melted cheese is a perfect way to encourage him to try a new taste.

INGREDIENTS | YIELDS 1 SERVING

½ cup cauliflower
2 cups water
2 ounces cheese

1. Wash the cauliflower, dice into small florets, and place in a steamer basket. Fill the bottom of a saucepan with water, place the steamer basket inside, then bring to a boil. Cook for 15 minutes, or until the cauliflower is tender.

2. Melt the cheese in a microwave-safe bowl. Heat in the microwave in 30-second intervals, stirring in between, until well melted.

3. Place the cooked cauliflower in a bowl and pour the melted cheese on top.

Pasta and Broccoli

Go as easy (or as heavy) on the garlic as your toddler seems to like. You can easily use part of a an entire clove if she seems to like it. This is also a perfect dish for serving to the rest of the family, and it won't require any additional seasonings.

INGREDIENTS | YIELDS 2 SERVINGS

½ cup broccoli
4 cups water
1 cup pasta
1 teaspoon olive oil
½ clove garlic, minced
1 teaspoon parsley
1 teaspoon grated Parmesan

1. Wash the broccoli and dice into small florets.

2. Bring the water to a boil. Add the pasta, and cook for about 10 minutes. Add in the broccoli and cook for another 10 minutes, or until both pasta and broccoli are tender. When cooked, drain.

3. Heat the olive oil in a medium skillet. Add garlic and parsley, sautéing for 2–3 minutes.

4. Add the pasta and broccoli to the saucepan. Sauté for 2–3 minutes, tossing the pasta and broccoli together with the garlic.

5. Sprinkle with Parmesan before serving.

Pear Pudding

Here's an unusual pudding, made with fresh or canned pears, that provides a healthy snack or dessert for your toddler. If you like a crunchy topping on your pudding, try sprinkling graham cracker crumbs on top before baking.

INGREDIENTS | YIELDS 2 SERVINGS

1 medium pear
1 egg, separated
1 teaspoon lemon zest
½ teaspoon cinnamon
2 tablespoons sugar
3 tablespoons all-purpose flour
2 tablespoons milk (regular or soy)

1. Preheat the oven to 375°F. Wash and peel the pear. Remove the stem and seeds, and grate the pear flesh.

2. Place the egg yolk in a bowl. Beat in lemon zest, cinnamon, and sugar. Mix in flour and milk; then stir in grated pear.

3. Whip the egg white to soft peaks using an electric mixer. Beat on high until small white peaks form. Fold the egg white into the pear mixture.

4. Pour into a greased baking dish. Bake for about 30 minutes or until pudding is set.

5. Allow to cool before serving.

Apple Nut Bake

Here's an easy recipe that makes good use of leftover apples. Any variety will do.
If using Granny Smiths, you may want to add a pinch more sugar.
If your apples are already sweet enough, feel free to omit the sugar entirely.

INGREDIENTS | YIELDS 2 SERVINGS

2 medium apples
4 cups water
1 tablespoon almonds
1 egg
1 teaspoon all-purpose flour
1 teaspoon sugar
Dash of cinnamon
Dash of nutmeg

1. Preheat the oven to 350°F. Wash, peel, and core the apples. Dice into chunks.

2. Bring the water to a boil in a medium saucepan. Add the apple chunks and cook for 20–25 minutes, or until the apples are tender. Drain the apples and fork-mash into a rough purée.

3. Place the almonds in a food processor or food mill. Grind until they are finely chopped.

4. Mix the apples, almonds, and egg together in a bowl. Add the flour and sugar, stirring to combine. Add nutmeg and cinnamon, and stir until the mixture is thoroughly coated.

5. Place in a greased baking dish and bake for 30 minutes. Allow to cool before serving.

Asparagus Cheese Dip

Asparagus dip is a great way to use up leftover asparagus. This dip is high in vitamin C, vitamin K, and folate, which is beneficial for your toddler's cardiovascular system.

INGREDIENTS | 1 SERVING

2 asparagus spears

2 cups of water

½ ripe avocado

1 tablespoon cottage cheese

Dippers

Toddlers may want to dip their fingers (or entire hands) into this recipe—and that's okay! But if you're looking for a cleaner dipper than a human body part, try whole-wheat crackers. Bread crusts make excellent tools for dipping. Also, try well-cooked baby carrots as dippers; they're firm enough for toddlers to handle, and soft enough to chew.

1. Bring the asparagus and water to a boil in a shallow saucepan. Steam for 10–15 minutes, or until the asparagus is soft.

2. Cut the avocado in half. Remove the pit and scoop the avocado out of the skin. Cut into chunks and place into a food processor or blender.

3. When the asparagus is cooked, chop into pieces and add to the food processor.

4. Add the cottage cheese to the food processor and purée until the mixture is smooth. If it's too thick, add cooking water from the asparagus, 1 tablespoon at a time.

5. Serve as a dipping sauce. Refrigerate the leftovers immediately.

Fish Chowder with Corn

Chowder is a type of thick, creamy soup that usually contains seafood and/or potatoes. The starch from the potatoes binds the soup into a stew, and the resulting smooth texture is great for young eaters. If fork-mashing leaves too many discrete pieces, purée in the food processor before serving.

INGREDIENTS | YIELDS 2 SERVINGS

½ medium white potato, diced

⅛ cup corn

⅛ cup peas

2 cups water

1 small whitefish fillet

1 tablespoon butter

¼ cup milk (regular or soy)

The Origins of Chowder

According to most sources, the soup we know as chowder originated in England in the 1700s. Fishermen would start a pot of water boiling in the morning and, as the day wore on, would add fresh fish, vegetables, bread, and any other available ingredients. By day's end, a thick soup was ready for all.

1. Combine potato, corn, and peas in a saucepan with 2 cups of water. Bring to a boil; then cook for 25 minutes, or until the potatoes are soft.

2. Wash the fish fillet, removing all bones. Place fish into the bottom of a microwave-safe dish and add enough water to cover the bottom of the dish. Cover with either a lid or microwave-safe plastic wrap.

3. Cook fish in the microwave on high for 3 minutes. Let rest; then cook for another 3–4 minutes. Fish is done when it flakes easily with a fork and is an opaque color.

4. Drain the vegetables. Add the fish, butter, and milk, stirring over low heat until the chowder thickens. Allow to cool; then fork-mash or purée before serving.

Baby's Peach Cobbler

Traditional peach cobbler is a baked fruit dish with a sweet biscuit topping. Because most toddlers wouldn't be able to eat the topping once it's baked and hard, here's a variation on an old favorite, and one that's tailored right to your child's developing abilities.

INGREDIENTS | YIELDS 2 SERVINGS

1 fresh peach
1 teaspoon brown sugar
1/8 teaspoon cinnamon
1/8 cup rice powder
2 cups water

Cobbling Together a Dessert

Cobblers are fruit desserts that are traditionally cooked in deep-dish pans. They're historically made with whatever fruits are in season; blueberry, blackberry, apricot, and apple are all popular cobbler flavors. Cobblers are distinguished from other baked fruit desserts because they're usually topped with a sweet biscuit dough.

1. Preheat oven to 350°F.

2. Wash the peach and cut into thin slices. Remove the skin.

3. Place peach into a small greased baking dish with brown sugar and cinnamon. Give it a quick stir; then bake for 30 minutes, or until peaches are completely soft.

4. In a small saucepan, bring 1/2 cup of water to a boil. Add the rice powder and stir for 30 seconds. Cover the pot, turn down the heat to low, and simmer for 7–8 minutes, or until the rice is a smooth, thick consistency. Stir occasionally to prevent sticking.

5. When the peach is cooked, fork-mash. Mix in the cooked rice cereal until the cobbler reaches the desired consistency.

Bell Pepper Faces

Here's a fun way to encourage your toddler to eat vegetables. Go for contrasting colors; reds, greens, and oranges will stand out nicely against a white or yellow tortilla. It doesn't matter if your tot's meal looks like a Rembrandt painting, but he'll be more excited about it if it's colorful.

INGREDIENTS | YIELDS 1 SERVING

1 flour or corn tortilla
1 cherry tomato
¼ green pepper
1 slice cheese
½ carrot
1 tablespoon peanut butter

Peppers

Red, green, or yellow bell peppers are sweet and crunchy. Their hotter cousins, such as the jalapeño or the cayenne, will bring tears to your eyes and do much worse for a toddler. Hot peppers contain capsaicin, an alkaloid that forms the basis of pepper sprays. Good for people who thrive on spicy food, but keep it out of your toddler's meal.

1   Place the tortilla on a flat plate. Slice the cherry tomato in half. Place on the tortilla for eyes.

2. Slice the bell pepper in half and remove all seeds. Cut 5–10 thin strips; place at the top of the tortilla for hair.

3. Cut the cheese into 2 half-circles. Place at the sides of the tortilla for ears.

4. Wash and peel the carrot. Grate several pieces and place on the tortilla for the mouth and eyebrows.

5. When the vegetables are all positioned the way you like them, affix each to the tortilla with a dab of peanut butter.

Potato Salad

Potato salad "dressing" can be made in any number of ways. For young eaters, go for simple ingredients, and fewer of them. Also, stay away from heavily seasoned, spiced, or salty variations, and avoid adding little bits of hard celery or pickles that toddlers could choke on. Stick to soft, easily recognizable ingredients.

INGREDIENTS | 2 SERVINGS

2 red potatoes

4 cups water

1 tablespoon mayonnaise

1 tablespoon yogurt

½ teaspoon sugar

½ teaspoon prepared mustard

Dash of garlic powder

Dash of salt

Hot or Cold?

Some potato salads are meant to be served hot, such as German potato salad. It's usually prepared with an oil-and-vinegar dressing, rather than the creamy dressing typical of cold potato salad. This variation may be a little too sour for your toddler, but it's certainly worth trying! Just be sure to serve it warm, not hot, to avoid burning your toddler's tongue.

1. Wash and peel the potatoes. Cut out any bad spots; then dice into small pieces.

2. Place the potatoes in a medium saucepan and cover with water. Bring to a boil and cook for 25–30 minutes, or until potatoes are soft.

3. Drain the potatoes and allow to cool.

4. In a small bowl, mix the mayonnaise, yogurt, sugar, mustard, garlic powder, and salt. Gently toss with the potatoes.

5. Chill before serving. Fork-mash if desired.

Cheesy Corn Nuggets

Sometimes known as fritters, corn nuggets are usually deep fried, but can be made healthier by pan frying in a small amount of oil. These fried delights, when made with buttermilk and cornmeal, are also called hush puppies in some southern parts of the United States.

INGREDIENTS | YIELDS 4 SERVINGS

1 cup corn (canned, or 3 ears fresh corn), cooked

1 egg

2 tablespoons flour

½ tablespoon butter, melted

¼ cup shredded Cheddar

2 tablespoons oil

1. Shave the corn kernels off the ears of cooked corn, yielding 1 cup of corn kernels. Mash them well with a fork or run them through the food processor.

2. Whisk the egg in a medium bowl. Add the flour, melted butter, shredded cheese, and corn, mixing thoroughly to combine.

3. Heat the oil in a frying pan. When hot, drop the batter into the pan by the spoonful, leaving enough space between them so that the fritters do not touch.

4. Let fry 2–3 minutes; then flip over with a spatula. Cook another 2–3 minutes, flipping again if necessary.

5. Drain onto paper towels. Serve as finger food once cooled.

Toddler Cordon Bleu

When making a stuffed chicken or stuffed beef dish, a meat mallet is important because it will both flatten and tenderize the meat. A meat mallet is basically a perforated wooden or metal block, usually attached to a wooden handle. Simply place the meat on an appropriate work surface, and pound it with the mallet.

INGREDIENTS | 2 SERVINGS

1 small boneless, skinless chicken breast (about 6 ounces)

2 thin slices of ham

2 ounces cheese, shredded

1 tablespoon butter, melted

2 tablespoons bread crumbs

1. Preheat the oven to 350°F. Wash the chicken breast and remove any skin or fat.

2. Slice the chicken breast in half horizontally. Pound with a meat mallet to make the chicken as thin as possible.

3. Place the ham slices over one piece of chicken. Sprinkle the cheese on top; then place the other piece of chicken on top.

4. Place the assembly in a greased baking dish. Brush with melted butter and sprinkle the top with bread crumbs. Bake for 40 minutes, or until the chicken's internal temperature reaches 170°F. The juice from the chicken should run clear when pricked with a fork.

5. Allow to cool, cut into small pieces, and serve.

Basic Chocolate Chip Cookies

Everyone loves chocolate chip cookies. The nice thing about this recipe is that you can sneak in the healthy nutrition of whole grains by adding powdered oats.

INGREDIENTS | YIELDS 6 SERVINGS

½ cup shortening
⅓ cup white sugar
⅓ cup brown sugar, packed
1 egg
¾ cup all-purpose flour
¼ teaspoon salt
½ teaspoon baking soda
1 cup ground oats
1 cup chocolate chips

Chewy Versus Hard

When making cookies for toddlers, try to bake them on the soft side (rather than hard and crunchy). Don't overdo it on the baking powder or baking soda, since those ingredients tend to make cookies more cake-like. Don't overcook; burning is a sure way to crisp a cookie. For really soft cookies, try using corn syrup instead of sugar.

1. Preheat the oven to 350°F.

2. In a medium bowl, cream the shortening, and sugars together. Mix with a fork until large crumbles are formed, or use an electric mixer.

3. Add the egg and mix well. Add in the flour, salt, and baking soda, continuing to stir until a dough is formed.

4. Add oatmeal and chocolate chips. Stir well; then drop spoonfuls onto a greased baking sheet, leaving about 2 inches between each cookie. Bake for 11–14 minutes.

5. Let cool on the baking sheet for 1–2 minutes, then remove and finish cool on wire racks.

Mini Meatloaf

Kids love things that are just their size. These pint-sized meatloaves are perfect single-serve foods for toddlers, and the leftovers make great school lunches.

INGREDIENTS | YIELDS 4 SERVINGS

¾–1 pound ground beef

1 egg

½ cup milk or water

3 tablespoons ketchup

2 teaspoons Worcestershire sauce

½ teaspoon oregano

½ teaspoon parsley

Dash of salt and pepper

½ cup bread crumbs

½ small onion, diced

½ cup Cheddar, shredded

1. Preheat the oven to 350°F.

2. In a medium bowl, mix the ground beef, egg, and milk together. Stir well.

3. Add in the ketchup, Worcestershire, oregano, parsley, salt, pepper, bread crumbs, and onions. Mix thoroughly to combine, using your hands if necessary.

4. Scoop equal portions into 6 muffin cups of a metal muffin tin.

5. Bake for 35–45 minutes, or until the meat is no longer pink. About 15 minutes before they're done, sprinkle Cheddar cheese on top of each mini meatloaf. Allow to cool before slicing and serving.

Turkey with Fruit

Turkey fruit salad is a fun way to get kids to eat their protein and vegetables, all in one serving, and you can use up leftover turkey in the process! Adjust the seasonings as necessary to suit your child's taste.

INGREDIENTS | YIELDS 1 SERVING

2 large lettuce leaves

½ cup cooked turkey

¼ cup grapes

¼ cup cantaloupe or honeydew melon

1 ounce mozzarella or Cheddar, shredded

1 teaspoon olive oil

1 teaspoon white wine vinegar

Dash prepared mustard

Grown-Up Salad Dressing

Many children will eat vegetables with the "modified" oil-and-vinegar dressing described here. To make this dressing more suitable for adult taste buds, add a dash of garlic powder, salt, pepper, sugar, and freshly diced herbs.

1. Tear the lettuce into small pieces and place in the bottom of a serving bowl.

2. Cut the turkey into small pieces, removing any fat and skin. Place on top of the lettuce.

3. Wash the grapes and cut in half. Cut the melon into small cubes. Mix grapes and melon in with the turkey.

4. Top with shredded cheese.

5. Prepare the dressing by mixing the oil, vinegar, and mustard. Stir well; then drizzle over the salad and mix gently.

Sweet-and-Sour Meatballs

Sweet-and-sour sauce doesn't need to be so powerful that it brings tears to your eyes, or makes you cringe. Especially when cooking for young children, it's important to introduce a variety of flavors—but not super-strong ones!

INGREDIENTS | YIELDS 2 SERVINGS

¼ pound ground beef

¼ cup bread crumbs

½ teaspoon soy sauce

2 teaspoons oil

½ cup canned pineapple chunks, diced

1 teaspoon cornstarch

2 tablespoons water

¼ cup bell pepper, diced

Keeping It Together

If your meatballs always fall apart when you cook on the stovetop, there are a few things you can try to help them maintain their shape. Add a little oil to the pan to keep them from sticking and falling apart when you roll them over. Also, adding more egg and bread crumbs (and pressing the meat very firmly into balls) will keep them from disintegrating into meat sauce.

1. Mix the ground beef, bread crumbs, and soy sauce together. Form into round 1-inch balls.

2. Heat the oil in a skillet. Add the meatballs, reduce heat to medium, and cook until the meatballs are no longer pink.

3. Put the pineapple chunks and juice (about ¼ cup) into a small bowl. Add cornstarch and water, and stir well to mix. Add in the bell pepper.

4. Pour the pineapple mixture into the skillet. Stir the meatballs around to coat in the sauce, and cook the sauce for several minutes or until it thickens.

5. Allow to cool before serving.

Chicken, Pasta, and Carrots

This recipe is a classic spring dish, and one that covers nearly the entire food pyramid! Farfalle pasta is a good choice, but any small pasta shape will cook quickly and be easy for self-feeders.

INGREDIENTS | YIELDS 2 SERVINGS

1 small boneless, skinless chicken breast (about 6 ounces)

2 teaspoons oil

1 medium carrot

½ cup pasta

½ cup chicken stock

Spoon, Fork, or Spork?

Your toddler has three main choices for eating utensils once her fingers no longer suffice. Rubber-tipped spoons are great for feeding purées, and dull-tined forks help more for stabbing discrete bites. Neither seeming to work quite well enough? Try a spork, or a spoon with tined edges. She can both scoop and stab at the same time.

1. Wash the chicken breast and remove any skin or fat. Cut into small pieces.

2. Heat the oil in a skillet. Add the chicken; then stir-fry for 10–12 minutes, or until the chicken is cooked.

3. Wash and peel the carrot; slice into thin coins.

4. Bring water to a boil. Add the carrots and cook for about 10 minutes. Add the pasta and cook for another 20 minutes, or until both pasta and carrots are tender.

5. Drain; add the pasta and carrots into the skillet with the chicken. Add chicken stock and cook at a high temperature for 4–5 minutes.

Mini Pizza Faces

*Bring a smile to your child's face with this smiling pizza meal! You can do any number of substitutions here—olives instead of pepperoni or green pepper instead of carrots.
Use whatever vegetables you have on hand.*

INGREDIENTS | YIELDS 2 SERVINGS

1 baby carrot
2 tablespoons peas
2 cups water
1 English muffin
2 tablespoons tomato sauce
4 thin slices pepperoni
1 ounce shredded Mozzarella

Super-Size It

If the whole family's in the mood for pizza, simply make a full-sized pie and serve your toddler a slice. Use the same fun ingredients to make a pizza face, but use pizza dough instead of English muffins.

1. Preheat the oven to 375°F.

2. Slice the baby carrot in half lengthwise. Place it and the peas in a saucepan with the water. Bring to a boil; then cook for about 10 minutes, or until the vegetables are tender. Drain and set aside.

3. Split the English muffin in half and lay the two pieces face-up on a baking sheet. Spoon tomato sauce over each muffin to cover it and lay a foundation for the pizza face.

4. On each muffin, place 2 pieces of pepperoni for eyes. Place half a baby carrot for a nose. Make a smile out of peas. Place the shredded Mozzarella around the top of the muffin for hair.

5. Bake for 10–15 minutes, or until the cheese melts.

Fish-Potato-Broccoli Pie

Most toddlers have difficulty with hard pie crust, so this "pie" recipe is minus the shell.
Baking it in muffin tins provides single-servings and easy leftovers.

INGREDIENTS | YIELDS 6 SERVINGS

1 boneless fillet whitefish

1 cup water

2 medium red potatoes, diced

1 medium carrot, diced

½ cup broccoli, diced

1 tablespoon butter

1 tablespoon all-purpose flour

½ cup milk (regular or soy)

Adding a Crust

For a more "adult" version of this recipe, try making it using a single-shell pie crust. A single pie crust is made by mixing 1 cup flour with ½ cup vegetable shortening. When mixed, slowly add 3 tablespoons of ice water. Once a dough is formed, roll out and use immediately, or store in the refrigerator (wrapped in plastic) until ready for use.

1. Rinse the fish fillet and remove all bones. Cut into small pieces.

2. Bring water to a boil in a medium saucepan. Add the potatoes, carrots, and broccoli, then cook for about 10 minutes. Add the fish and cook another 10–15 minutes or until the fish flakes easily. When cooked, drain and return the fish and vegetables to the saucepan.

3. In a separate small saucepan, melt the butter. Stir in the flour. Once mixed, add in the milk and stir constantly until a thin sauce is formed. Mix this sauce in with the fish and vegetables, stirring to combine.

4. Divide the fish and vegetables into a 6-cup muffin tin. Bake at 350°F for 30 minutes. Let cool before serving, and fork-mash if desired.

Carrot and Squash Soup

If you're looking for a creamed squash soup, that variation can easily be added to this recipe. After puréeing the soup, add ½ cup heavy cream and simmer over low heat for 5 minutes. The soup can also be made a little richer by substituting a cup of milk for the vegetable stock.

INGREDIENTS | YIELDS 5 SERVINGS

½ small butternut squash

1 tablespoon butter or margarine

½ small onion, diced

1 small clove garlic, minced

2 medium carrots

6 cups water or vegetable stock

⅛ teaspoon oregano, crushed

⅛ teaspoon thyme, crushed

Squash Too Difficult to Peel?

If you're having a struggle peeling the squash, bake it in the oven before combining with the other ingredients. The peel will be easier to remove. Slice the squash in half and place cut surfaces down on a lightly oiled baking sheet. Bake at a medium temperature until tender. Then remove the peel.

1. Peel the squash, remove the seeds and pulp, and cut into chunks.

2. Melt the butter in a large saucepan. Add the onion and garlic, sautéing until the onion becomes translucent.

3. Add the squash, carrot, and vegetable stock. Bring to a boil; then add oregano and thyme. Reduce to a simmer and cook for 1–2 hours, or until the vegetables are tender.

4. When the soup is done, purée in a food processor or blender before serving.

Chocolate Pudding

*Ye olde standby. Chocolate pudding is as basic as it gets, and is a
favorite when all other mealtime foods seem to flop.*

INGREDIENTS | YIELDS 2 SERVINGS

1 ounce unsweetened chocolate

1 tablespoon butter

1 cup milk

¼ cup flour

½ cup sugar

1 egg yolk

¼ teaspoon vanilla extract

Roll with the Pudding

This is a good recipe for older children to practice their cooking skills with, but don't be too fussy about the end result! If it doesn't end up gelling into pudding, just call it hot chocolate. Toddlers can eat it with a spoon or drink it through a straw.

1. Put the chocolate and butter into a microwave-safe dish. Microwave on low, in 30-second intervals, until the chocolate is melted. Stir well after each microwave interval to see if the chocolate is sufficiently melted.

2. Combine the melted chocolate and milk in a medium saucepan. Stir in the flour and sugar. Heat almost to boiling, and reduce heat to a simmer. Cook for 5–6 minutes or until the pudding starts to gel together.

3. Give the pudding a good stir, and add the egg yolk. Stir well, then continue cooking over low heat for 2–3 minutes. Stir constantly to keep lumps from forming.

4. Remove the saucepan from the heat. Add in the vanilla and mix thoroughly.

5. Allow to cool before serving.

Peanut Butter Goodies

Peanut butter and chocolate is a devilishly delicious combination—treat your child's sweet tooth with this no-bake recipe. For variety, try substituting peanut butter chips or butterscotch chips for the chocolate.

INGREDIENTS | YIELDS 8 SERVINGS

½ cup crushed graham crackers

3 ounces semisweet chocolate

1 tablespoon shortening

1 cup powdered sugar

½ cup peanut butter

¼ cup chocolate chips

Making Parents Feel Better

If the thought of gooey treats makes you want to run for the toothpaste, you can mitigate the health concerns by adding a tablespoon of wheat germ to these peanut butter goodies. Also, instead of chocolate chips, try throwing in a few "twigs" of an oat bran cereal.

1. Place the graham crackers in a sealing plastic bag. Crush with your hands or a mallet to make coarse crumbs (this is a great task for toddlers).

2. Put the chocolate and shortening into a microwave-safe dish. Microwave on low, in 30-second intervals, until the chocolate is melted. Stir well after each microwave interval to see if the chocolate is sufficiently melted.

3. Mix the chocolate and sugar together until they're combined. Stir in peanut butter.

4. Add graham cracker crumbs. Mix gently until they are completely incorporated. Add chocolate chips and stir until thoroughly mixed.

5. Press into a loaf pan; then cut into cookies about 1" × 2".

Resources

Books for Your Toddler

Barrett, Judi. Illustrated by Ron Barrett. *Cloudy with a Chance of Meatballs.* New York: Aladdin Paperbacks, 1982.

Breeze, L., and A. Morris. *This Little Baby's Bedtime.* New York: Little Brown, 1990.

Bridwell, Norman. *Clifford the Big Red Dog.* New York: Scholastic Books, 1963. There are many other *Clifford* books.

Brown, Margaret Wise. *Goodnight Moon.* New York: Harper Festival; board edition, 1991.

———*The Runaway Bunny.* New York: Harper, 1942.

Carle, Eric. *The Very Hungry Caterpillar.* New York: Philomel, 1994.

Christelow, Eileen. *Five Little Monkeys Jumping on the Bed.* New York: Clarion Books, 1998.

Eastman, P. D., illus. *Are You My Mother?* New York: Random House Books for Young Readers; board edition, 1998

Frankel, Alona. *Once upon a Potty.* New York: HarperCollins, 1999.

Gomi, Taro. *Everyone Poops.* New York: Kane/Miller Book Publishers, 1993.

Keats, Ezra Jack. *The Snowy Day.* New York: Viking Books; board edition, 1996.

———*Goggles!* New York: Viking, 1998.

———*Peter's Chair.* New York: Viking, 1998.

————*Whistle for Willie*. New York: Puffin Books, 1977.

Kingsley, Emily Perl. *I Can Do It Myself*. New York: Western Publishing Co., Inc., 1980.

Kunhardt, Dorothy. *Pat the Bunny*. New York: Golden Books; reissue edition, 2001.

Martin, Bill Jr., and Carle, Eric. *Brown Bear, Brown Bear, What Do You See?* New York: Henry Holt and Company, 1983.

Paterson, Bettina. *Potty Time*. New York: Grosset & Dunlap, 1993.

Potter, Beatrix. *The Tale of Peter Rabbit*. New York: Frederick Warne & Company, 1902.

Rey, Margaret, and H. A. Rey. The *Curious George* books. New York: Houghton Mifflin, 1941–2003.

Sendak, Maurice. *Where the Wild Things Are*. New York: HarperCollins, 1988.

Dr. Seuss. *Green Eggs & Ham*. New York: Random House, 1960.

————*Dr. Seuss's Sleep Book*. New York: Random House, 1962.

————*Hop on Pop*. New York: Random House, 1963.

————*Fox in Socks*. New York: Random House, 1965.

————*One Fish Two Fish Red Fish Blue Fish*. New York: Random House, 1981.

Viorst, Judith. Illustrated by Ray Cruz. *Alexander and the Terrible, Horrible, No Good, Very Bad Day*. New York: Aladdin Paperbacks, 1987.

Westcott, Nadine Bernard. *I Know an Old Lady Who Swallowed a Fly*. New York: Little Brown & Co., 1988.

Books for Parents

Alvino, James. *Parents' Guide to Raising a Gifted Toddler: Recognizing and Developing the Potential of Your Child from Birth to Five Years*. Boston: Little, Brown, and Company, 1989.

Brazelton, T. Berry. *Touchpoints: Your Child's Emotional and Behavioral Development*. Cambridge, MA: Perseus Publishing, 1994.

Douglas, Ann. *The Mother of All Toddler Books*. New York: John Wiley & Sons, 2004.

Eisenberg, Arlene, Heidi E. Murkoff, and Sandee E. Hathaway. *What to Expect: The Toddler Years*. New York: Workman Publishing, 1994.

Faber, Adele, and Elaine Mazlish. *Siblings Without Rivalry: How to Help Your Children Live Together So You Can Live Too*. New York: Avon Books, 1987.

Feldman, Robert S. *Child Development*. Upper Saddle River, New Jersey: Prentice Hall, Inc., 2001.

Galbraith, Judy. *You Know Your Child Is Gifted When . . . : A Beginner's Guide to Life on the Bright Side*. Minneapolis, MN: Free Spirit Publishing, 2000.

Hewitt, Deborah. *So This Is Normal Too?* St. Paul, MN: Redleaf Press, 1995.

Iovine, Vicki. *The Girlfriends' Guide to Toddlers*. New York: Perigee Books, 1999.

Kohl, MaryAnn. *First Art: Art Experiences for Toddlers and Twos*. Beltsville, MD: Gryphon House, 2002.

Margulis, Jennifer, ed. *Toddler: Real-Life Stories of Those Fickle, Irrational, Urgent, Tiny People We Love*. New York: Seal Press, 2003.

Murphy, Jana. *The Secret Lives of Toddlers: A Parent's Guide to the Wonderful, Terrible, Fascinating Behavior of Children Ages 1–3*. New York: Perigee Trade, 2004.

Nathanson, Laura Walther. *The Portable Pediatrician for Parents*. New York: HarperPerennial, 1994.

Osit, Michael. *Generation Text: Raising Well-Adjusted Kids in an Age of Instant Everything*. AMACOM: New York, 2008.

Schiller, Pam. *The Complete Resource Book for Toddlers and Twos: Over 2000 Experiences and Ideas*. Beltsville, MD: Gryphon House, 2003.

Shonkoff, Jack P., ed. *From Neurons to Neighborhoods: The Science of Early Childhood Development*. Washington, DC: National Academies Press, 2000.

Smutny, Joan Franklin, ed. et al. *The Young Gifted Child. Potential and Promise, an Anthology*. Cresskill, NJ: Hampton Press, 1998

Smutny, Joan Franklin, et al. *Your Gifted Child: How to Recognize and Develop the Special Talents in Your Child from Birth to Age Seven*. New York: Ballantine Books, 1994.

Spock, Benjamin. *Baby and Child Care*. New York: Pocket Books, 1976.

White, Burton L. *The New First Three Years of Life*. New York: Fireside, 1995.

Winn, Marie. *The Plug-In Drug: Television, Computers, and Family Life*. New York: Penguin Books, 2002.

Zand, Janet, et al. *Smart Medicine for a Healthier Child*. Garden City, New York: Avery Publishing Group, 1994.

Films for Young Children

Bambi. Walt Disney, 1942.

The Chronicles of Narnia. Walden Media, 2005, 2008, 2010 (for mature, gifted toddlers).

Clifford the Big Red Dog. Scholastic Books and PBS series.

Elmo's Musical Adventure; The Story of Peter and the Wolf. Sony Wonder, 2001.

Elmo's World: Flowers, Bananas & More. Sony Wonder, 2000.

The Lion King. Walt Disney, 1994.

Little Bear: Little Sherlock Bear. Paramount Studio, 2001.

Richard Scarry's Best Sing-Along Mother Goose Video Ever. Sony Wonder, 1994.

Spirited Away. Distributed by Disney's Buena Vista, 2001.

Thomas Trackside Tunes and Other Thomas Adventures. Anchor Bay Entertainment, 2001.

Winnie the Pooh. Walt Disney, 1966, 1968, 1974, 1977. There are several Pooh films, based on the stories of A.A. Milne.

Zoboomafoo: Play Day at Animal Junction. PBS Home Video, 2001.

Magazines for Parents

Parents. www.parents.com
Parent & Child. www.scholastic.com
Parenting. www.parenting.com/parenting
Mothering. www.mothering.com

Organizations and Websites

National Association for Gifted Children
1701 L Street, NW, Suite 550
Washington, DC 20036
202-785-4268
www.nagc.org
This organization helps parents and teachers of gifted children.

Supporting the Emotional Needs of the Gifted (SENG)
405 White Hall
Kent State University
PO Box 466
Poughquag, NY 12570
845-797-5054
www.sengifted.org
This organization offers helpful articles about the unique emotional needs of gifted adults and children.

GT World
This site is generally helpful for those with an interest in gifted children.
www.gtworld.org

Hoagies' Gifted Education Page
This site offers general support and help for parents and teachers of gifted children.
www.hoagiesgifted.org

The Gifted Child Society
This organization offers information about gifted children.
www.gifted.org

National Association for the Education of Young Children
1313 L Street, NW, Suite 500
Washington, DC 20005
202-232-8777 or 800-424-2460 or 866-NAEYC-4U
www.naeyc.org
This is a professional organization for teachers of young children. It would be helpful to parents of older toddlers.

National Health Information Service
Clearinghouse on Disability Information, Office of Special Education and Rehabilitative Services
550 12th Street, SW, Room 5133
Washington, DC 20202-2550
202-245-7307
202-205-5637 (Voice – TDD)
This government branch of the Department of Education offers legal and educational material for parents and teachers of children with special needs.

March of Dimes National Office
1275 Mamaroneck Avenue
White Plains, NY 10605
914-997-4488
www.modimes.org
This national charity helps to prevent birth defects and assist parents with children of special needs. There are branch offices in every state in the United States.

Resources for Children with Special Needs
116 E. 16th Street, 5th Floor
New York, NY 20003
212-677-4650
www.resourcesnyc.org
This special-needs organization primarily assists families in the boroughs of New York City.
There are national organizations for each special need.

The following sites are helpful in evaluating toys:
Oppenheim Toy Portfolio (*www.toyportfolio.com*), the Toys section of About.com (*http://toys.about.com*) and The Toy Guy (*www.thetoyguy.com*).

Another source to check out is *Consumer Reports*, which evaluates everything from toddler toys and furniture to the pesticides in store-bought vegetables. Subscribe to the magazine by calling (800) 208-9696, or to the online service at *www.consumerreports.org*.

You might want to investigate the following sites:
www.parents-choice.org: Parents' Choice website.

www.4everythingnanny.com: Learn the ins and outs of in-your-home child care at a website devoted to nannies.

www.abcparenting.com: Get help on thorny issues like day care, weaning, and potty training. There's also information for parents of multiples and discussion groups for everyone.

http://babyparenting.about.com: Here's a website with great smoothie recipes, potty training tips, and the chance to network with other online moms and dads.

www.disney.go.com: Check out the activities, music, and stories. Games teach toddlers basic concepts like matching, but the sounds and graphics provide great sensory stimulation whether or not they care to play.

www.drsonna.org: Read the online articles and get personal answers to your toddler questions at this website.

www.kidsdr.com: This site contains a wealth of information on health, nutrition, parenting, and behavior.

www.kidsfree.com: Check the toddler section to download free software for kid-friendly games, stories, and keyboard bangers. Well, maybe not that kid friendly; parents will still need to supervise.

www.kidsource.com: If you have a toddler health-and-wellness question, they've got the answer. Read the articles or post your question to a forum.

www.nccic.org: When you want child care information, go for the best at the National Child Care Information Center. It has a searchable database, too.

www.parentcenter.com: Here's a site that offers a wealth of tips and how-to's to enhance toddler learning, health, and better behavior.

www.parents-choice.org: Find out which books, toys, videos, software, and TV shows get the thumbs-up from other parents.

www.parentstv.org: Parent's Television Council Green Light Seal of Approval identifies TV shows that exhibit positive values and/or educational content for families. Phone: (213) 629-9255.

www.pbskids.org/barney: Color with BJ, make music with Baby Bop, and play games with Barney.

www.pbskids.org/rogers: Hear the songs, learn the facts, listen to the stories, and color in the online coloring book while visiting Mr. Rogers Neighborhood.

www.pbskids.org/teletubbies: Make Tinky Winky, Dipsy, Laa-Laa, and Po talk while touring their Teletubbie homeland.

www.tnpc.com: Before you buy a children's product, check the recommendations and recalls at the National Parenting Center's Seal of Approval website.

Programs and Associations

- Achievement of Human Potential has educational products and programs that teach toddlers to read, do math, and acquire knowledge. It has a program for brain-injured children, too. (800) 344-MOTHER, *www.iahp.org*
- The International Parenting Association offers free, downloadable educational materials and publishes *Child Genius* magazine. Contact P.O. Box 1152, Emigrant, MT 59027, *www.ycsi.org*
- The National Association for Gifted Children, 1707 L Street, NW Suite 550, Washington, DC 20036, (202) 785-4268, *www.nagc.org*
- To join an e-mail list in which parents and educators discuss the needs of gifted children, see *www.ri.net/gifted_talented/lists.html*
- If you are interested in genius, learn more about Mensa, the exclusive international group, (800) 66-MENSA, *www.mensa.org*
- National Association for Down Syndrome, P.O. Box 4542, Oak Brook, IL 60522, (630) 325-9112, *www.nads.org*
- National Association of the Deaf, 814 Thayer Avenue, Silver Spring, MD 20910, (301) 578-1788, *www.nad.org*
- National Federation of the Blind, 1800 Johnson Street, Baltimore, MD 21230, (410) 659-9314, *www.nfb.org*
- United Cerebral Palsy, 1660 L Street, NW, Suite 700, Washington, DC 20036, *www.ucpa.org*

Sites for Software Programs and Apps

www.apple.com

www.appolicious.com The developer of Toddler Teasers, apps for two-year-olds and older toddlers.

www.dailynoggin.com

www.duckduckmoosedesign.com Educational iPhone apps, including Itsy Bitsy Spider, Fish School, Wheels on the Bus, Baa Baa Black Sheep, Old Mac-

Donald. There is a link on their site of moms who review and recommend apps for toddlers.

www.juiceboxsoftware.com

www.kidsource.com The developers of Jump Start Baby and Jump Start Toddler

www.larryloveland.com Cyberstart for young children, freeware that explores size, shape, colors, and order. Uses a mouse, not a keyboard.

www.leapfrog.com

www.nickjr.com Online games, such as Dora the Explorer, Thomas the Tank Engine, Winnie the Pooh, and Finding Nemo.

www.PBSkids.org

www.storyplace.org

www.storyreaderbooks.com Books with sound accompaniment, encouraging very young children to read.

www.superkids.com

www.wartoft.nu/software/sebran Sebran's ABC, developed by Marianne Wartoft of Sweden.

www.educationalgamer.com Offers educational software.

Developmental Tasks

Age Twelve to Eighteen Months

Language

Responds to own name.
Knows the meaning of "mama," "dada," and "no"
Communicates needs by pointing and making sounds
Repeats words and imitates sounds
Points to a part of the body
Jabbers, hums, and "sings"
Responds to one-step commands (e.g., "Come here.")
Identifies two pictures in books

Cognitive/Intellectual

Understands that a hidden object still exists
Repeats actions to learn cause and effect
Explores via touch and taste
Sorts simple objects by shape
Dumps things out
Does 3-D puzzles (e.g., insert a block into a square hole)
Takes things out of a container and puts them back in again
Remembers some things he saw or heard hours or days ago
Tears paper

Physical/Motor

Stands alone
Puts an object in a container
Lowers herself from standing to sitting

Scribbles

Walks alone

Opens drawers and cabinets

Walks while carrying toys

Tosses or rolls a ball

Bends over and picks something up

Throws a ball

Claps

Stacks two to four blocks

Points with index finger

Stirs with a spoon

Picks up small objects with thumb and index finger

Climbs 1- to 2-foot objects

Social

Imitates demonstrations

Signals a need for help

Initiates simple games

Waves "bye-bye"

Looks to caregiver for praise

Shows affection

Is proud of accomplishments

Smiles at favored objects and people

Self-Care

Washes hands

Drinks from a cup with a lid

Takes off an article of clothing

Uses a spoon

Age Eighteen to Twenty-four Months

Language

Understands the meaning of "don't"
Speaks in gibberish that has the cadence and rhythm of speech
Knows names for familiar people and objects
Uses fifty words (if talking)
Identifies four pictures in a book with words (if talking)
Makes two-word sentences ("Go bye-bye")
Follows a two-step command ("Get your coat and come here.")
Listens to short books and nursery rhymes
Points to six parts of the body when asked

Cognitive/Intellectual

Categories (e.g., "toys," "books," "foods," "people")
Pretends (e.g., the piece of play dough is a snake)
Points to specific pictures in books when asked
Focuses on an activity for five minutes
Tries different ways to do something
Chooses (between two things)
Figures out how to do things by trying different strategies
Inspects something by looking (not tasting or touching)
Learns from looking at books

Physical/Motor

Runs
Walks up steps
Stacks six blocks
Kicks a ball forward
Rides a toy by pushing on the floor with alternating feet

Social

Has an impact by saying "no" or resisting
Handles simple responsibilities

Feels concerned when someone is crying
Is interested in other children
Tries to comfort someone who is very upset
Feeds a doll

Self-Care

Drinks from a cup without a lid
Takes off some clothes
Uses a spoon and fork (still has trouble turning the hand)
Puts on an article of clothing
Puts arms and legs through holes when being dressed
Washes and dries hands

Age Twenty-four to Thirty Months

Language

Speaks in two- to three-word sentences (if talking)
Has short conversations (if talking)

Cognitive/Intellectual

Listens to books with simple stories
Identifies one color
Understands the concepts "one" and "two"
Plays make-believe and fantasy games

Physical/Motor

Draws
Kicks a ball forward
Matches objects that are the same
Throws a ball
Makes play dough or clay snakes and balls
Stands on one foot (briefly)
Stands on tiptoes

Climbs low ladders
Stacks eight blocks
Leans forward without falling
Pedals a tricycle
Goes up and down stairs using alternate feet
Jumps forward

Social

Plays next to other children
Participates in interactive games
Categorizes people as boy or girl
Identifies a friend

Self-Care

Puts on a pull-over shirt
Puts on or pulls up pants

Age Thirty to Thirty-six Months

Language

Says the names of pictures in a book when asked (if talking)
Names six body parts (if talking)
Describes what two objects are used for (if talking)
Makes three- to four-word sentences (if talking)
Speaks so that others understand him most of the time (if talking)
Says fifty words (if talking)
Understands most of what is said to him

Cognitive/Intellectual

Follows a two-step command ("Find your hat and put it on.")
Reasons through problems by herself
Counts to two
Identifies four colors

Physical/Motor

Copies a straight line

Balances on one foot (two seconds)

Copies a circle

Stacks eight blocks

Confines coloring to the paper

Social

Says "please" and "thank you" when prompted

Negotiates and compromises

Takes turns (with guidance)

Asks for information

Asserts rights with peers

Approaches other children to play in daily care setting

Knows not to bully other children

Plays with other children

Contributes to joint activities and discussions

Self-Care

Uses the potty

Dresses himself

Eats with minimal assistance

Fixes a bowl of cereal

Index

We Have

EVERYTHING
on Anything!

With more than 19 million copies sold, the Everything® series has become one of America's favorite resources for solving problems, learning new skills, and organizing lives. Our brand is not only recognizable—it's also welcomed.

The series is a hand-in-hand partner for people who are ready to tackle new subjects—like you!

For more information on the Everything® series, please visit *www.adamsmedia.com*

The Everything® list spans a wide range of subjects, with more than 500 titles covering 25 different categories:

Business	History	Reference
Careers	Home Improvement	Religion
Children's Storybooks	Everything Kids	Self-Help
Computers	Languages	Sports & Fitness
Cooking	Music	Travel
Crafts and Hobbies	New Age	Wedding
Education/Schools	Parenting	Writing
Games and Puzzles	Personal Finance	
Health	Pets	